BY APPOINTMENT

BY APPOINTMENT

150 Years of the Royal Warrant
and its Holders

TIM HEALD

Photographs by Jorge Lewinski and Mayotte Magnus

Queen Anne Press

A Queen Anne Press BOOK

First published in Great Britain in 1989 by
Queen Anne Press, a division of
Macdonald & Co (Publishers) Ltd
66-73 Shoe Lane
London EC4P 4AB

A member of Maxwell Pergamon Publishing Corporation plc

British Library Cataloguing in Publication Data
Heald, Tim *1944*
    By appointment: 150 years of the royal warrant and
    its holders
    1. Great Britain. Royal warrant holders
    I. Title
    381'.1

ISBN 0 356 17099 3

Typeset by Angel Graphics, Islington, London N1
Printed and bound in Great Britain
by BPCC Paulton Books Ltd, Paulton, Bristol

FACING TITLE PAGE Goldfingers – Royal porcelain restorer Clive Swindle gilds the lily

CONTENTS

*The Mayfair Window Cleaning Company at work. J.D. Howard, the Warrant Holder, looks on
from the roof as cleaner Fred hangs in a thirteenth-floor cradle*

PREFACE

The officially sanctioned celebratory book is one to be wary of. The odds are that it will have been commissioned with fierce provisos about vetting procedure, stern injunctions about causing no offence and a general sense of slow strangulation by committee. In the case of anything to do with the Royal Family these misgivings are even more justifiable. I know from past experience that no one worth listening to will say anything about them unless it has first been cleared by Buckingham Palace. Even then people can be almost unbearably discreet. Years ago, when I was researching a book about The Prince of Wales, a deer-stalking companion agreed to lunch with me for an off-the-record briefing. After the initial pleasantries I asked what sort of rifle The Prince used. My guest was scandalised. 'I couldn't possibly talk about anything like that,' he said.

This is not, therefore, a book of revelation in the sense that it uncovers the most intimate secrets of the Royal cellar-book, let alone bedchamber. 150 years ago the Royal tradesmen banded together to form an association. This book tells the story of those 150 years, as well as giving a picture of the Warrant Holders as they are today. I have found my researches quite fascinating and I hope I have managed to convey some of this fascination to the printed page, but this is not what is called, in the hideous argot of the age, a 'Kiss 'n' Tell' book.

In the past there have been similar books at appropriate moments and they have always been put together like some sort of trade directory, with each Warrant Holder given his separate entry and a small box of fulsome prose. It might be that in this day of the thirty-second attention span this would have been sensible, but I have tried instead to write old-fashioned English prose in chapters which continue without pause from one paragraph to another.

I have not given equal prominence to each Warrant Holder. There are between 850 and 900 of them and to have done so would have made a seriously deranged book. Each and every one of them has been invited to send in whatever details of their company they have thought appropriate. In addition I have gone visiting all over the British Isles, though again I haven't been to every grantee. Indeed, I would be at least half inclined to argue that in some cases I have learned more from a succinct correspondence or telephone conversation than from a sub-state visit where, after a while, one vast hall full of humming machinery controlled by a bank of cool computers tends to blur into another and one is hard put to remember whether the place is manufacturing boiled sweets, cashmere sweaters or pharmaceuticals! To those friendly and cooperative Warrant Holders who seem to have less space than they think they deserve, I can say only that I wanted to write a book that was interesting to read and therefore had to be selective. Someone had to lose out, but each Warrant Holder is listed alphabetically in an appendix at the back of the book. Otherwise I have been deliberately serendipitous.

I won't deny that there has indeed been a small committee of Warrant Holding scrutineers. We haven't agreed about everything but they have been considerate and helpful and, above all, they have understood that despite all the caveats and provisos a book is ultimately the responsibility of the author whose name appears on the cover. My thanks to them, and especially to Commander Hugh Faulkner, Secretary of the Royal Warrant Holders' Association, and to his Assistants, Ann Wycherley and Patricia Norsworthy. My thanks also to all those many Warrant Holders who gave up their valuable time to assist me in a variety of ways. It would be invidious, I think, to mention most of them by name and they will, I hope, find their reward in the text, but I should particularly like to acknowledge the support and help of the Association's Treasurer, Sir Edward Rayne, of next year's President, Barry Reed, and a number of his predecessors, in particular

Graeme Wilson, Timothy Sandeman, John Marks and Comte Alain de Vogue.

It was the last of these who was perhaps most instrumental in seeing that this book happened at all and its genesis may tell you something about what to expect. Some years ago Maurice Buckmaster, former head of the French Section of the wartime Special Operations Executive, invited me to join a party on a visit to Champagne, where he was the Public Relations Consultant to the local industry. In the course of that visit Veuve Clicquot offered to make a member of our party a 'Friend of the Widow', one of whose perks is a gift of a bottle of the Widow every birthday. Because I was the youngest of the group and therefore likely, on an actuarial basis, to get the most bottles, I was the lucky man. A year or so later Comte Alain became President of the Royal Warrant Holders' Association and was confronted with the problem of making after-dinner speeches at vast and intimidating banquets. As a professional writer and Friend of the Widow, I was wheeled in to act as his speech-writing assistant, and in the course of this I met Commander Faulkner, who just happened to mention that the 150th anniversary of the Association was looming. At which I responded that a book might be a good way of marking the event. And the rest is history.

It was always important that the book should be an impressive artefact in itself, quite apart from the words and pictures it contains. As the author I think the words are important, but I happily concede that they are more than complemented by the exquisite photographs of Jiri Lewinski and Mayotte Magnus, who have been a great support during my research. Some people think that photographers 'just take photographs', but that is emphatically not so in this case.

I hope the result speaks for itself but there are two particular points I feel I should stress. The first is that holding the Royal Warrant is universally regarded as an extraordinary honour. One really cannot overemphasise the pride and pleasure that every single Warrant Holder I met expressed in serving the Royal Family. It is easy to get a distorted view of the Royal Family from much modern media coverage and it was a revelation to find such luminous and universal loyalty among their servants in real life. The second point is that so much of British trade and industry is in such manifestly good shape. The briefest glance at the list of Warrant Holders will demonstrate an extraordinary variety of companies, from individual craftsmen to vast corporations. Their skills differ from the most ancient, inherited artistry to the highest of high tech. Everywhere I went I found that the Royal Warrant Holders were a living demonstration of the Best of British and it was heartening to find that the Best of British still seems – here at least – to be synonymous with the Best in the World.

The first part of this book broadly describes the history and evolution of the Royal Warrant, while the second deals with the modern holders of the Warrant. It puts them into both a British and a Royal context, and it tries to demonstrate how and why they are all, in their different ways, the Best of Britain.

PART

THE WARRANT EVOLVES

Tempered steel – Derek Brooks of Wilkinson Sword at work on a dangerous blade

THE ROYAL SERVANTS

'His deedes obligatory to serve the court'
(Letters patent, 1430)

The idea behind the Royal Warrant is almost as old as time itself and certainly as old as the Monarchy. The King and his court always had to be provided for. From the very beginning someone had to make the robes, the crowns, the orbs and the sceptres; someone had to provide the wine and the food, the cutlery and the dining-tables themselves; someone had to fix the Royal roof and clear the Royal drains.

The King, being King, did not have to pinch pennies. He could afford whatever he wanted. In order to make sure that he had only the best, he cornered the market wherever possible, ensuring that he always had first call on the services of the most proficient in the land, from goldsmith to butcher. The said goldsmith or butcher was proud to serve his King and saw that being known to do so could confer certain trading benefits denied to his less favoured competitors. It is no secret, though one does not broadcast it too loudly, that to be known to supply the Royal Household with marmalade or mutton, computers or candles, suggests to the world at large that your marmalade, mutton, computers and candles are quite simply the best available. Why else would the Royal Court grant you a Warrant and the right to display the Royal coat of arms – discreetly – on your products and your shop front and your writing-paper?

Written evidence of such relationships in England goes right back to mediaeval times, although the very earliest records apply to groups rather than individuals. In 1155, for example, the Weavers Company received a Royal Charter from King Henry II, and various other livery companies followed suit. The Drapers got theirs from Edward III and the Mercers from Richard II. These Charters gave the companies the right to discipline anyone within their trade who produced substandard goods or workmanship or offended against the rules which the companies themselves drew up.

At the time Richard II was granting a Charter to the Mercers, there were similar relationships with individual tradesmen. From The King's Wardrobe accounts for 1395–6 we learn that a London goldsmith named Thomas Polle had provided 'divers' gallon pots of white silver, inscribed with the arms of England and France. In return he had received a number of similar but broken old vessels from The King. Another goldsmith, William Fitzhugh, made six pots weighing more than 17 lb and a silver water pot. With his colleagues George Cressy and Reymund Standelf, Fitzhugh also produced eight silver gilt candelbra. William Lucas, yet another London goldsmith, made twelve plain white silver cups with a leopard on the bottom, and Nicholas Twyford made a dozen silver gilt chargers weighing 65 lb 1d.

These records suggest that transactions were conducted on an *ad hoc* basis and were not part of the continuous relationship that would be expected if the tradesman was a Warrant Holder in the modern sense. By the next century, however, that principle had been properly established in writing. On 29 July 1430, a year after the coronation of the boy-king Henry VI, William Staunton received the following Royal letter:

It having been shown to The King and Council by The King's servant WILLIAM STAUNTON that the letters patent dated 22 May last, whereby he was appointed purveyor of furs and pelts, are invalid because they do not mention what wages he is to receive nor by whose hands, The King at his request and by advice of the council, has granted him from 22 May last, during pleasure, the said office of purveyor in the Port of London and other ports, of furs and pelts for The King, which furs and pelts he is

Royal printer Caxton shows proofs to King Edward IV

to deliver when purchased to the Keeper of the Great Wardrobe by whom he is to receive yearly wages of 12d a day and his liveries for summer and for Christmas last, and so from year to year as Henry Barton, the last purveyor, received them.

When Staunton died he was succeeded by Christopher Wartre. Wartre's letter confers on him the office 'Skinner' rather than 'purveyor of furs and pelts', but they presumably meant the same. Wartre was granted the office for life 'with wages of 12d a day and livery of vesture and all other daily fees and wages'.

A more famous fifteenth-century Warrant Holder was William Caxton, who was appointed the King's Printer after setting up his press at Westminster in 1476. His successor under Henry VIII was Thomas Berthelet, who was responsible for the printing of the Statutes of Eltham which dealt with the 'good order of his household'. The 'Lord Great Master, Mr Treasurer, Mr Comptroller and others' were identified as those responsible for maintaining this good order and a wide variety of Royal servants were listed, together with their duties and emoluments. Thus:

Thomas Hewytt who hath bound himself by his deede obligatory to serve the Court with Swannes and Cranes,

price the piece two shillings. The said Hewytt shall serve The King with all kinds of Wildfoule, in every degree according to the articles specified. It is ordeyned that the said Purveyor shall have authority by The King's Commission to make his provision of Poultry within this Realme.

Elizabeth I refined the Statutes of Eltham by instituting a Household Book, which listed 'Purveyors of Beeves and Muttons', who were to have £13 13s 4d a year together with riding charges; the 'Purveyor of Veales', who received a 100s a year and 20d a day 'Board Lodging'; and the 'Purveyor of Fish', who had £10 a year 'entertainment' plus £22 11s 8d a year 'for losses and necessaries'.

It all seems rather haphazard, but despite appearances some systems did exist and some traditions were established. Not the least of these was the office of Royal Skinner, which had obviously been going continuously since William Staunton's day. In 1554 Elizabeth's elder half-sister, Mary, made a grant for life to Thomas Percy. He was to be paid 12d a day – just as Staunton had been more than 100 years earlier – and he was to be described as 'The Queen's skinner or serjeant of the Peltry'.

Percy was certainly required to make items rather more exotic than anything that has ever been asked of J. G.

Links, the present Queen's original furrier. A 'warrant for the Queen's apparrell' refers to the 'furring of a louse Gowne of blacke damaske with eight blake Conye skinnes with white heares and fourscore and eleven blacke conye skynnes to the same Gowne of our greate wardrobe'. Even the Royal fool, William Somer, had a majestic 'Turquey Coate' with 'vi blewe conyes and gresseled clowdes and fortie and eighte gresseled coneyes all of our great wardrobe'.

The following century, saw the birth of companies such as Firmin, the button makers (1677), and Toye, Kenning, whose founder was a Huguenot lace weaver who fled to England in 1685, Today, both companies hold Warrants to supply Queen Elizabeth II.

Betty Whittington, who wrote a valuable short history of the Royal Warrant in 1967, mentions Edward Chamberlayne, the seventeenth century's equivalent of Anthony Sampson who published several editions of *The Present State of England*. In this he listed tradesmen who supplied goods and services to the Palace. At first he rather disparaged them, talking of 'those that live by buying and selling, people of the baser sort'. Later, however, he curbed this snobbery and conceded that 'many of these Offices and Places are of Good Credit, Great Profit, and enjoyed by Persons of Quality.'

The 1684 list consisted of a Haberdasher of Hats, a Button Maker, a Joyner, a Locksmith, an Upholsterer, a Sword Cutter, a Watchmaker in Reversion, an Operator for the Teeth, a Corn Cutter and a Goffe-club Maker. As Betty Whittington points out, it was the Scottish King James I who first introduced the game of golf to England.

In 1671 a Warrant from Charles II – a parchment measuring two feet square – identified all the Royal Tradesmen and their duties, even down to the embalming of the body of the Duke of Albemarle. The Master of His Majesty's Great Wardrobe paid a total of £1,348 18s 4¾d.

An eighteenth-century button bill from Firmin

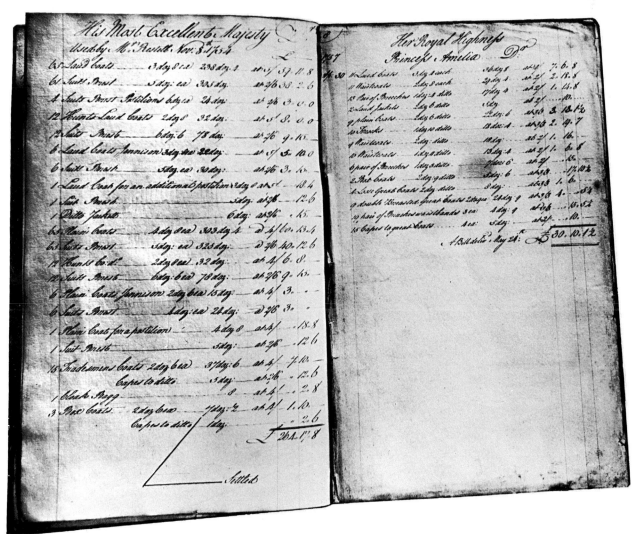

Breastbeating – Household Cavalry cuirasses are still made at their Birmingham factory by Firmin, who have been in business since 1677

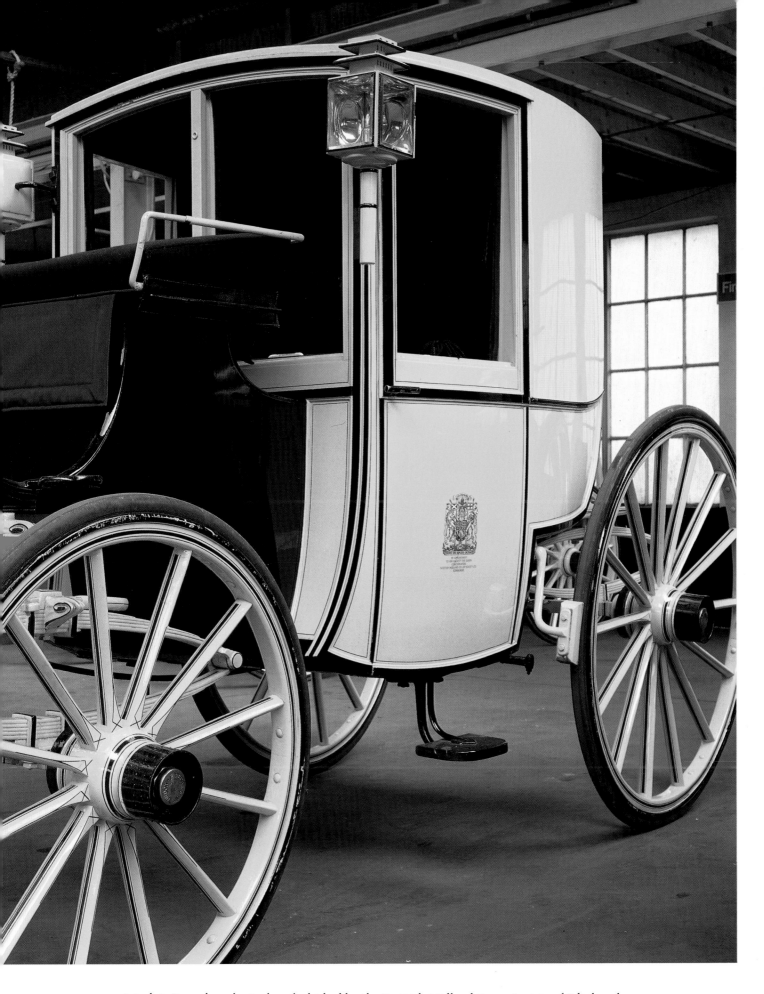

A Lady's Brougham lovingly refurbished by the Scottish Midland Co-op Society of Edinburgh,
Royal Coach Painters

The Wardrobe was situated at Puddle Wharf and had come a long way from its origins as a mere clothes closet. By the reign of King John it had been transformed into a Third Treasury. It was known as the 'Great' as opposed to 'The King's' Wardrobe because of the size of its contents. The Great Wardrobe provided the court with beds, hangings, clothes of estate, carpets and 'all Linens and Laces for His Majesty's Person'. Much more than a wardrobe, it was in fact a small factory, turning 'metal into arms and cloth into clothes'.

Not that The King's largesse was limitless. Indeed, at times his purse was decidedly pinched. On 1 August 1682, for instance, the Lord Steward, the Duke of Ormond, recorded in his Warrant Book that the office of King's Grocer (Purveyor of Grocery ware, to give him his full title) was 'altogether unnecessary and useless, especially at this time, when the expense of Sugar, Fruite, Oranges, Lemons, Spices and other grocery wares is very small, as the expense of His Majesty's House is retrencht to a very low rate'.

The 1700 edition of *The Present State of England* included a list of purveyors to William and Mary, coming under the Officers of the Board of Green Cloth, 'below stairs'. The Board was originally a court of justice with green cloth under it and above it, 'The Arms of the Compting House, signifying their Power to Reward or Correct'. These purveyors included a Purveyor of Bacon, a Purveyor of Poultry, a Purveyor of Fish, a Purveyor of Butcher's Meat and a Purveyor of Oysters. This last, unusually, was a woman – Anne Bridge. There was also a Linen Draper, a Wine Merchant, a Brewer, with the apt name of John England, and another Brewer described as 'Brewer at Hampton Court'.

Throughout the eighteenth and nineteenth centuries there was an annual *Royal Kalendar*, which listed the Royal tradesmen. Despite mentioning the Royal Rat-Catcher and the Royal Mole-Taker, it does not, Betty Whittington observes, list the Royal Bug-Taker. This was hard on Andrew Cooke, of Holborn Hill, who claimed in 1775 that he had not only removed bed bugs from a number of Royal apartments but had also 'cured' a total of 16,000 beds 'with great applause'. He was very irritated, therefore, to find that there was a rival Bug-Taker passing himself off as 'Bug-Destroyer to His Majesty'.

A year later the Lord Steward's Warrant Book contains a Warrant dated 1 August 1776 which states that one Mr Savage Bear was 'Purveyor of Greens, Fruits and Garden Things'.

There was much abuse of Royal patronage in the eighteenth century and in 1782 George III was forced to rationalise a number of court practices. As a result the Great Wardrobe was abolished by act of parliament. 'The care and management of all Services formerly done by the Late Great Wardrobe Office are committed to the care and Management of the Lord Chamberlain,' says a Warrant of the day, signed by Lord Salisbury, the Lord Chamberlain. That Warrant, incidentally, was granted to Mr Richard Thresher of the Strand and confirmed him as one of His Majesty's Hosiers. Today the firm of Thresher and Glenny is still in the Strand and still holds the Royal Warrant.

To this day it is the Lord Chamberlain of the Household who takes overall charge of the granting of Royal Warrants. Nowadays all Warrants are similar. In those days the only thing they had in common was that they were handwritten. This was Firmin's, the button makers':

By Virtue of the Powers invested in me by His Majesty, I do hereby constitute and appoint Philip Douglas Firmin to serve His Majesty's Stables in Quality of Buttonmaker (in the room and place of Samuel Firmin deceased) and as both the Goodness and Price of the Buttons delivered will be strictly examined into, so for the Encouragement of such Tradesmen as shall have the Honor of serving His Majesty in this Department, it is ordered that their Bills shall be regularly paid at the End of Each Quarter, and that no Poundage Free, nor Perquisite, shall be given to the Clerk of the Stables, or to any other Person whatsoever.

Westmoreland.

As Betty Whittington points out, it sounds as if the Clerk of the Stables was in the habit of making 'a little on the side'. If so, this was the end of his profitable sideline in perks and poundages. The Crown was cleaning up its act.

By the late eighteenth and early nineteenth centuries, the Warrant system was beginning to resemble the one we know today in a number of important respects. There was a move towards standardising the wording of Warrants and the Royal coat of arms began to be used by proud – or opportunist – tradesmen on bill-heads and shop fronts. In 1779, for instance, Johnson and Justerini (ancestor of the modern Justerini & Brooks) had a bill-head with the famous three-feather crest and the inscription 'Foreign Cordial Merchants to H.R.H. The Prince of Wales'. In the reign of William IV a brewery at Brentford received a perpetual grant to use the Royal arms.

This perpetual grant is one of only three (Gillon's William IV whisky and the Brighton Dome are the

Heraldic Artistry demonstrated by G.C. Francis at his studio in West Sussex. The painting in the foreground was by his father, who also held the Warrant

Bryan Toye, the latest in a very long line of Toyes, with a range of Toye Kenning insignia

Copes, chasubles, tapestries, damasks and brocatelles from Watts and Co., Ecclesiastical Furnishers to The Queen

A Council Meeting of the Royal Warrant Holders' Association. Members sit round the table while Commander Hugh Faulkner RN, the Secretary of the Association, and his Assistants, Ann Wycherley and Patricia Norsworthy, lurk discreetly in the background

others). It was given to the brewer Sir Felix Booth, as much in recognition of his services to polar exploration as of his beer. He financed the Ross voyage which discovered the magnetic pole in 1837.

After a series of mergers and acquisitions 'The Royal Brewery, Brentford Limited' is now a subsidiary company of Courage, who no longer brew in Brentford. Nevertheless, the right to perpetual use of the arms of William IV continues.

There are several other ancient Warrant Holders whose descendants still serve the Royal Family. James Swaine (now Swaine, Adeney, Brigg & Sons Ltd) made George III's

whips. James Wilkinson was his Gunmaker and Wilkinson Sword Ltd are now Her Majesty's Sword Cutlers. Richard Wall, George Prince of Wales's Pork Butcher, has his name preserved in Mattessons Wall's Ltd of Malthouse Walk, Banbury, Suppliers of Sausages and Meat Pies. Charles Chubb, George IV's locksmith, lives on in three separate modern Warrant Holders: Chubb Alarms Ltd, Installers of Intruder Alarms; Chubb & Son's Lock and Safe Co., Ltd (Patent Lock and Safe Makers); and Chubb Fire Ltd, who make fire extinguishers. Robert Garrard was William IV's goldsmith and Garrard & Co. Ltd are still goldsmiths, though they are now under different ownership. Caleys of Windsor, who now supply Household and Fancy Goods, were represented at the court of Queen Charlotte by Mrs M. Caley, who was The Queen's Milliner and Dressmaker.

This list, random though it seems to be, shows how a cross-section of British companies has changed and evolved over the last two centuries. Locks have become burglar alarms; a lone milliner a department store; an individual sausagemaker a mass-producer of bangers and pies. Of them all, perhaps only gold remains a constant.

In 1830 the Tradesmen of The King's Household occupied less than a page in the *Royal Kalendar*. There were just under 100 of them and many, like George Halfhide, the Seal Engraver, or Robert Rogg, the Chinaman, sound as if they were individuals in business on their own account. Others, like Garrard – R. J. and S. Garrard and T. Hawley – were plainly companies even though they were small ones. The Crown Jewellers are one of the very few entries in the 1830 list which have a contemporary ring.

The list has an essentially domestic flavour. It is replete with cabinet makers and upholsterers, joiners and paper-hangers, tailors and turners, opticians, floor-cloth manu-facturers, pen-cutters and lamp and lustre makers. Only an occasional entry suggests pomp or circumstance: the eight different 'goldlace-men'; William Webb, the Robe-maker; Mrs Elizabeth Clarke, the Plumassier; and above all, T. and W. Clarke, the Globe Makers.

Queen Victoria came to the throne in 1837 and two months after her accession she began issuing her own Warrants. The form was very similar to that in use during Charles II's reign. They were dated and signed by the Lord Chamberlain, who then gave them to Her Majesty's Gentleman Usher in Daily Waiting, who administered an Oath to the Grantee. This was taken upon the Bible for all except for Jews, who swore on the Old Testament, and Quakers, who affirmed.

The new Warrant Holder had to say:

I hereby solemnly swear that I will be a true and loyal servant to our Sovereign Lady Victoria, of the United Kingdom of Great Britain and Ireland Queen, and that I know nothing that may be hurtful or prejudicial to Her Royal Person, State, Crown or Dignity but I will hinder it all maybe in my Power, and reveal the same to the Lord Chamberlain of The Queen's Household or one of the Most Honourable Privy Councillors. That I will serve The Queen truly and faithfully in the Place and Quality of... and will obey the Lord Chamberlain at all times.

King William IV – first Monarch to allow tradesmen to use the Royal Arms

One of these pioneer Victorian Warrant Holders was Richard Twining, whose Warrant for supplying The Queen's tea was dated 2 September 1837. Today Twining's still sell tea from the same shop in the Strand and they still have the Royal Warrant. The present holder, Sam Twining, a former President of the Royal Warrant Holders' Association, is the ninth generation of a family which has held the Warrant for over 150 years.

Three years after Queen Victoria came to the throne those who held her Warrant decided that the time had come for them to band together into some sort of formal organisation. They were not motivated by greed or snob-bery, but Victorian society did practise a social ostracism of trade. For example, while city and professional folk might attend a Royal levee, 'At retail trade the line is drawn, and very strictly so, were a person actually engaged in trade to obtain a presentation, his presentation would be cancelled as soon as the Lord Chamberlain was made aware of the nature of his occupation.' That judgement from *Manners and Rules of Good Society*, by 'A member of the Aristocracy', represented an attitude which was, obviously, anathema to the Royal Tradesmen, who took great pride in their calling and particularly in their associ-ation with Royalty. Forming an Association was their way of celebrating both.

Robert Gieve of Gieves and Hawkes Limited with samples of the naval uniforms they have provided for Royalty for generations

THE USUAL HONOURS

'An association for the celebration of her Majesty's birthday'
(Mr Hunter's proposal, 1840)

The original minute book of the Royal Warrant Holders' Association is kept at the office in 7 Buckingham Gate, London, where it lives in a special plum-coloured box with brass clasps. It has to be kept in something like that because after 150 years it is showing signs of wear and tear. Nevertheless, it is still perfectly legible, written in that copperplate handwriting which only a professional calligrapher can manage in this word-processing age.

The foundation of the Association is announced on the very first page, but it is clear from the phrasing that an informal group of Royal Tradesmen already existed and met for dinner once a year to celebrate the Royal birthday. The birth of the new, more formal organisation took place on one of these occasions at the Freemasons' Tavern in Great Queen Street. It was 25 May 1840. The toasts were drunk with the 'usual honors' (*sic*) and when the last one was finished the chairman, a Mr Hunter, 'begged leave to submit to the company present a proposition he had made to his Brother Stewards, and which had met with their concurrence, viz. that of Her Majesty's Tradesmen forming an Association for the celebration of Her Majesty's Birthday, which proposal was agreed to by all present'.

Mr Hunter further proposed that this organisation should be called 'The Royal Tradesmen's Association for the Annual Celebration of Her Majesty's Birthday. Established 1840'.

In other words, they were establishing that fine old Victorian institution the dining club. Membership was restricted, naturally, to those supplying goods to any department of the Royal Household or to the department of Woods and Forests. Anybody who qualified could pay a guinea and be entitled to attend the annual dinner. If he wished he could send his son instead. You could invite a friend but that would cost 25s. The dinners, and therefore the Association, were exclusively male, although it was agreed that if 'a lady or firm of ladies' held a Royal appointment they should be allowed to 'appoint a Gentleman to represent them'.

At first the membership was a mere twenty-five, but in the second year it was 'agreed unanimously that Dinner should be ordered for 80', and the numbers stayed at around that figure for years. The members were unhappy at this, feeling strongly that if you were privileged to be a Royal Tradesman then you should have the courtesy to dine on The Queen's birthday. From the very first, The Queen – or rather the Lord Steward or Board of Green Cloth – sent over a couple of bucks so that the tradesmen could eat Royal venison. The stewards of the Association obviously felt that this turned the dinner into something of a command performance and in 1851 they decided to send out a letter to 'the General Body of Gentlemen who held appointments for the Crown requesting them to belong to the Association'.

Three hundred of these letters were sent and anyone not replying got a personal call from Mr Scarman, one of the stewards. Words were not minced. The stewards 'cannot but feel it only requires their application to enable you to obey Her Majesty's Commands in celebrating Her Majesty's Birthday by dining together on 31st May, the appointed day'. And again, 'The stewards ... feel the condescension so great on the part of Her Majesty in presenting the Association with venison for the occasion that the tradesmen so greatly favoured can do no other than gratefully accept and do honour to the gift.'

The tradesmen were surprisingly unbiddable, however. In fairness it should be remembered that a great many

The 1899 banquet at the Hotel Metropole

lived abroad, but even so membership of the Association was far short of the total number eligible. In view of the close interest The Queen took in the dinners, this is surprising. In 1861 the Association had a note from the Palace saying that the date they had chosen to dine was not 'consonant with the feelings of Her Majesty'. It was therefore postponed to 10 July, which was the day 'specially appointed for its [the birthday's] celebration'. The following year the dinner was cancelled 'in consequence of a communication from the Lord Chamberlain's office'. Prince Albert had died.

The dinner was remarkably good value. More to the point it was remarkably steady value – a reflection of the stability of the times. In the beginning Mr Cuff was able to provide 'Dinner, Dessert, wine including twice of champagne' for a guinea. Twenty years later a surcharge

of a shilling a head was levied for 'Real Turtle and Punch', but as late as 1877 it was 'agreed to supply the Dinner on the same terms as last year at one Guinea per head including the Turtle soup and the usual wines, tea, coffee, ices etc.' It was still a guinea a head in 1889. Imagine what the world would be like if in 1989 we were still able to dine at the prices of 1940.

You got a lot for your guinea, quite apart from wine and food. The fact that it was a prolonged evening of entertainment is reflected in the time of meeting. The invitation said 'Five for half past five o'clock'. The earliest programme in the archives is for 24 June 1884, and there is every reason to think that it was entirely typical. It includes no fewer than eleven separate toasts. The minute book is full of such lines as 'The usual loyal and fratristic toasts were given and responded to', so it's safe to assume that eleven was par for the course. They drank to The Queen first, and then to the rest of the Royal Family, and then to the Army, Navy and Auxiliary Forces. They toasted the Mistress of the Robes singly and alone and the Lord Steward, the Lord Chamberlain and the Master of the Horse as a trio. Then they dealt with the Chairman; the Association of Her Majesty's Tradesmen; the Stewards and the Stewards Elect; the Honorary Secretary; the Visitors; and finally, the Ladies.

Many of these toasts were proposed in what one can safely assume were quite long speeches. At least half of them would have also had another speech, just as long, in response.

And then, of course, there was the music. For years this was under the direction of Mr Chaplin Henry, who appears to have made an annual charge of ten guineas and to have brought along three or four other singers, together perhaps with Miss Kate Chaplin to play violin, or Miss Nellie Chaplin and Mr F. R. Kinkee to play at the pianoforte.

They always started with a sung grace from the 'Laudi Spirituali' of 1545. Then came two verses of the national anthem, after which there was a variable potpourri of patriotism, romance, jingoism and sentiment. You might have 'The Old Brigade':

> Where are the boys of the old Brigade
> Who fought with us side by side,
> Shoulder and shoulder and blade by blade
> Fought till they fell and died?

Or a humorous song, like the very curious 'Happy Fatherland', which began:

> The Germans are a noble race,
> And of that race I'll sing:
> They love their Pa's and adore their Ma's
> And they idolise their King.

A Scottish song – 'The Sand of Dee', perhaps, or 'Charlie Is My Darling' – seems to have been *de rigueur*, but it is the romantic ballad which most surely evokes the scene in the Freemasons' Tavern at the height of Queen Victoria's reign. Imagine that all-male gathering of Royal tradesmen in white ties and tails as they listened to Miss Henden-Warde giving them 'Friends or Lovers?'

> They stood beneath the beeches where the sunlight
>   never reaches,
> And the road beneath them lay;
> There had been some idle chatter o'er a very
>   little matter,
> And what won't people say?

So she drew a ring from her dainty hand,
And then fitted it on once more:
'Of course we shall always be friends,' said she,
'Tho' our dream of love is o'er.'
'Oh yes! we shall always be friends,' said he;
'The truest and best of Friends,' sighed she,
And the twilight shadows grew dim and grey,
As they stood and talked on each side of the way.

It seems horribly prosaic to pass from that to the question of food and drink, but it has to be recorded that the Victorian tradesmen were prodigious trenchermen. A typical menu has The Queen's picture on the front of a tiny card folded in two. The toasts are on the back and on the inside you have drinks to the left and food to the right. The wines went Chablis, Punch; Hock; three different champagnes – Moët and Chandon, Georges Goulet and Wachter; Liqueurs; Port and Claret. The food consists of seven different courses, *excluding* cheese,

Taylor's, sometime lensmen to the Prince and Princess of Wales, but now, alas, no more

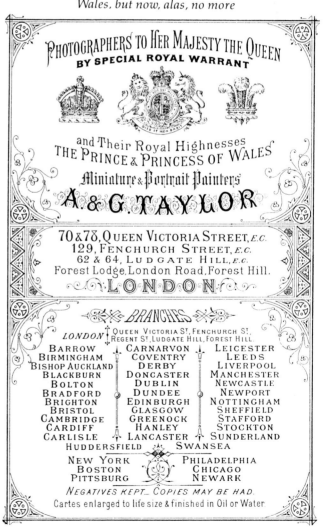

A full hand of historic banquet menus

salad, fruit and nuts, and coffee with cognac. They began with anchovies, olives and shrimps and then ran through soup, fish (sole, salmon, whitebait) on to sweetbreads, guinea fowl and a Prince of Wales sorbet, designed presumably to clear the palate. Then, under the heading 'Relevés' – the menu was entirely in French – they were offered lamb with mint sauce and new potatoes, York ham braised in champagne, French salad, Her Majesty's haunch of venison and lobster mayonnaise. After that there was a 'Roti', which was Aylesbury duckling with asparagus, and then there were four different puddings, which with names like Timbales à l'Impératrice and Pudding Glacé Diamond sound quite exotic.

All this for a guinea!

Throughout the nineteenth century and beyond, the Association was to all intents and purposes a dining club, but gradually it began to change its character. Various straws in the wind suggest some of the changes.

The first was its increasing politicisation. It never became political in the party sense, but its members did begin to concern themselves with the rights and privileges involved in serving the Monarch. Some of them even went so far as to use the dinners to try and make protests about Royal patronage. On 10 November 1891, for instance, there were ugly scenes at The Prince of Wales's birthday banquet at the Criterion. A man in the body of the hall got up and tried to speak. Frankly, reading the press reports it is difficult to work out the precise burden of his complaint, but it sounds as if he was complaining about The Prince's relationship with the stores. Whatever it was, it greatly upset the other diners. 'He was met with cries of "traitor" and other unpleasant noises... At length The Prince of Wales's tradesmen at dinner got tired of simply yelling, and commenced throwing at their obnoxious colleague at first champagne corks and then nuts, apples, oranges and bananas.'

Coupled with this, and perhaps even stemming from it, came an increasing sense of self-importance. Until 1840 there had simply been an almost entirely informal annual gathering of tradesmen wanting to wish their sovereign a happy birthday. From 1840 onwards this was codified and organised into an Association, but in 1895 it became 'The Incorporated Association of Her Majesty's and Other Royal Warrant Holders Limited'. In 1902 it changed again to the simpler 'Royal Warrant Holders' Association Limited'. In 1907 it underwent the final change and

Royal champagnes – not so much a drink as a festive celebration

became what it is today: 'The Royal Warrant Holders' Association', incorporated as such by Royal Charter.

Not everyone approved of this transformation from 'tradesman' to 'Warrant Holder'. Mrs Sala, a Victorian predecessor of Nigel Dempster, who wrote a column called 'Table Talk', said:

This is an age of humbug! Why do the tradesmen of The Prince of Wales when they send to the daily papers that on such and such a date they will hold their annual banquet at the Hotel Splendide call themselves 'Warrant Holders' to His Royal Highness? Surely these fortunate men are proud of providing our future king with all the necessaries of life, therefore, why not call themselves tradesmen instead of Warrant Holders?

The late Victorian list of Royal Warrant Holders represents an extraordinary transformation from the rather austere one published in the reign of her uncle George IV. The Queen herself had 807 Warrant Holders – more than eight times as many as her uncle. The Prince and Princess of Wales had 736. And then there were the Duke of Saxe-Coburg and Gotha with 271 and Princess Mary Adelaide, Duchess of Teck, with a more modest forty-two.

The first point that strikes one about Queen Victoria's list is its apparent frivolity and exoticism: biscuit makers from Biarritz, confectioners from Cannes, fruit preservers from Nice, gardeners from Darmstadt. It is not at all what one associates with that austere Monarch. Many names are familiar even though not all of them are still Warrant Holders: Thomas Goode for china and glass; Fry's for chocolate; Garrard inevitably, for gold and silver, but Mappin and Webb as well; Twinings for tea; Schweppes for you know what; Fortnum and Mason and Crosse and Blackwell for – quaintly – 'Oilery and Provisions'; T. Wall and Sons for pork; and Bollinger for wine.

Others have succumbed to the ravages of time, progress and circumstances: Beal, French and Co., of Crutched Friars, were the Royal wine cork suppliers; Wyckoff, Seamans and Benedict were the 'Type Writing Machine Makers'; W. Mabey and Son were responsible for turtle; the Welch Whiskey Distillery held the Warrant for spirits; and so on. Nor is it just the companies themselves that have passed away. Fashions, technology, taste – life itself – have, in certain areas, changed almost beyond recognition in the last ninety years. In those days there were Warrant Holders for lamp oil, starch, snuff, wax (six separate Warrants for The Queen alone!), steel pens, tricycles, wigs and chemical compounds.

Royal 'dip' pens – a casualty of time and progress

One can detect a distinct shift in style after the death of Edward VII. At the first banquet of George V a familiar item is missing. There is no haunch of Royal venison, and although venison has featured on subsequent menus, that ancient Victorian tradition of sending two bucks for the birthday party has never been revived. It is also noticeable that whereas the last Edwardian banquet was 'In honour of the *birthday* of His Majesty The King', the first neo-Georgian banquet was simply 'In honour of H.M. George V'. The loss of the birthday banquet strikes one as a definite move away from the quite intimate association which the tradesmen had previously enjoyed with the Monarch. It is not being unduly flippant to observe that the Edwardian banquet menu was in French and began with 'Royal Native' oysters whereas the Georgian one was in English and started with melon.

In the reign of Queen Victoria's grandson *The Royal Warrant Holders' Who's Who* listed over 1,400 Warrant

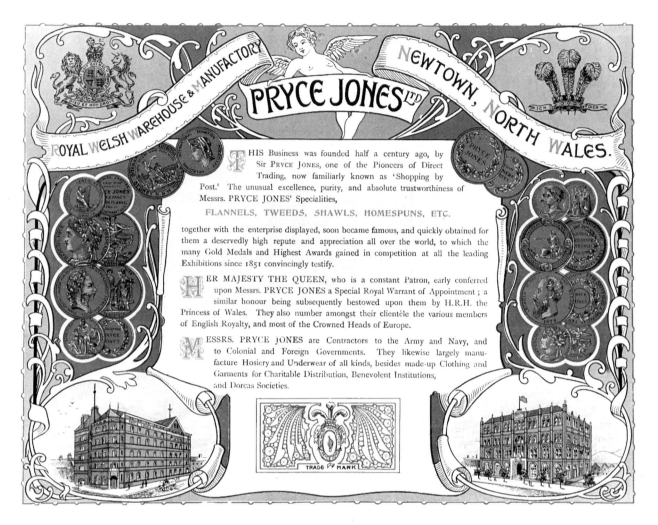

Another Warrant Holding ghost – Pryce Jones' good Welsh homespun tweeds

Holders. This seems remarkable for a generally conservative and frugal Monarch like George V, who had only been on the throne eleven years when this volume was published. The list is extraordinarily far-flung and eclectic. W. Abernethy, photographer, was from 29 Belfast High Street, but who were the Baggs Brothers of Canal Walk, Portsmouth? History does not relate. Das Gopinath Bhagwan of Benares was a brocade and shawl merchant, goldsmith and silversmith to Queen Alexandra. Miss Kate Braun of 94 Wigmore Street, London, made lace for Queen Alexandra; James Brown of Aberdeen provided fish and poultry for The King. The Caesar Brothers of Aldershot were builders and decorators. Carlo Calderai of Florence was in 'comestibles' and Mrs Duncan of Shetland was a haberdasher. Heaton, Butler and Bayne of 14 Garrick Street, London, painted stained glass. Herzog and Higgins of Mhow, India, took photographs for Queen Alexandra. Charles Jasper Hill was a Canadian florist.

Occasionally an address gives a clue to occupation. Joseph Mansfield's address in Kenmare, Ireland, is 'The Spinning Wheel'. He was responsible for The King's 'Irish homespun'. John Mitchell could be found at the Newhall Pen Works in Birmingham, where he held the Warrant for making The King's steel pens. Gustave Morlock of the Hotel Bristol in Paris was presumably that establishment's manager, though for once the Warrant Holders' Archives say nothing about him. Señor Don Joaquin M. Rivero of Jerez de la Frontera was, as you might expect, responsible for the Royal sherry.

A relatively small number of Warrant Holders have short essays in this volume and others have taken advertisements at the back. You do not have to be unduly cynical to think that most of the entries have been written by the Warrant Holders themselves. They are without exception exceedingly flattering. Readers are asked to consider a silver epergne made by the founder of Hemings

*ABOVE Richard Skinner in one of his company's silver frames alongside his father, his grandfather
and his grantor, Her Majesty The Queen*

*OPPOSITE Downstairs – William Summers, the Warrant Holder at Garrard's the Crown Jewellers,
together with his team*

the jewellers and to 'marvel at the infinite skill that has produced it, the geometrical precision of the hand-cut lattice work and its beautiful proportions and delicate handling'. Mr George Gregory, the antiquarian bookseller of Bath, was 'President of the International Association of Antiquarian Booksellers, 1915 to 1918, and although the rule of this body is to elect a new President every year from town and country alternately, he was strongly urged to continue in office throughout the last war, which he patriotically agreed to do'. And so on.

In the thirty-year interval between this and the late Victorian era, some of the requirements of the Monarch appear to have remained precisely the same, while others had changed out of recognition. Motorised transport had arrived. Humber Ltd recorded that 'His late Majesty King Edward rode a Beeston-Humber tricycle for a considerable period.' Shell took an advertisement with a picture of a bi-plane and a sailing ship with the legend, 'In times past the pioneer depended on trade winds – to-day he depends on SHELL AVIATION'. Shell, in those days, was 'the dependable spirit for all motors'.

Already the curious paradoxes of contemporary Monarchy were beginning to emerge. On the one hand Royalty espoused the very latest inventions and on the other they stayed loyal to the very oldest traditions. Even under the As you find Adam and Co., with their floral tributes 'so beautiful and appropriate that they are like embodiments of "sympathy and hope proclaiming the triumph over the grave".' On the page after this statement of the florists' timeless craftsmanship, you find a puff for the Aeolian Company Ltd, whose latest 'Vocalian's tone has been scientifically demonstrated to be nearer any voice it reproduces than has hitherto been possible in phonographic production'.

And so it goes on. Beer from Burton, 'famed' for the beverage since the thirteenth century; radiator tablets from 'Boilerine'; walking sticks from Briggs and their new Parisian partners ('a combination of French cleverness in design and British solidity of workmanship'); 'motor spirit' from British Petroleum; pianos from Broadwood . . . the juxtaposition of ancient and modern persists right through to the end of the alphabet, where Windovers's 'world renowned "Ralli" car' and Yost's typewriters are cheek by jowl with Mr Yapp's boots and the Zaehnsdorfs' bookbindings.

They were a wide-ranging and cosmopolitan collection, though united in their patriotism and loyalty to the Crown. That question of French or English on menus, for example, might seem trivial to some, but it was clearly significant for an organisation of Royal tradesmen. In 1925 the Council formally decided 'that the menu should as far as possible be printed in the English language and in old English type'. Unfortunately, this resolution was ignored and the following year a member of the council, Mr Verney Drew, wanted to know why. No satisfactory answer seems to have been forthcoming.

Although the dining and social aspect of the Association remained important, other issues began to interest it. Not only did it change its name after the Emergency General Meeting of 1896, but it assumed new functions. In an important change in wording the Association pledged itself to act 'against the representation by any person or persons, company, society or body without the authority of Her Majesty or other sufficient authority, that such person or persons company, society or body enjoys or enjoy Royal patronage or the patronage of a Government Department'.

Stripped of its Victorian bureaucratese, this means that the Association was assuming a watchdog role. Anyone pretending to be a Royal tradesman would be taken to task by the Warrant Holders and prevented from doing so.

At times this acquisition of power seems to have gone to their collective head. At the council meeting of 29 February 1912, for example, the following motion was passed: 'That the government be urgently requested to bring in legislation (with the knowledge and assent of His Majesty's Opposition) that shall terminate this most disastrous coal strike.' One copy was to be sent to Mr Asquith, the Prime Minister, and another to the Lord Chamberlain to be forwarded to The King. This curious *folie de grandeur* appears to have been a one-off. There is, needless to say, no evidence that it had any effect whatever on the coal strike, or indeed any other aspect of government policy!

The question of false pretences, however, crops up again and again. Indeed, the basement archives of the Association are full of dusty boxes containing files of evidence for presentation in court.

In 1927, Martin and Company of the Burlington Arcade were found to be displaying a Royal coat of arms by virtue of the fact that the father of the present Mr Martin had been 'honoured at the Great Exhibition of 1862'. The Council said he should take it off. That same year they ordered that the Emblem of Empire Industry issued by the 'All British Campaign' should be withdrawn.

From time to time a code was issued to explain the rules and regulations precisely. In 1938 one of these was issued

Upstairs – Garrard's staff craft exquisite jewellery high above the Regent Street showroom

A classic display in Simpson's of Piccadilly

*Game, set and match – the ultimate carnivore's cornucopia, presided over in traditional style at
Harrods' Food Hall*

to 'every advertising agent whose name is in the Advertisers Blue Book'. But still there were transgressions. In 1947 Daish's Hotel in Shanklin, Isle of Wight, was admonished for displaying the Royal arms. The proprietor sent an unsatisfactory reply. The same year there was an improper use of the arms on a pamphlet relating to the Portuguese International Industries Fair.

A publisher proposing a volume called *Royal London: Where Royalty Shops* was warned that it proceeded with the book at its own risk. A company marketing Royal Bittersweet Chocolate with reproductions of the orb, sceptre and crown was asked to desist.

When taken to court the miscreants were invariably found guilty and made to pay costs, though not usually fined. The charge was that by displaying the 'Royal Arms or Arms so nearly resembling the same' they were carrying on trade in a manner 'calculated to deceive' the public into thinking they were doing so under 'such authority as aforesaid'.

At times these cases gave rise to courtroom scenes worthy of Mr Justice Cocklecarrot himself. In 1907, for example, a firm of confectioners was prosecuted for displaying the arms on the labels of their toffee tins. Counsel for the defence deployed an original line of argument. 'The use of the Royal Arms', he said, 'you will see every day in the common form at the head of the *Daily Mail*, for instance, and at the head of *The Times* and many of these papers, not that anybody imagines there is any Royal Warrant for that. The Royal Arms, by themselves, do not amount to a representation.'

The prosecution were not having this.

'*The Times* is a registered Trade Mark,' they pointed out.

The defence were not to be dissuaded.

'*The Times* may be, but that does not apply to the *Daily Mail*'.

The prosecution was nonplussed.

'Well, I don't know. I cannot answer that.'

In Britain there has been a falling-off in such prosecutions as people have become aware of the principles involved. Only very occasionally does the Association have to take a stand and these days a gentle reprimand is all that is required.

Abroad, however, it has long been a rather different story. The writ does not run overseas in quite the same way and foreigners have always tended to play rather fast and loose with their claims to Royal 'endorsement'. The Association still retains a paid adviser in the United States, but one of the longest-running and most curious cases comes from France and involves a company called Old England of 12 Boulevard des Capucines, Paris.

In 1936 Old England was engaged in selling a line of country-wear which, as the name suggests, was extremely English in style and appearance. Their motto was 'Quality First' and they bolstered this claim with widespread and illegal use of the Royal coat of arms.

This was drawn to the attention of the British Embassy in Paris, who duly informed the Royal Warrant Holders' Association in London. Correspondence started, but before any satisfactory solution was reached, it was terminated by the advent of the Second World War and the German occupation. The case of Old England was consigned to the archives.

Some fifty years later, when the files were reopened in the course of researching this book, it transpired that the matter was technically still unresolved. In 1988, when the Secretary of the Warrant Holders, Commander Hugh Faulkner, looked into the matter he suddenly remembered that he himself had recently acquired an Old England garment. On inspecting the label inside the collar his worst fears were confirmed. Old England were still using something that looked terribly like a Francofied version of the Royal coat of arms. The Commander accordingly wrote to 12 Boulevard des Capucines and received a swift response from Old England's Managing Director, M. J. M. Henriquet. Yes, he said, Old England had indeed modified their business paper as requested by the Warrant Holders. The coat of arms used on their products had now been modified and a sample was enclosed. The stained-glass window at the top of the staircase at 12 Boulevard des Capucines, bearing a Royal coat of arms, had been there since 1886 and was registered as an ancient monument. During the war the Germans occupied part of the Old England premises and tried to get the window removed – but without success.

M. Henriquet concluded by saying that he hoped the above explanation was satisfactory and after due consideration the Association decided that on balance it was. Indeed, he has subsequently been to a Warrant Holders' banquet as the guest of Barry Reed, President of the Association in the year of its 150th anniversary.

So, the matter has finally been laid to rest, but the case of Old England should serve as a warning to all that the Royal Warrant Holders' Association has a long arm and a long memory, even if it is magnanimous and even humorous in protecting its interests.

Stuffed shirt – Gentleman's formal evening wear, suitable for Royal Warrant Holders' banquets, from Thresher and Glenny in the Strand

Mr Stephenson and Mr Brine at Lock's the Royal hatters in St. James', no more than a hat's throw from the Palace

THE WARRANT TODAY

'Guarded with jealous care'
(*The Official History of the Aberdeen Warrant Holders*)

Today, 150 years after that inaugural dinner at the Free-masons' Tavern, the Royal Warrant Holders' Association is still a dining club. That is not the same as saying that it is just, or only, a dining club. It is not the same as saying that it does not do fine charitable work. It is not the same as saying that it does not have what the historian of the Aberdeen Branch has described as 'a tendency to-wards the conservation of its special privileges' nor to deny that, in the same author's words, 'the Royal Arms and badge of membership are guarded with jealous care'. It is certainly not to suggest that the Association is com-posed of anything other than the very best of British trade and industry.

Nevertheless and notwithstanding, it is certain that the high point of the Royal Warrant Holders' year is the annual banquet, held every autumn in the ballroom of Grosvenor House in Park Lane. This is the Warrant Holders – or, to use the more prosaic and descriptive term still in use north of the border, the Royal tradesmen – at their most clubbable, their most loyal and their most proud.

On one recent November night a keen social historian would have done well to be a fly on the wall at Grosvenor House to try to make sense of the gathering of some 1,500 guests: the ladies – a significant minority in long dresses; the gentlemen in white tie and tails save for those Scottish members, the President foremost among them, who favoured the kilt. In recent years some gentlemen had taken to coming in black tie and dinner jacket. This was felt to be lowering the tone and the council sent round a stiff edict reminding members that it was a white-tie dinner. Nearly everyone complied.

As in Victorian days, there was not just a menu but a slim volume of significant details. On the cover the simple badge of the Association, a Royal coat of arms, circled with the words 'The Royal Warrant Holders' Association'. Under the arms it says, simply, 'By Authority'.

The President for this dinner was Graeme J. Wilson, a builder's merchant from Aberdeen. Ebullient, extrovert, short, stout and jolly, he had created, as all good presidents of all dining clubs are wont to do, an evening in his own image.

Item: the menu. The food was entirely Scottish, to wit: poached darne of salmon in sorrel sauce; haggis wi'chappit tatties and neeps and auld critter sauce; medallions of venison in a juniper-berry sauce, new pota-toes in their jackets and creamed spinach; iced drambuie parfait; Orkney and caboc cheeses and oat cakes. Wine is not a Scottish product, though they have always had a nose for good claret, and the Château la Combe des Dames 1982 was shipped by Findlater Mackie Todd. Whisky is entirely Scots and it was a twelve-year-old Highland Park which took the place of liqueur or cognac.

It is not mere frivolity to linger over such food and drink, for lives depend on it. There are many Scots Warrant Holders who earn their living from it, whether they are large companies such as Baxters of Fochabers or Pinneys, the smoked fish people from Dumfries, or small village grocers, butchers or fishmongers. This was not only a dinner to enjoy but a dinner which served as a shop window.

Item: the toasts. Not as many nor as long as in Victorian times, but still demonstrably loyal. The Queen, Queen Elizabeth The Queen Mother, The Prince Philip Duke of Edinburgh, The Prince and Princess of Wales and the other members of the Royal Family. It is traditional too for the President, early in the proceedings, to announce that loyal greetings have been sent to Her

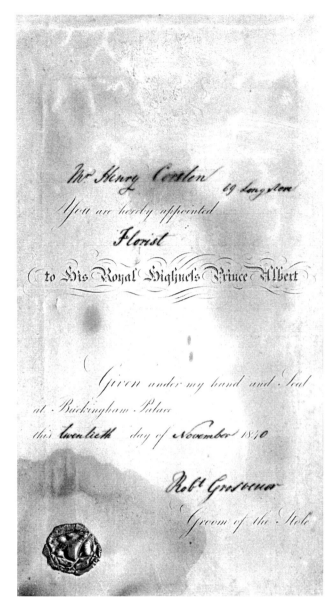

*Letter of appointment to Prince Albert's Florist signed by
'The Groom of the Stole'*

Majesty and that these have been gracefully acknowledged. It is a reminder that this is not any old white-tie dinner but one one with a truly regal significance.

Immediately after the loyal toasts there was a toast which reminded one that despite the flummery there is a steely edge to modern Warrant Holding. 'British Trade and Industry' was the proposition put with some eloquence by the Business Editor of the *Yorkshire Post* and responded to by John Marks, the Vice-President and boss of Edward Sharps, the confectioners. After that the Association's health was proposed by the Chief Scout, who was there primarily because Graeme Wilson is a

passionate scouter. The Warrant Holders have no great problem attracting the great and the good to their table.

Item: music. Not as extensive and elaborate as in Victorian days but a medley of mainly Scottish airs provided by the Regimental Band of the Argyll and Sutherland Highlanders. This is not, perhaps, tremendously significant in itself, but a well-informed fly on the wall would, of course, be aware that the trim military figure at Table 30 was John Weatherston, MBE, BEM, formerly Pipe Major of the Argylls and now a Royal Warrant Holder as the joint owner of R. G. Hardie and Co. of Glasgow, 'Maker of the World's Finest Bagpipes'. Warrant Holders are everywhere.

Item: the guests. At the top table the mixture was essentially Royal Household and Warrant-Holding top brass. Among the past Presidents one noticed Veuve Clicquot Champagne, Twinings Tea and Roberts Radios. Among the Royal Household, the Lord Chamberlain, the Manager of the Royal Studs, the Keeper of the Privy Purse, the Master of the Household, the Queen Mother's Treasurer and the significant, though to outsiders unknown, figure of John Titman Esq., CVO, who is Secretary of the Lord Chamberlain's Office and of the Royal Household Tradesmen's Warrants Committee.

As for guests in the body of the church, there were 148 tables, each seating ten, and perhaps the only way to hint at the diversity of those present is to play scrupulously fair and light on those at the first and last tables as well as those in the absolute middle. Table 2 was composed of the Ardath Tobacco Company Ltd; Mrs Valerie Bennett-Levy, who makes the posies for the annual Maundy Thursday service; Joseph Allen, the proprietor of the specialist Horseman's Bookshop just behind Buckingham Palace, and Stanley Gibbons Ltd, the stamp people. All with guests. Table 74 was ten from Greenaway-Harrison, the printers, and you get an even clearer idea of the range of Warrant Holders when you consider that they were sandwiched between ten from Whitbread on Table 75 and representatives of Sandicliffe Garage, Slumberland Ltd and the Royal British Legion Poppy Factory at Table 73. Table 148 was ten from Kango Wolf Power Tools.

The banquet is a rare and precious opportunity to catch so many Warrant Holders on the hoof. The only other comparable event is the Hilton luncheon in May, which is traditionally attended by the Lord Mayor of London. The other Associations, centred on Edinburgh, Aberdeen, Sandringham and Windsor, also have annual celebrations, but these are necessarily on a much smaller scale.

Coffeemen and woman – the Higgins family behind the counter of their coffee shop in London's Duke Street

ABOVE Before: Tables laid at Grosvenor House in anticipation of the annual banquet of the Royal
Warrant Holders' Association. The Monarch's tradesmen have been dining together every year
since 1840

OPPOSITE And after: Bibbed and tuckered Warrant Holders – white tie and tails are de rigueur – animate the
previous page's still life. The High Table with President, Council members and honoured guests is
on the right

It is tempting to generalise on the basis of this great dinner, but as one looks down from the balcony on the hundreds of starched shirt fronts fogged by a light-blue haze of post-prandial cigar smoke and accompanied by the convivial hum of well-dined chatter, it is difficult to be too sure. The differences are so acute. There are great companies represented here and small; ancient firms with genteel premises in the heart of London's West End and modern ones with functional factories in the furthest reaches of the realm; one-man bands and multi-nationals. There are competitors and rivals from within the same trade or industry and others whose lives do not impinge on one another except at times like this.

It is only the Warrant that really unites them. It gives them a profound sense of privileged loyalty and a sense of being singled out as among the very best in Britain and, therefore, the world. Having a Warrant makes them special. And though everyone is careful not to say so, especially on a night like this, it isn't at all bad for business.

In the cold light of day the holding of a Royal Warrant still seems glamorous and exciting. Travelling about the British Isles in search of the essence of what that resplendent coat of arms and those magic words 'By Appointment' actually mean to the holders of a Warrant, it is impossible to find anyone who is blasé about it.

Warrant Holders often find it difficult to describe precisely what the honour means to them. This is partly a result of that ancient British habit of stiff upper lip, inability to show emotion and an obsessive horror of being caught 'showing off' or 'swanking'. To take too much obvious pleasure in holding the Warrant is 'bad form'.

But the pride is always there – often understated, inarticulate or even silent. At least one Warrant Holder was so shy that he pleaded not even to be mentioned in this book. Yet for a start there is scarcely a Warrant Holder in the land who does not display the Royal coat of arms prominently at the entrance to the premises. This is the entitlement of every Warrant Holder, even though some are surprisingly hazy about the rules. At least one Warrant Holder did not put up the Royal arms by his front door until recently because he did not think it was allowed. A quick word with the Secretary of the Association assured him that it was.

Apart from putting the coat of arms outside their shop, factory or office as a public demonstration of their Royal Appointment, Warrant Holders are also entitled to display the Royal arms inside provided you can't see more than one example at any one time.

In addition they can display the Warrant itself on the wall. The modern Warrant is an impressive document which now follows an unwavering standard form. In the example of the notional case of a fishmonger named Fish, the Warrant would be signed by the Lord Chamberlain and would say, in beautiful copperplate print: 'By command of The Queen the firm of "Frederick Fish and Sons Ltd" has been appointed into the place and quality of fishmongers to Her Majesty.' Note, however, that the Warrant itself is not granted to Fish and Sons but to an individual within that company. Fish and Sons may be The Queen's fishmongers, but the Warrant will be held by Mr John Smith. The rules stipulate that Mr Smith must be a director of Fish and Sons and if Fish abuse their Warrant in any way it is Mr Smith who will be held to account for it.

Warrant Holders are also allowed to put the Royal arms on their writing paper, though they are expected to do so discreetly. The same is true of commercial vehicles and packaging. It is quite instructive to make a swift check of the kitchen store cupboard and see with what good taste and discretion Warrant Holders do display the coat of arms. I have in front of me, as I write, five items you'd expect to find in any self-respecting British kitchen.

One jar of mustard where the arms, black on gold, are minutely stamped below the 's' and 't' of mustard with a tiny legend to say 'By appointment to Her Majesty Queen Elizabeth II, Manufacturers of Mustard and Sauces, Colman's of Norwich'.

One jar of mango chutney with the arms immediately above the word Sharwood in gold on green with similar wording ('Manufacturers of chutney and purveyors of Indian curry powder').

One tin of Cadbury's drinking chocolate with the arms, gold on magenta, very small and just above the note saying that if you don't like the chocolate you must complain to the Consumer Services Manager.

One jar of marmalade with the arms, in black on white, above the words 'Frank Cooper's'.

One box of Earl Grey teabags, with the arms in white on black just above the word 'Twinings', which is itself black on gold.

In every case the position and colour scheme is different and in every case the arms and the legend beneath are tiny and occur only once per package. In other words, no vulgar exploitation of the Warrant is allowed. You would not be allowed to produce 'Royal Oxford Marmalade' with a coat of arms several times bigger than the word 'Marmalade'; much less include a line that said 'As eaten by Her Majesty The Queen on toast for breakfast daily'. That would be very bad form and you would be struck off instantly. Yet the implication of the discreet, tiny coat of arms which *is* allowed is very much the same. Potential consumers are expected to assume that The Queen is indeed in the habit of using all these items regularly. And the message, however subliminal, is that if you too consume them, then an infinitesimal part of the magic of Monarchy will rub off on you. Of course, the message must be imparted with the utmost good taste, lest the Crown be thought to be endorsing a commercial product for commercial gain. But provided the taste is good – in every sense – the message may be sent.

Royal service involves absolute discretion. The official press brief issued by the Royal Warrant Holders' Association states that 'Warrant Holders are never allowed to reveal any details of the service given to the Royal Household or to contribute to any article concerning The Queen or the Royal Family. So naturally you will find that Warrant Holders are never prepared to discuss their Royal Warrant with members of the Press or indeed, any persons unknown to them.' In practice, of course, individual Warrant Holders *do* commit minor indiscretions and even the most respectable of them have let slip minor – and quite

Don't leave home without it – Gerald Bodmer and staff in S. Launer and Co's London workshop where they make handbags for The Queen

OPPOSITE *A lasting memorial – Eric Lobb of Lobb's, the shoemakers, standing amid a veritable Who's Who of customers' wooden feet*

ABOVE *High rise with Heinz – 57 varieties of Warrant Holding tin cans*

All the better to eat you with – Arthur Price of England, The Queen's Cutler and Silversmith, with his knives and forks

harmless – revelations with the proviso that they must under no circumstances appear in print. And the rule is not as absolute as it looks. It is perfectly proper and is, indeed, perfectly accepted for Valerie Bennett-Levy to give the ingredients of the nosegays that she makes annually for the Maundy Thursday service. It is perfectly proper and accepted for Her Majesty's kiltmakers to give chapter and verse about the famous Balmoral tartan or even the provenance of the kilts worn by The Queen's grandchildren.

There are other things about which it would be grossly improper for a Warrant Holder to talk. So much so that they cannot even be mentioned in a book like this. In between there is an enormous and difficult grey area which has to be governed by individual and corporate common sense and good taste. It is a curious paradox, however, that the more someone knows about the Royal Family, be he Warrant Holder or not, the less he will tell you. This should, incidentally, serve as a warning to anyone who expects to find tabloid tittle-tattle in these pages. Being 'authorised' means having access one would not otherwise enjoy, but it also imposes constraints of a sort one would not normally have to conform to.

At the time of writing there are some 870 Warrant Holders, but the numbers fluctuate constantly. Every year some twenty or thirty companies are granted a Warrant for the first time, while a similar number lose it for reasons such as bankruptcy, amalgamation, take-over (the coat of arms must *never* be used in a take-over), death or other 'change of character'. And, of course, as often happens, a Warrant Holder may lose his Warrant because his company ceases to supply the goods or services for which he was originally granted the Warrant.

Four members of the Royal Family grant Warrants and of these Her Majesty The Queen is by far the most prolific, with more than 600. The Duke of Edinburgh, by contrast, grants only a twelfth of that number. Part of the reason for this is that, as far as Warrants are concerned, The Queen and The Duke operate the Monarchical equivalent of a joint account wherever appropriate. Thus, for example, Roberts Radios have a Warrant to supply radios to The Queen, The Queen Mother and The Prince of Wales. Prince Philip also listens to a Roberts radio, but he does not issue a separate Warrant on the grounds that the radio to which he listens is The Queen's too. He does, however, grant his own Warrant to Artistic Iron Products, who make his carriages for competitive driving, to Stephens Brothers, who make some of his shirts and

Balmorality – The Queen Mother with young Princesses Elizabeth and Margaret in tartan from Kinloch Anderson

socks, and to Autoscan Ltd, who make his power filing systems.

The Prince of Wales has granted his own individual Warrant only since 1980. He has now granted more Warrants than his father.

Queen Elizabeth The Queen Mother has over 200, a reflection of her longevity and the fact that she continues to maintain residences at Royal Lodge in Windsor Great Park, Birkhall near Balmoral and the Castle of Mey in Caithness as well as Clarence House in London.

The Queen's Warrants are further subdivided into five separate categories: the Privy Purse, the Royal Household, the Lord Chamberlain's Office, the Royal Mews and the Royal Collection.

The Privy Purse, under the Keeper of the Privy Purse, also The Queen's Treasurer, deals with those items in the Royal budget classified as 'private expenditure as Sovereign'. The Royal finances are almost impossibly

Sheila Pickles of Penhaligon's, Manufacturers of The Duke of Edinburgh's Toilet Requisites, with bottles of same and her very own scented book of 'Love'

*Anne Cocker of Cocker's Roses in Aberdeen with a porcelain replica of the Company's unique rose
'Silver Jubilee', specially created for the occasion*

complex, but the Privy Purse is financed by the revenue from the Duchy of Lancaster. This is exempt from tax and covers such items as robes and uniforms which are necessary for The Queen's personal wear but only because she has to wear them in her role as Monarch. It also covers the maintenance of Sandringham and Balmoral, which are 'private' Royal residences, unlike Windsor Castle and Buckingham Palace.

In practice this means that all those firms dealing with agriculture come under the Privy Purse. So do bagpipes, boilers and builders, and nearly all the fuel merchants, apart from John Mackaness, who makes the charcoal for the Royal barbecues and comes under the Royal Household. When you come to tailors, however, you will find firms serving all four different departments. S. Redmayne Ltd of Wigton, Cumbria, make the jackets for the Royal gamekeepers and come under the Privy Purse; Horne Brothers are under the Royal Household because they make livery for the Royal servants at Buckingham Palace; J. Dege and Sons Ltd of Savile Row come under the Lord Chamberlain's Office; Redwood and Feller of Rochester Row deal with the Royal Mews.

The Master of the Household's department used to be the Lord Steward's Department and is financed by the Civil List, which is the annual grant made by act of parliament for the upkeep of the Monarchy in its official as opposed to private capacity (which, as we have seen, is dealt with by the Privy Purse). This is a difficult distinction but on consulting the Warrant Holders' official blue book we find, for instance, that the Royal Household deals with baggage labels, bedding, biscuits, breakfast cereals and butchers.

The Lord Chamberlain's office used to deal with booksellers (antiquarian), bookbinders, button makers, calligraphers, computers and the crown jewellers, though some of these have now been hived off into the new Royal Collection's department. The Lord Chamberlain is officially the Head of the Household, although other departments are more or less autonomous. His multifarious duties used to include the censoring of plays (the last time this right was exercised was in 1968, when he banned *Hair*) and now includes the appointment of the Poet Laureate and the Queen's Bargemaster, and the appearance of the Court Circular. As we have seen, it is his signature which appears at the foot of all Royal Warrants, irrespective of which department they are issued through. But his own department is directly responsible for comparatively few Warrant Holders.

The Royal Mews is probably the most clearly defined department of all. The man in charge is the Master of the Horse, though this is largely a ceremonial position which involves riding as close to the Queen as possible whenever she is travelling on horseback or in a carriage. Mastership is an honorary position and the day-to-day running of the Mews is the responsibility of the Crown Equerry. His job is to deal with the horses, the carriages and the motor cars. Those whose Warrant means that they deal with the Mews include the Horseman's Bookshop, a number of bootmakers, five coach and carriage painters, two paint makers, a farrier and sundry motor vehicle manufacturers, including Austin Rover, Ford, Jaguar, Land Rover, Rolls Royce and Vauxhall. After the labyrinthine intricacies and overlaps in the other three departments, the purchasing of the Royal Mews seems mercifully straightforward and clear-cut.

In 1987 twenty-nine new Warrant Holders joined the Association: two held The Prince of Wales's Warrant, five The Queen Mother's and twenty-two The Queen's; there were no new members holding The Duke of Edinburgh's Warrant. This breakdown reflects the trend of the moment quite accurately. The Prince of Wales's two Warrants were for fine bone china and gardening materials; The Queen Mother's for calendars, radios and TVs, protein balancers, vitamins and mineral supplements, biscuits and agricultural machinery. The Queen's ranged from printers to quilters, from suppliers of diamond-braced field gates to suppliers of glass table-tops. Many of the new Warrant Holders were obviously small local tradesmen and only one – Royal Doulton, who were awarded The Prince of Wales's Warrant – could be described as a grand household name.

In order to qualify for the Royal Warrant a trader must supply the Warrant Grantor with goods over a period of at least three years. The key word in this context is 'substantial'. If our fishmonger, Fish and Sons, provided only one or two salmon over the three years, then he would not receive the Warrant. If, however, he had been sending in regular supplies of cod, whiting, roes, salmon and exotic foreign species for the Royal table, as well as supplying the staff dining-room with more run of the mill comestibles, then he would have every likelihood of success. He would, of course, have to complete a lengthy application form and supply as many receiptts as possible. This formal application would then be considered at the annual meeting of the Royal Household Tradesmen's Warrants Committee. This committee, whose delib-

A policeman's lot – helmet badges being assembled by Firmin, the Royal buttonmakers

erations are extremely confidential, would consider not just the receipts but the quality of the goods provided and the standard of the service given. It is axiomatic that a Warrant is an honour and not just a statement of fact. If the committee were to find in Fish's favour, then a recommendation would be made to the head of the relevant household. The final decision on a Royal Warrant is made by The Queen, The Queen Mother, The Duke of Edinburgh or Prince Charles and in that sense it is and always has been a personal recognition of personal service, and not just a rubber stamp on a committee vote.

In the normal course of events a Warrant will be reviewed after ten years.

In both theory and practice, therefore, a newly appointed Warrant Holder has only to maintain his standards and to continue to supply the Royal Family's needs in order to retain the Warrant. As a Warrant Holder he can display, if not flaunt, the Royal coat of arms; wear a Royal Warrant Holders' Association tie or headscarf (tasteful gold monogram on dark blue); and attend the formal luncheon and dinner – not to mention the Association Open Golf Day. On his behalf the Association sends loyal greetings to members of the Royal Family on their birthdays, and flowers on special occasions, such as The Queen and Prince Philip's Ruby Wedding.

The Association also has a charity fund. The tradition is for the Lord Mayor of London to be presented with a cheque for his Appeal Fund at the annual luncheon and also for the President of the RWHA to direct a donation towards a charity of his choice. The local Associations also raise money for charity. In 1987, for instance, the Sandringham Branch gave £1,650 to the Sail Training Association.

Today's Warrant Holders are a remarkable cross-section of trade and industry. 'British' trade and industry might be nearer the mark, but it would not be wholly accurate.

John Gamble of Kleen-Way, Royal Chimney Sweeps, up a chimney somewhere near Windsor

The world's most distinctive radiator grille bar – surely? – none

Although the number of foreign Warrant Holders has greatly diminished since Queen Victoria's time, there are still some things the British cannot do. Making champagne is one. There are a number of French companies who hold Warrants as 'Purveyors of Champagne' – a legacy of King Edward VII's well-known preference. Cherry Heering of Copenhagen have the Warrant for Cherry Brandy and Hine for Cognac. Roger & Gallet have it for soap. Siegert and Sons of Trinidad still make The Queen's Angostura bitters. Rochelle Thomas, the Bermuda art dealers, have a Warrant and so do Hardy Brothers, the Australian silversmiths.

Most Warrant Holders, however, are British and the few non-British grantees serve to prove the rule. It may seem chauvinistic to claim that the Royal Warrant is a synonym for 'Best of British', but that is not so far from the mark. It would be surprising if it was. If the British Royal Family is in the business of handing out accolades, one would expect them to be handed out only to the best.

One or two oddities have explanations; one or two others defy them. There are no solicitors, no surgeons and no stockbrokers among the Warrant Holders. This results from the ancient distinction between the professional person and the man in trade. The Warrant Holders are trade. 'Professionals' have, in their time, been admitted to Warrant Holders' functions, but they are not and cannot be Warrant Holders themselves.

The geographical distribution is not precisely what you might expect. It is odd, for instance, that there should be so few Welsh Warrant Holders. This is partly because there is no Royal palace, official or unofficial, in Wales.

Apart from London, where there are almost 250 Warrant Holders, the biggest concentrations are around the Royal residences at Windsor, Sandringham, Balmoral and Holyroodhouse. The Queen Mother has Warrant Holders as far north as Wick, Thurso and even Kirkwall in the Orkneys – all within striking distance of her home at the Castle of Mey in Caithness.

The map of British Warrant Holders reflects the position of the Royal homes – heavy concentrations in the South-East, in East Anglia and in Scotland; comparatively little in the South-West and Wales until you hit an emerging pocket of local tradesmen in Prince Charles's Cotswolds; not a lot in the North of England either.

More important than geography, however, is the way in which the Warrant Holders reflect every aspect of modern Royalty: Royalty as a symbol of the national spirit; Royalty as landowner and farmer; Royalty as racehorse owner and breeder; Royalty as custodian of ancient and historic houses; Royalty as – almost – showbiz! In a sense, too, the Warrant Holders mirror many of the characteristics of modern Britain: traditional craftsmanship on the one hand, high-tech on the other; dynamic entrepreneurial skills in some places, innate and unchanging conservatism in others.

Today the Royal Warrant Holders' Association operates from offices immediately opposite the back entrance to Buckingham Palace. It is a particularly appropriate headquarters for the Royal tradesmen, making for mutually simple access which helps to ease an already smooth and well-oiled relationship between the Royal Household and those who supply it.

The small permanent secretariat is presided over by Hugh Faulkner, a retired Naval Commander, who has been in the job since retiring from active service in 1979. As the Assistant Secretary, Ann Wycherley, served in the WRNS there is a distinctly senior service sense about the place. One feels, visiting the Warrant Holders' headquarters, almost as if one is calling in on the Flag Officer, Malta, in the days when the island was still the HQ of the Mediterranean Fleet.

The Commander's room, with Royal portraits and long mahogany table, doubles as a boardroom. The secretaries sit outside and there are records in the basement, well catalogued and ordered some years ago thanks to the good offices of the Business Archives Council.

Apart from the permanent staff there is a President and a Vice-President, who both hold office for a year only. The Vice-President is the heir to the President and both are drawn from the 'Council'. As ex-Presidents automatically retain their seat on the Council and as Warrant Holders seem to be remarkably long-lived, this body is expanding regularly and at the time of writing comprises thirty-four.

The only other permanent officer is the Honorary Treasurer, a post held by Sir Edward Rayne, who first joined the Council in 1959. For many years he was Chairman and Managing Director of H. and M. Rayne Ltd and held the Warrant for making The Queen's shoes. He was President of the Association in 1964 and has taken a close interest in its affairs ever since. 'His advice,' says the Commander, 'is freely available and frequently sought by successive Presidents as well as the Council.'

Today the Association rationalises its activities under three main headings. First, it helps the Lord Chamberlain to 'police' the use of the Royal Warrant. They have to ensure that those who have it use it correctly and also see to it that those who don't do not try to deceive people into thinking that they have. If legal action is needed to prevent tradesmen using the Royal arms illicitly, then it is the responsibility of the Association to take the offender to court. Luckily this seldom happens nowadays. 'A polite but firm letter from the Association's office usually does the trick,' says the Commander.

Role two is to act as the official channel of communication between member firms and the Royal Household on everything to do with their Royal Warrant. The Association helps firms get the Warrant, helps them use it properly and helps them keep it, provided they continue to provide the high standard of goods or services which is expected of Royal Warrant Holders, both by their Royal clients and by the general public. This means that there has to be a very close working relationship with the staff of the Households who issue Warrants. This has been achieved for years now, notably through the principal Palace 'linkman', John Titman, Secretary of the Royal Household Tradesmen's Warrants Committee.

'Finally,' says the Commander, 'the Association is charged with promoting the interests of Royal Warrant Holding firms generally.' This is mainly done at the large and rather grand London luncheon and annual banquet. 'Each of the four local associations,' he continues, 'Windsor, Sandringham, Aberdeen and Edinburgh, has its own President and Honorary Secretary and organises its own functions, but each comes under the umbrella of the London-based National Association. The National President visits all the local associations during his term of office.'

One of the provisions in the 1907 Royal charter was that members should look after those less fortunate than themselves. In the ten years up to the time of writing the Association gave almost £200,000 to charity. In addition, there is a loyal tradition of making special gifts to members of the Royal Family to mark Royal Weddings, birthdays and other notable dates.

But the essential function of the Association is a serious constitutional one. 'We are the representatives of the Crown whenever there are commercial transgressions involving the use of the Warrant,' says Sir Edward, 'and it is our duty to maintain the prestige and position of suppliers to the Royal Family.'

Hi-tech hattery – Mr Parker of Lock's, the Royal hatters, steaming a hat before stretching it

Royal brushmaker David Coward at Mere, Wilts., bestrides the whole process of making one of his brushes from the very beginning

Three generations of Bodenhams at the Jermyn Street shop of their company, Royal perfumers
J Floris Ltd

THE BEST OF BRITAIN

Mrs Moony constructs The Queen's Remembrance Day wreath at the Royal British Legion Poppy Factory in Richmond-upon-Thames. The Duke of Edinburgh's and The Prince of Wales's are in the background

POMP AND CIRCUMSTANCE

'The balm, the sceptre and the ball
the sword, the mace, the crown imperial'
(Shakespeare: *Henry V*)

There is one moment in the annual calendar of the United Kingdom when what Walter Bagehot described as the mystic reverence and religious allegiance which no legislature can manufacture are more closely focused on the Royal Family than at any other. On the second Sunday of every November the muted massed bands play the sad songs to which the young men of 1914 marched away to Flanders and to death. The disabled and blinded, old comrades, leaders of the political parties, foreign ambassadors and a great host of ordinary people gather in Whitehall by Lutyens's bleak Cenotaph to pay their respects to the dead of Britain's wars. And under the remorseless scrutiny of the television cameras the national mourning is led by The Queen, Prince Philip and Prince Charles. In every button-hole there is a red poppy and when the Royal Family walk to the Cenotaph each member places an individual wreath of those same red poppies.

All these, from the grand personal Royal wreaths to the humblest individual boutonnière, have been made at a factory in Richmond, Surrey, once described, aptly, as 'a truly human war memorial'. The factory is deliberately run in an old-fashioned way with as much as possible being done by hand, often slowly and painstakingly by people who would otherwise be unable to find work. In this way almost 1,500 disabled men and women have been assisted since the prototype factory was set up with five disabled men in a small room in Bermondsey in 1922.

The first Poppy Appeal was in 1921, when artificial French poppies were used. It raised over £106,000. Today it raises millions.

The idea began during the second Battle of Ypres, in 1915, when a Canadian Medical Officer, Colonel John Macrae, pencilled a poem into a leaf from his despatch book.

In Flanders' fields the poppies blow
Between the crosses, row on row
That mark our place: and in the sky
The larks, still bravely singing, fly
Scarce heard among the guns below.

We are the dead. Short days ago
We lived, felt dawn, saw sunset glow,
Loved and were loved, and now we lie
    In Flanders' fields.

Take up our quarrel with the foe;
To you from failing hands we throw
The torch: be yours to hold it high.
If ye break faith with us who die
We shall not sleep, though poppies grow
    In Flanders' fields.

In 1918 Macrae was brought, wounded, to a hospital on the French coast. One evening the nurses wheeled him out on to a balcony to look across the Channel towards England. 'Tell them this,' he said to his doctor. 'If ye break faith with us who die, we shall not sleep.'

That night he died.

An American, Moina Michael, responded to his challenge, first in verse and later in practice. Two days before the Armistice Miss Michael was given a sum of money by the overseas War Secretaries of her employers the YMCA, who were meeting in her house. She immediately said that she was going to spend the money on twenty-five red poppies, and when she had bought them she distributed them among the secretaries, all of whom wore them in remembrance of Macrae and the Flanders dead.

So the custom was born. Over the years many members of the Royal Family have visited the poppy makers in Richmond. In 1926 The Prince of Wales laid the foundation stone of a block of flats for employees nearby; in 1933 The Princess Royal opened a new factory; and in 1972 the organisation was allowed to incorporate the prefix 'Royal' into its title, so that it became 'The Royal British Legion Poppy Factory', entitled to display the Royal coat of arms as 'Poppy Manufacturers and Suppliers of rosettes to Her Majesty The Queen'.

And every November at the Cenotaph as The Queen steps forward with her hand-crafted wreath from Richmond, that special link between the Monarchy and those who died or were disabled in the country's wars is there for all to see.

On really grand ceremonial occasions no Royal male is really complete without his sword. This will naturally come from Wilkinson Sword, who have held the Warrant since Victorian days, although their history dates back to the eighteenth century when George III's gun maker took on an apprentice named James Wilkinson and turned to sword cutlery. The modern company, whose name is perhaps more popularly associated with razor blades, makes swords for all the British armed services and for those of innumerable foreign governments. The Queen, of course, uses a Wilkinson sword for dubbing knights at investitures. But do not be fooled by their ceremonial beauty. Wilkinson are proud of the fact that they are weapons too. A Wilkinson sword is made to kill.

Another annual ceremony, with different traditions and different Warrant Holding suppliers, is Maundy Thursday. This is one of those customs whose origins are, as its official historian has observed, 'veiled in obscurity'. It is said to derive from the Last Supper, after which Jesus 'took a towel and girded himself', washed the feet of his disciples and said, in the words of St John's Gospel, 'If I then, your Lord and Master, have washed your feet, ye also ought to wash one another's feet. For I have given you an example that ye should do as I have done to you.' This was an order and in Latin order is *mandatum*, which became corrupted into Maundy.

The first reference to the British Maundy comes from St Augustine in around AD 600. In 1213 King John distributed thirteen pennies to thirteen men at Rochester Castle and thereafter most of the Royal Family seem to have come together every Maundy Thursday to distribute thirteen pennies and some clothing to thirteen needy men. An account of Queen Mary I's Maundy in 1556 shows that she not only washed people's feet but also made an uncomfortable perambulation on her knees to decide who should receive her beautiful purple fur-lined gown.

Henry IV began the custom of relating the number of recipients to the sovereign's age. Elizabeth I appears to have continued her brother Edward's notion of 'ransoming' her gown rather than giving it away, so that each person received twenty shillings. There is a full account of Elizabeth's 1572 Maundy in which her laundress, Sub-Almoner and Lord High Almoner all washed feet before The Queen entered the room and did the same – kissing the poor people's feet into the bargain. Afterwards The Queen gave each poor person enough broadcloth to make a gown, a pair of sleeves, half a side of salmon, the same of ling, six red herrings and six loaves.

Charles I did not wash feet; Charles II, despite the plague, did and so did William III.

In 1724 the rules were changed so that women no longer got clothing but received money instead. The reason was that they had insisted on trying their clothes on then and there, thus creating 'a most unseemly bustle'. In 1731 forty-eight poor men and forty-eight poor women were given boiled beef, shoulders of mutton and money to the value of £4 a head. Their feet were washed by the Archbishop of York but not by The King.

In 1891, after a long period in which the ceremony was held in Whitehall, it moved to Westminster Abbey, where it stayed for sixty years. By now all gifts had been translated into money in small leather purses, which for some two centuries had been handed out not by the Monarch but by a representative – usually the Lord High Almoner. In 1932, however, King George V attended in person and since then the Maundy has nearly always been distributed by the Monarch. In the present reign the custom grew of holding the service in great churches – mainly cathedrals – throughout the kingdom.

Feet washing was discontinued in the nineteenth century but the officials still wear the old linen towels over the right shoulder. For centuries now the principal actors in this pageant have carried nosegays to ward off disease. For thirty years these have been made up by Mrs Valerie Bennett-Levy of Haslemere in Surrey. In recognition of this annual service Mrs Bennett-Levy has, for more than a quarter of a century, held the Royal Warrant as The Queen's 'Supplier of Nosegays'.

Maundy Thursday – Her Majesty The Queen holding the traditional posy made by Warrant Holder Valerie Bennett-Levy

Mrs Bennett-Levy does not run a business. 'Since it is both an honour and a great joy,' she says, 'I refuse to accept payment.' The nosegays are always made up the night before the service and each one consists of nine daffodils, fifteen pieces of white stock, twelve of Cheerfulness, fourteen bunches of violets, twelve bunches of thyme and twenty bunches of cupressus. Every herb and every flower is separately wired.

The traditional Maundy purses are produced every eight or nine years at Barrow Leather Ltd's Corunna Works, just south of the River Thames in Battersea. They took on the purse-making when, in 1963, they bought a company called Clarke's, who had themselves taken over after the previous makers, James and Co. of Old Bailey, disappeared. Much of Barrow Hepburn's work is in the safety equipment line, making belts and harnesses for construction, oil and mining industries, but happily for the traditionalists they still keep a toehold in traditional leather-making. Apart from the purses they make saddles for the Household Cavalry and the famous Despatch boxes for Her Majesty's Ministers.

Few companies are more steeped in ceremony than Ede and Ravenscroft, who hold all four Warrants as Robe Makers. Their premises in Chancery Lane, the very heart of legal London, seem totally Dickensian, but the company goes much further back than Dickens. They claim to be 'probably' the oldest tailors in the world and have held the Warrant of thirteen successive British Monarchs. Ravenscrofts were making robes in 1689 just after the Glorious Revolution.

Perhaps the most significant breakthrough in the company's fortunes came in the early nineteenth century when Humphrey Ravenscroft designed and patented the modern 'forensic' wig. The barrister's wig came in 1822 and the full-bottomed wig in 1839. Hitherto the wig had been cumbersome and time-consuming, always having to be dressed and powdered and otherwise adjusted, but Ravenscroft's invention revolutionised wig-wearing. 'Making a forensic wig,' he explained, 'the curls thereof are constructed on a principal [sic] to supersede the necessity of frizzing, curling or using hard pomatum and for forming the curls in a way not to be uncurled, and also for the tails of the wig not to requiree tying in dressing; and further the imposssibility of any person untying them.' Wigs such as this have survived every attempt at legal reform – including the latest.

Maundy Purses for the Royal Maundy being hand-stitched at Barrow Leather's Corunna Works in South London

Valerie Bennett-Levy and her helpers bringing the Maundy posies to Lichfield Cathedral after working on them through the night

A legal whig under construction at Ede and Ravenscroft of Chancery Lane. They are outfitters to the bar and robe makers to Royalty

Nowadays their horsehair wigs, specially treated as a precaution against diseases such as anthrax, are said to be 'the most durable and therefore the most economical item of legal attire that a barrister can buy'. Every year they give a prize of a full barrister's outfit to one student from each of the Inns of Court.

As far as robes are concerned, Ede and Ravenscroft claim that 'most university and civic gowns and judicial gowns and wigs' have been made by them. They are impressive exporters and one of their specialities is designing brand-new academic or ceremonial outfits. The Prince of Wales's Investiture robe was an Ede and Ravenscroft original. So are the robes of most University Chancellors and much academic dress. They made the robes for the first woman judge, the first woman recorder and the first City Aldermen. They offer 'quality footwear and hosiery' as well as hats. Indeed, when it comes to hats

they say, 'In addition to academic and municipal hats, special hats are made to order for diplomatic and ceremonial wear – tricornes, cocked and top hats of silk plush, trimmed with gold lace and plumes.' And just to add the finishing touch, they can provide 'jabots, stocks and cuffs, bands, collarettes, mourning bands and weepers'. If one ever needed a truly impressive outfit in which to process or preside, it is difficult to see where else one could possibly go.

There are moments when it seems that the Warrant Holders are as much of a dynasty as the Monarchy itself. M. W. G. Skinner holds The Queen's Warrant as Managing Director of J. Dege and Sons, the tailors of Clifford Street, Savile Row. His father held King George VI's Warrant through Wilkinson and Son and his father-in-law, W. R. Vincent of Vincents of Reading, once made The Queen's motor horseboxes. As for Dege and Sons, with their logo of sardonic fox mask surmounting crossed hunting horn and brush, they are relatively new Warrant Holders in this reign, but their forbears made robes for William IV, Queen Victoria and King George V, as well as making Queen Mary's coronation robes. Nowadays they are not only tailors to The Queen but to the Sultan of Oman as well.

Another very old Warrant Holder much concerned with ceremony is the company of Firmin and Sons, who hold the Warrant to The Queen and Queen Mother as button makers. Michael Amey, the grantee, says that they have 'apparently dealt with the Royal Household continuously since the seventeenth century and have held Royal Warrants since the reign of George II, although there are only extant Warrants since George III'. Note the 'only'! Their 1796 Warrant contains the sound commercial note that 'for the honour of serving His Majesty in this Department, it is ordered that their bills shall be regularly paid at the end of each Quarter'.

Until the late seventeenth century buttons, usually of French manufacture, were made of silk or woven metal thread. But in 1680 the Royal Regiment of Artillery broke with tradition and appeared in smart brass buttons made by the City firm of Thomas Firmin. Since then Firmin's buttons have been worn by soldiers in almost every campaign in history. Marlborough's men wore Firmin

buttons at Blenheim; so did Wellington's at Waterloo. And so did both sides in the American War of Independence and in the War Between the States. In the Second World War at least eight of the Allied forces were buttoned by Firmin. It is extraordinary that there is no ode to Firmin by Rudyard Kipling.

Today they are not only the Royal button makers; they also, at their factory in Birmingham, make the helmets and cuirasses for the two regiments of Household Cavalry, and can and do provide almost any item of uniform from ceremonial helmets to epaulettes, aiguilettes and swagger canes, regimental cap badges and, of course, buttons. Buttons of brass; buttons of silver; base-metal buttons; composition buttons; plated buttons; shanked or pierced buttons in any shape or size with raised or indented patterns; and badges. Truly, it can be said that over 300 years Firmin and Sons have proved themselves 'the button of the cap'.

Royal tailors divide roughly – very roughly – into those who supply livery and uniform and those who supply civilian garments. Prince Philip's 'naval tailors' are Gieves & Hawkes Ltd, who amalgamated in 1975 shortly after the IRA planted a bomb in Gieves's shop window in Bond Street. Gieves were used to this because during the war the Germans had bombed the same shop, as well as branches from Portsmouth and Devonport to Malta. In

Cadets embark for the former Royal Naval College at Osborne, Isle of Wight

Robes and wigs at Ede and Ravenscroft, who have been making Royal robes since the reign of William and Mary. Royal wigs are now a thing of the past but they still make them for the legal profession

The Royal handmaiden – Kathy Pow, Manicurist to Her Majesty The Queen Mother

any case, the merger had already been agreed. Nevertheless, it seemed an omen that the time was right to move into Hawkes's famous shop at 1 Savile Row. It was an appropriate union, for Gieves, who had once dressed Lord Nelson, are still the pre-eminent Royal Naval tailors, and Hawkes, who used to make Wellington's caps and helmets, are still the official tailors to officers in forty regiments and corps of the modern army. Notwithstanding this continuing tradition, Robert Gieve, the grantee, says, 'It is the home and overseas civilian market that represents our future.'

As far as the Royal Family are concerned, Hawkes first held a Warrant from George III and Queen Charlotte as Velvet Cap Maker, though his real breakthrough came when he discovered a method of 'jacking' leather so as to make it sword resistant. This led him to invent the 'shako', which became a standard head-dress in the army of the day. Gieves's first Warrant came from George V, whose naval uniform had always been made by the firm. The company obviously benefited from the Royal connection with the Navy. George V's sons Prince Edward, Prince Albert and Prince George were all kitted out by Gieves. Prince Philip first became a customer when he joined the Royal Navy and granted Gieves his Warrant in 1956 and they now also hold The Prince of Wales's Warrant. At the Prince's wedding in 1981 the pages were in uniforms with dirks and accessories which were exact replicas of those made by the company for the 1863 wedding of the then Prince of Wales and Princess Alexandra.

One of the four 'livery tailors' is Henry Poole and Co. of Savile Row, who, in a history that began in 1806, must be among the all-time record holders for the number of Warrants held. They designed a mulberry velvet or bottle-green court dress for Queen Victoria which was worn until 1939 – and they were also granted the Warrant by her son, The Prince of Wales, in 1865. That, however, is only the tip of the Royal iceberg. They held the Warrant of the Emperor Napoleon III, and King Amadeus I of Spain, and Haile Selassie, and the Czar, and the Shah. Not to mention the 1923 Warrant from the Imperial Household of Japan and the 1936 one from King Boris of Bulgaria. They had a Warrant from Friedrich the Grossherzog of Bavaria in 1891 and a year later they were granted one by Prince Emmanuele Filiberto di Savoia. Then there was the King of the Belgians and the Khedive of Egypt and the Prince of Teck and Prince Oscar of Sweden and Norway. The Emperor of Brazil gave them one in 1874, as did the Maharajah Gaekwar of Baroda in 1905. But here one must,

I think, cease before the recital begins to sound like Gilbert and Sullivan. Almost as impressive is the tribute from Benjamin Disraeli, who described Poole, under the fictitious name Mr Vigo, as 'the most fashionable tailor in London... consummate in his art... neither pretentious nor servile, but simple and with becoming respect for others and for himself'.

More recently they have made uniforms for Field Marshal Montgomery and the Free French Air Force in the last war, and they kitted out Rex Harrison for his role as Professor Higgins in the original West End production of *My Fair Lady*.

Attention to detail gives substance to ceremony. It matters – particularly in the age of television and telephoto lens – that the smallest, tiniest bits and pieces receive as much attention as the overall grand design. Leather, for instance. The Queen's leather tanners and curriers are Connolly Bros., the descendants of two brothers who came into leather via a boot repair business

Connolly's, The Queen's leather tanners and curriers, had their factory immortalised by the great cartoonist W. Heath Robinson for the firm's 50th anniversary

so prosperous that in the late nineteenth century their windows were broken by resentful opposition.

At first they specialised in harness leather; then in 1902 they made the leather seating and C springs for Edward VII's Coronation coach. As the motor industry grew so Connolly's did more and more leather upholstery. Between the wars the Cunard liners, *Queen Mary* and *Queen Elizabeth*, were both upholstered in Connolly leather. In the Second World War they made the seat leathers for Spitfires, Lancasters and Hurricanes. Subsequently they upholstered the *QE2* and now some 50 per cent of their production goes into top-range motor cars, including three Warrant Holders – Rolls Royce, Jaguar and Aston Martin. Today if you sit on the Speaker's Chair in the House of Commons, Norway's equivalent in the Storting, Boodle's, the Jockey Club, the Central Criminal Court, 10 Downing Street, the Banqueting House or the Transport and General Workers' Union the odds are that you will be sitting on leather from Connolly's, The Queen's leather tanners.

If chair seats are among the least visible parts of a ceremony, then jewellery is the most prominent, and in the case of Royalty the most symbolic. Several of the great names in jewellery are the proud possessors of the Warrant, but in this sphere of Royal service there is one jeweller who is *primus inter pares*: Garrard, the Crown Jewellers – note, not just Warrant Holders but Crown Jewellers. Every February a team from the Garrard's workshop high above Regent Street travels east to the Tower of London. There they spend a fortnight cleaning the crown jewels by hand in the time-honoured traditional way, just as they have been doing since they first became Crown Jewellers in 1843. Henry Phillips, the Workshop Manager, was part of the team that prepared the Royal regalia for the Coronation in 1953. One of his ambitions is to still be part of the Garrard team at the next Coronation. If he is, he will be the only jeweller in history to have been involved in two.

The founder of the firm was George Wickes, who registered his mark at Goldsmiths' Hall in 1722 but did not set up his own shop until 1735, which is the date Garrard generally cite as their foundation year. From the beginning Wickes was patronised by Frederick, Prince of Wales, who lived just round the corner in Leicester Square. In 1745 he made him an elaborate twenty-nine-inch-high centrepiece, embellished by Robert Garrard II more than 100 years later, which is still one of the treasures of the Royal collection.

For a while the relationship prospered and Wickes described The Prince's purchases of an eighty-pound cup and cover and fifty-pound 'bread baskett' as 'fine'. For 'a black eboney Handle for tea kettle and a Button for a teapot' he made no charge at all. After The Prince was banished to Kew, however, Wickes was left with unpaid plate to the value of £500, but before long things were back to normal and The Prince was commissioning as avidly as before.

As time went on Wickes took on partners, but it was not until 1792 that the first Garrard became one. He had been working for the firm since 1780 and by 1802 he seems to have been in sole charge of the company. In 1830 he and his son, Robert, were awarded King William IV's Warrant. The former Crown Jewellers, Rundell, Bridge and Rundell, were in decline at this point and in 1843 Queen Victoria conferred on Garrard's the title the firm still holds today.

Apart from Royal regalia the Victorian Garrard's became famous for their grand and intricate sporting trophies, of which the best known is probably the America's Cup, the yachting trophy made in 1848 and won by the schooner *America* three years later. As far as Royalty is concerned, the list of assignments is seemingly limitless.

In 1850 the East India Company presented The Queen with the fabulous Kohinoor diamond, a monster stone of 191 carats whose name means literally 'mountain of light'. It is supposed to date back to the fourteenth century. When it was shown at the Great Exhibition in 1851 many people thought it lacklustre, so Garrard were commissioned to recut it. Special cutters were brought in from Amsterdam, a 2.4 horsepower steam engine was employed and the Duke of Wellington rode to Garrard on a white horse and helped cut the first facet. Afterwards Queen Victoria wore it as a personal ornament. At Edward VII's Coronation Queen Alexandra wore it. At George V's Coronation Garrard incorporated the Kohinoor into a crown for Queen Mary. Finally they made another crown for the Coronation of King George VI and the present Queen Mother. This, incorporating the Kohinoor in a Maltese cross, is still The Queen Mother's crown and has detachable arches so that it can be worn simply as a circlet.

Another great diamond which links Garrard and the Monarchy is the Cullinan, 3,106 carats, presented to Edward VII by the government of Transvaal. It was cut into nine major gems and ninety-six small 'brilliants'. Garrard built one of the biggest gems into the Imperial State Crown and moved the thirteenth-century Stuart

The Shiva of West One – Kenneth Snowman of Wartski's, jewellers to The Queen, The Queen Mother and The Prince of Wales, demonstrates his wares

More than a chestful of gongs at Spink and Son, the Royal Medallists. Their book British Battles and Medals *is the definitive word on the subject*

Sapphire to the back. The other big Cullinan stone was incorporated into the Sceptre with Cross which was first made for King Charles II.

Garrard adapted the Imperial State Crown for the 1953 Coronation, with help from Mr Lock, the hatter, and made engagement rings for The Princess of Wales (sapphire and diamond cluster) and The Duchess of York (ruby and drop diamonds). Garrard also make the badges for the select Royal Family Orders, worn by members of the Royal Family on the left shoulder. Queen Elizabeth II's, suspended from a bow of chartreuse yellow silk, has a miniature portrait of the Queen within a border of brilliants and baguette diamonds, and shows her in the Order of the Garter and a necklace given to her by the Nizam of Hyderabad.

Not that Garrard are the only Royal jewellers to marry ancient and modern or to be involved with repairs to national symbols. In Edinburgh, Hamilton and Inches, who hold a Warrant as silversmiths and clockmakers, specialise in modern versions of ancient Celtic quaiches, or drinking bowls, as well as the silver accoutrements of Highland dress. And when, in 1987, the historic Calcutta Cup was used as an after-dinner rugger ball by some of the England and Scotland players, it was to the craftsmen of Hamilton and Inches that it was sent for repair.

The Queen's medallists are Spink and Sons, who were first established in 1666. Although they were given the privilege of manufacturing the Order of St Michael and St George in the mid-fifties and later the Military Division of the Order of the Bath, their main Royal work is connected with the mounting, supply and renovation of medals. The actual manufacture is now mainly for foreign countries. The mounting of medals and the construction of ribbons for less formal occasions is a task which not only requires a degree of expertise but also calls for detailed knowledge of the Order of Precedence. Even if you do know it there are still some dubious grey areas to trap the unwary.

Spink's is perhaps best known for the innumerable treasures, particularly Victoria Crosses and other medals, which have passed through their hands. Of these the most important are probably the Juxon Medal presented to Bishop Juxon by King Charles on the scaffold just before his execution; the Drake Cup; various pieces of Nelson Plate; the red lacquer throne of the Emperor Chi'en Lung; and the Nemi Bronze – the Emperor Caligula's votive bronze statue of Diana, which was purchased from Spink's in 1915 and presented to the British Museum.

Other jewellers tend to divide their work between public and private – an uneasy distinction – but when you consider a dazzling decoration like the Diamond Garter Star, made by Collingwood of Bond Street for Earl Mountbatten of Burma while he was Viceroy of India, you know that you are in the public domain. The diamond necklace designed by the same company as a wedding present from Queen Victoria to Princess 'May' of Teck for her wedding to the Duke of York, later King George V, in 1893 is essentially a private piece. Collingwood now hold The Queen's, The Queen Mother's and The Prince of Wales's Warrants and can trace their Royal connection back beyond their formal foundation in 1817 to a pub in Streatham run by a man named Tom Gray. Gray was obviously a man of parts because he not only provided good beer but also put on popular cockfights which attracted, among others, The Prince Regent. Gray was also a keen amateur jeweller and when Prinny discovered this he announced that if Gray set up shop professionally he could rely on Royal patronage. The Royal link has remained unbroken ever since, though Henry Collingwood, after whom the company was named, joined only in 1853.

Wearing it is not the only way of displaying gold and silver, and some of the Royal Warrant Holders who work in these precious metals tend to make objects which stand on their own.

Gerald Benney, at one time Professor of Silversmithing and Jewellery at the Royal College of Art, is one of the rare men who hold all four available Warrants. For more than thirty years now he has been supplying beautiful custom-built artefacts from the Georgian house in the Kennet Valley which is his home, design studio and workshop.

Benney has exhibited all over the world and is recognised as one of the country's finest artists, yet he got off to an inauspicious start with what he concedes was a rotten degree from the Royal College of Art. His earlier training was at the Brighton College of Art, where his father was Principal. Then he studied under the late Dunstan Pruden, the ecclesiastical silversmith, at Eric Gill's Guild of St Joseph and St Dominic at Ditchling, before doing military service and going to the Royal College with a scholarship. He was not a natural academic and dissipated his energy on collecting motor cars and bikes (a total of fifty-six in four years) and multifarious activities including furniture design and glass blowing. When it came to his submission for a degree in industrial

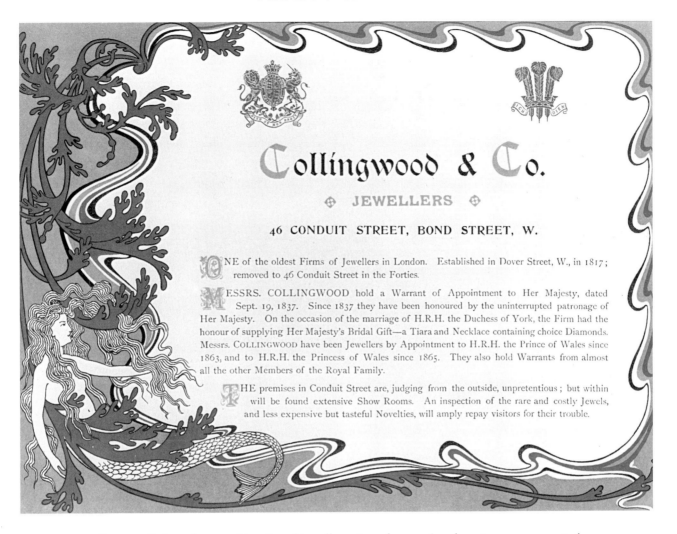

Collingwood & Co.

✠ JEWELLERS ✠

46 CONDUIT STREET, BOND STREET, W.

ONE of the oldest Firms of Jewellers in London. Established in Dover Street, W., in 1817; removed to 46 Conduit Street in the Forties.

MESSRS. COLLINGWOOD hold a Warrant of Appointment to Her Majesty, dated Sept. 19, 1837. Since 1837 they have been honoured by the uninterrupted patronage of Her Majesty. On the occasion of the marriage of H.R.H. the Duchess of York, the Firm had the honour of supplying Her Majesty's Bridal Gift—a Tiara and Necklace containing choice Diamonds. Messrs. COLLINGWOOD have been Jewellers by Appointment to H.R.H. the Prince of Wales since 1863, and to H.R.H. the Princess of Wales since 1865. They also hold Warrants from almost all the other Members of the Royal Family.

THE premises in Conduit Street are, judging from the outside, unpretentious; but within will be found extensive Show Rooms. An inspection of the rare and costly Jewels, and less expensive but tasteful Novelties, will amply repay visitors for their trouble.

Collingwood's have been making Royal jewellery since they produced anniversary presents for King George's IV's daughter, Princess Charlotte, and her husband, Prince Leopold

design and silver one of his prize exhibits was a self-balancing deckchair of his own invention. His professor praised its appearance and then made the mistake of sitting in it. Immediately the chair collapsed, pinning the professor between its twin jaws like some sci-fi monster. The professor did not forgive.

Subsequently he made ends meet by electroplating Hoover irons and headlight reflectors and, almost in his spare time, he began to earn commissions for original silver. One of the first was a piece commemorating Sir John Cockcroft, whom he had met while delivering small parts he had made for the Atomic Energy Commission, of which Cockcroft was the first head. Then Sir Basil Spence commissioned him to make the church plate for the new Coventry Cathedral and Vickers and ICI commissioned pieces for their boardrooms. He did a forty-six-piece table

service for the Ionian Bank and, after becoming consultant designer for Viners, his 'Chelsea' cutlery pattern became a world bestseller in stainless steel.

In 1968 he broadened his work to include enamelling. His first commission, for a bowl, was from Edward Heath when he was Prime Minister. More recently he has gone back to drawing and painting and has found ways of transferring some of this work on to his enamel ware.

At one time he did a lot of church ware but the vogue for low-church austerity has diminished demand for chalices and candlesticks and his work is now more popular in synagogues. Private clients outnumber his corporate ones and he produces an array of relatively small items such as wine coasters and coolers, bowls and vases, trays and pepper mills to set beside the more elaborate pieces for such institutions as Oxford colleges.

All that glitters here is gold – Mr and Mrs Lingwood, The Queen's Gold Leaf Makers, with some tools of their trade

Surrounded by silver, Professor Gerald Benney at home in Berkshire with examples of his craft

He feels there is more interest now in silver than at any time since the fifties and he still believes in satisfying a demand for what he once described as 'modern design with an eighteenth-century feel, for elegance and "comfiness", for handwork which gives an object a soul, a peculiar Englishness which is very hard to achieve'.

Another Warrant-Holding goldsmith and silversmith who works for himself and enjoys a worldwide reputation is Stuart Devlin, an Australian, who has lived in London since 1965. While barely thirty he designed Australia's new decimal coinage. Since then his awards and commissions speak volumes and a number have involved the Royal Family. They include the Australian Jockey Club Derby Gold Cup, presented by Princess Marina; the Civic regalia for the London Borough of Brent (an interesting item in view of the Council's more recent political reputation!); the common seal for the Greater London Council (another commission to suffer from the vagiaries of politics); two alms dishes for Canterbury Cathedral; three Australian motor-cycling trophies commissioned by Prince Philip; the cutlery used during The Queen's state visit to France, commissioned by President Pompidou; Prince Charles's silver wedding present to his parents; the World Driving Championship Trophy commissioned by Prince Philip; the regalia for the Order of Australia; gifts for the Australian Premier to give to visitors and for The Queen to give to her hosts on a visit to the Middle East; crowns to go on the domes of the Malaysian Royal Palace in Kuala Lumpur; a silver bowl for The Queen to give to the Sultan of Oman; a sword for the Royal Armouries – the only such commission this century; and a surprise egg for the Tote to present to Queen Elizabeth The Queen Mother.

Mr Devlin is not the only Royal jeweller from Australia. Hardy Brothers Ltd are also and have been Warrant Holders since 1929. The Sydney-based jewellers, founded in 1853, had always worked for the Governor-Generals of Australia. Then in the 1920s they were asked to supply silver, glass and other tableware to Yarralumla, the Governor-General's official residence in Canberra. When The Queen was presented with a yellow and white diamond wattle brooch it came from Hardys. Hardys also made the gold mallet and trowel used for laying the foundations of the new federal capital.

Kenneth Snowman has said that Stuart Devlin 'exults in a laudable love of luxurious materials and the richness of his imagination is matched by its technical expression'. He also says that comparisons with Fabergé – inevitable because of Devlin's fondness for surprise eggs, like the one for The Queen Mother – are 'unfair to both Devlin and to Carl Gustavovitch at the same time'.

This is high praise because Mr Snowman is the grandson of Morris Wartski, founder of Wartski of Grafton Street. Wartski were the first jewellers, under the aegis of Mr Snowman's father, Emanuel, to import Fabergé jewellery to the West after the Russian Revolution. The company has held the Warrant since the time of Queen Mary, who inherited the Fabergé collection of Edward VII and Queen Alexandra.

My instinct tells me that much of what Fabergé made could be described as *objets d'art*. The *Concise Oxford Dictionary* describes an *objet d'art*, not altogether helpfully, as a 'small artistic object'. Be that as it may, most of us would probably claim to know one when we saw one. If in any doubt, go to 14 Brook Street, London, where Mrs Susan Benjamin holds all four Warrants for supplying such *objets* to the Royal Family. She started the business in 1950. Tole, *papier-mâché*, Tunbridge Ware, fans, Staffordshire pottery: these are the objects which are Mrs Benjamin's stock in trade, but it is for English enamels that she is best known. Her mother had a collection and Halcyon Days has always featured English eighteenth-century enamels.

The demand for such miniature *objets* died out in the early nineteenth century but Mrs Benjamin always had a strong wish to see it revived. In 1970 she set up a partnership with Bilston and Battersea Enamels, a company specialising in enamel powder for cookers and refrigerators whose factory was in Bilston, one of the centres of the eighteenth-century enamel trade.

Since then Halcyon Days Enamels have revived this traditional English form with a whole series of small boxes, clocks, musical boxes and... perhaps *objets d'art* is the only word. Apart from her own team Mrs Benjamin has commissioned eminent artists such as Sir Hugh Casson, Fleur Cowles and Peter Blake as well as forging links with any number of institutions like the Royal Academy and the Royal College of Art. The company can undertake original work to order. Among the *objets* on sale to the public there have been a sequence of five commemorative boxes to mark the first five birthdays of Prince William, a 'changing the Guard at Buckingham Palace Box', a 'Glory of the Garden Box' with a suitable quotation from Kipling and (my favourite) a replica of the Albert Hall, three inches in diameter, which plays 'Rule Britannia'.

Halycon Days are here again with Susan Benjamin and some typical objets d'art

Elephantine artistry – handpainting Queen Victoria at Royal Doulton's China Factory

An equestrian Elizabeth I at Royal Worcester

A Warrant Holder who has an affinity with these craftsmen is Richard A. Lingwood, who supplies The Queen's gold leaf from an industrial estate at South Ruislip, Middlesex. His company, formed in 1977, buys its gold bullion in grain form, which is then melted and hand-beaten into books of gold leaf, each one of which contains twenty-five three-and-a-quarter-inch-square leaves. Lingwood's Gold Leaf is everywhere, from the calligraphy on heraldic scrolls to the gilded finery of London's great Roman Catholic Church, the Brompton Oratory. Perhaps their greatest monument is the newly restored Big Ben clocktower at Westminster, for which Lingwood supplied 6,300 books of gold leaf.

From time to time the Royal Warrant Holders present gifts to members of the Royal Family, and on the occasion of The Princess of Wales's twenty-first birthday it was an attractive 'Plume of Feathers' brooch which probably dated from Edwardian times. It was found by Paul Longmire, who has a small shop in Bury Street, which, like a number of Warrant Holding premises feels more like a grand private house than anything quite as vulgar as a shop. Two of his specialities are custom-built cuff-links and jewel-sleuthing for pieces like The Princess's birthday present. He has even been able to satisfy the demands of a customer who has a particular interest in jewelled skulls. Apart from making cuff-links for the Royal Family and the Houses of Lords and Commons he has been known to be so personal that one pair were decorated with the owner's thumbprints. An interesting item for anyone trying to incorporate an original clue into a whodunnit. When Yehudi Menuhin lost a cuff-link of which he was particularly fond he asked Longmire to make him a replica. The only basis for this was a video of Menuhin playing the violin, so Longmire and his experts had to scrutinise the video and freeze-frame whenever there was a close up of the maestro's cuff. He was delighted with the result.

The great banquets at which The Queen entertains visiting Heads of State are occasions on which the Monarchy is seen at its most majestic. These are moments for the finest china and cutlery and food and drink, though one should remember Royalty can be informal too. Cross of Dunstable hold a Warrant as 'Manufacturers of Disposable Tableware to The Queen'.

The Royal patronage of china is one of the most long-standing of all. William Duesbury, who founded the original Derby porcelain factory, seems to have been allowed by George III to incorporate the crown into his 'backstamp' as early as 1775 and today three china companies – Derby, Doulton and Worcester – incorporate the word 'Royal' in their full formal title.

The Royal Doulton Group now includes four Warrant-Holding companies – Doulton, Minton, Royal Albert and Crown Derby. The Derby Royal connection was the earliest with, among others, a 1776 order from Queen Charlotte for items amounting to £12 6s 2d and another from The Prince of Wales in 1787 for muffin and water plates. In 1794 just before his marriage The Prince of Wales placed an impressively grand order for a service of eight dozen plates.

By Queen Victoria's reign Minton and Doulton were supplying the Royal Family too. In 1840, through Mortlock of Regent Street, Minton supplied Queen Victoria with a 'bone china dejeuner service' on a deep blue ground, painted by Joseph Wareham and enriched with tooled gilding. At the Great Exhibition of 1851 The Queen paid 1,000 guineas for the 'Victoria' dessert service. It consisted of 116 pieces dominated by two flower stands with figures representing the four seasons. Queen Victoria presented it to the Emperor of Austria and three years later she commissioned twelve models of a 'Highlander and Hound', which formed the bases of candelabra for Balmoral. The firm made some 'below stairs' artefacts too. In 1858 they supplied cooling fountains and tiles for the Royal Dairy at Frogmore. As the century proceeded Minton's popularity with the Royal Family grew ever greater, until there came a point in the 1870s when they were producing Royal dinner services on an almost annual basis, culminating in the 1896 Kiln blue service traced in gold with the Garter emblem and motto finished in blue, red and gold.

Doulton had begun their Royal services more prosaically with a set of stoneware spirit barrels for the Great Kitchen at the Brighton Pavilion, but by the end of the century they too were producing large and elaborate dinner services for the Royal table, notably a dessert service painted by Samuel Wilson commissioned by Princess Louise when she visited the Doulton works in 1894. It was presented to Queen Victoria to mark her Diamond Jubilee.

At the very beginning of his reign Edward VII 'was graciously pleased to grant permission to you to use the title "Royal" in describing your Potteries and manu-factures'. This was for Doulton, who supplied a large quantity of nursery-rhyme china for Queen Alexandra in 1905. The nursery theme proved consistently popular: Doulton supplied a miniature dinner service for Queen Mary's doll's house in 1924; Queen Mary bought 'This

The 1930 Royal Visit to Royal Doulton

Little Pig' in 1937, just as Queen Elizabeth The Queen Mother did in 1951. Nor was children's china from Doulton a purely Royal prerogative. At the beginning of his reign George V ordered 10,000 mugs to present to schoolchildren on his Coronation Day.

Mugs and cups have latterly tended to be the speciality of Paragon (now Royal Albert), whose 'Two Got Joy' design, incorporating a brace of magpies, so captivated The Duchess of York – who had seen magpies at Princess Elizabeth's christening – that she gave the company permission to incorporate photographs of the infant Princess into their china. Paragon made the commemorative Coronation Cup for the Coronation that never happened – that of King Edward VIII – but they were able to adapt the design for the subsequent Coronation of King George VI. As a child Prince Charles was given two large jumbo cups and a mug decorated by a seven-year-old boy called Barry Irving.

Relatively small items such as this crop up continually. Doulton gave The Princess of Wales a Bunnykins, a figure from the Oompah Band and an egg cup, mug and plate for Prince William when she visited the factory at Burslem, Staffs (immortalised in the novels of Arnold Bennett) in 1984. The Queen Mother commissioned a new shape called 'Queen's Gadroon' from Crown Derby and cast the first cream jug, which was later delivered to her at Clarence House.

But the truly significant items in the relationship between Royalty and the china industry are the great services. These continue to be made. Minton produced a comprehensive service with crowns and ciphers for the Royal yacht, *Britannia*, when she was commissioned in 1954. They also supplied gold-edged, crimson-banded place settings for The Queen's aeroplane and replacement pieces for the Royal train in green cheviot with laurels printed in brown and coloured yellowish green.

Cutting material at the Royal Flagmakers, Black and Edgington

Denis de Vere Collings, fourth generation Royal calligrapher, filling in a 'By Appointment' Royal Warrant. Also in the picture are examples of work for Lords Callaghan, Hailsham and Leverhulme

In recent years Royal Doulton have made gold-lined dinner and breakfast services for Buckingham Palace as well as a St Paul's dinner service as a wedding present for The Prince and Princess of Wales. Crown Derby has made a 120-piece service called 'Royal Pinxton Roses', which was presented to The Queen by the Derby Corporation; a service showing scenes from Shakespeare for Princess Alexandra; forty-eight plates and special dishes which Texaco gave The Queen Mother for use at the Castle of Mey; a Derby green panel service as a wedding present for Princess Anne; a service to commemorate Benjamin Britten's operas at the Aldeburgh Festival – again for The Queen Mother; and a set of thirty-six coffee cans and stands, six sugar bowls and six cream jugs, which Govan Shipbuilders gave The Queen Mother after she launched the flagship of North Sea Ferries in 1986.

Spode and Royal Worcester also hold Royal Warrants and Spode Copeland proudly proclaim themselves 'Potters to the Royal Family since 1806'. Josiah Spode founded his company in 1770 and it was his son Josiah Spode II who was first granted the Royal Warrant when, in 1806, The Prince of Wales visited the showroom and factory workshops on 12 September. The Prince conferred on him the title 'Potter and English Porcelain Manufacturer to his Royal Highness' and from then on the company has been supplying fine bone china and other ceramic wares to the Royal Household.

From time to time promoters of raw materials commissioned special pieces to give to members of the Royal Family. Thus the Cornish Clay Industry commissioned four bowls. In 1821 the Middletown Hill Company commissioned a special lidded vase for King George IV to help promote their Felspar Porcelain. The King was also presented with a pair of New Shape French Jars painted with figures of Aeneas and Andromeda which are considered the finest example of figure painting ever done on Spode ware.

But Spode, in the words of Robert Copeland, now the company's historical consultant, was 'not only Potter to the Royal Family but to Everyman'. The nineteenth-century output included 'potpourri or scent jars, incense burners, spittoons, vieilleuses or pap-warmers, invalid feeding pots and pap boats, syrup jars for pharmacies, bidets, chamber pots, ladies' slippers and bourdaloues'. Spode made bread crocks and egg separators for the kitchen, a Stilton cheese container and a complex stand for home-grown pineapples. Even Royalty's china was not all grand and ceremonial. Spode supplied toilet ware and

Perseus and Andromeda on a jar from Spode. A Royal Commission in 1822

chamber pots to Buckingham Palace and Windsor Castle throughout the reigns of William IV and Queen Victoria. They also made porcelain panelling, door handles and other fittings for Osborne House in 1846.

The Copeland family took over from the Spodes in a series of mergers and acquisitions through the early to mid-nineteenth century. In 1847 W. T. Copeland, who had been Lord Mayor of London, was allowed to market half-size busts of Queen Victoria's children, sculpted by Mary Thorneycroft. In 1863 The Prince of Wales ordered a vast dessert service to mark his wedding. It was not completed until 1866, when it went on public display and attracted a 'most ecstatic' review in the *Art Journal*.

In recent years Spode has produced cups to celebrate The Prince of Wales's wedding and the christening of the latest Royal Princes. In 1976 they merged with another Royal Warrant Holder, the Royal Worcester Company, which suffers nothing in comparison with the other great china-making Warrant Holders. King George III in 1789 was the first to grant them his Warrant, followed by The Prince of Wales, Victoria as Princess and Queen, and all subsequent crowned Monarchs.

Ever since George III and Queen Charlotte visited the Royal Porcelain Factory in 1788 there has been a stream of Royal visitors both there and to the former showrooms in Curzon Street. The first full Royal table service of Royal Worcester was made for The Duke of Clarence in 1792 and another thirteen had followed by the Coronation of Edward VII in 1903.

In 1947 the company made a special statuette of Princess Elizabeth, as she then was, to mark the first occasion on which she took the salute at the Trooping of the Colour. It showed her in the uniform of Colonel-in-Chief of the Grenadier Guards, mounted on the charger Tommy.

If they wished, The Queen and Prince Philip could entertain all day using Royal Worcester. On their wedding they were given a breakfast service by the Corporation of Worcester, tea services by the Worshipful Company of Carpenters and the Corporation of Cheltenham, and separate dinner and dessert services by the Brigade of Guards!

The food and drink consumed from these priceless artefacts has for the most part been relegated to a different part of the book. But there is one exception. Comte Alain de Vogue, Holder of Her Majesty's Warrant and the only foreigner ever to be President of the Royal Warrant Holders' Association, once repeated George Bernard Shaw's assertion that, while he might have been a total abstainer from the demon drink, he was not a 'champagne teetotaller'.

Champagne is not just a drink; it is a celebration. The Monarchy recognises this by granting Warrants to Bollinger, Heidsieck, Lanson, Roederer, Krug, Moët and Chandon, Mumm and Veuve Clicquot.

This tribute, like so many, is in effect a legacy of King Edward VII, whose liking for champagne was such that he is believed to be the only English Monarch ever to allow his effigy to be placed on the neck-label of a bottle. This was the special cuvée produced by Moët and Chandon in honour of his Coronation. It is a measure of the special *entente* that exists between champagne and the British Monarchy that the industry still produces cuvées such as this in honour of practically every important Royal anniversary or event.

Not that one should view the French gift of champagne through too rosy a tint. When the English were blockading France during the Napoleonic Wars one of the great Veuve Clicquot's salesmen, a German named Bohn, declared: 'The more I detest the English, the more I want to corrupt their habits. May the good God give us peace so that we can take vengeance on their throats for the evil they have done us, by giving them over to total drunkenness.'

This, too, is a remark much quoted by the Comte de Vogue, who has for some years held the Warrant on behalf of the Widow. But he quotes very much tongue in cheek.

It was Queen Victoria, with her devotion to Balmorality, who reinvested the Monarchy with elements of its Celtic past and made it arguably for the first time a truly British institution. Nothing symbolised this more than the ritual playing of the pipes every morning at breakfast time wherever Her Majesty was in residence. The tradition remains to this day and the Royal Piper, like practically every piper in the world, is supplied by R. G. Hardie and Co. of Glasgow, where the grantee is the dapper John Weatherston, MBE, BEM, formerly of the Argyll and Sutherland Highlanders and a world champion in his own right, having led his own pipe band to victory in the 1962 World Pipe and Drum Band Championships.

Royal tartan – George V and Queen Mary wearing the Highland Dress popularised at the time of Victoria and Albert

David Kinloch Anderson, Royal Kiltmaker and keeper of Prince Albert's own Balmoral Tartan,
with a regal array of Highland cloth

John Weatherston, of R.G. Hardie and Co. in Glasgow, holds the Royal Warrant as maker of The Queen's bagpipes. He is also a champion piper himself

'Makers of the world's finest bagpipes' is the company's proud claim and, indeed, the cramped and ancient little workshop in Renfrew Street despatches pipes all over the world. They even make the pipes for the band of a correction school in Papua New Guinea, not to mention doing a lot of work in Tokyo and Saudi Arabia. 'We had a big order in from Gaddafi the other day,' said Mr Weatherston, as he demonstrated a set of pipes.

Around the turn of the century the company made the only known set of gold-mounted bagpipes. They were commissioned by the Sultan of Morocco for 'Mad' Kaid Maclean, whose real name was Lieutenant Sir Harry Aubrey De-Vere Maclean, from Kirn near Dunoon. Maclean had helped the Sultan reorganise his army and the gold pipes were his thank-you present. Nothing has been heard of them since.

Today's pipes come in any number of guises but the best use real silver, real ivory and African blackwood, alias *Dalbergia melonoxolin*, though for lesser breeds almost anything can be imitated. The Warrant dates back to the early years of Queen Victoria's reign and one of their proudest possessions is a telegram, dated 1933, which says, 'Please send one practice chanter price one guinea to HRH The Prince of Wales at York House, St James, London, to arrive on Thursday morning next.' It was handed in at Sandringham at 10.07 and arrived in Glasgow eight minutes later. Anyone wishing to send a telegram today would use the simple and evocative address: 'Bagpipes Glasgow'! In 1986 Hardie and Co. refurbished the pipes originally made by Queen Victoria's piper, Pipe Major Ross. 'He was,' says John Weatherston, 'an excellent bagpipe maker, silversmith and engraver to boot.' His work has stood the test of time, for although the wood has swollen and cracked the pipes are now back in service and played daily by The Queen's Piper, Brian MacRae.

As evocative of Scottishness as the bagpipes is Highland dress. Kinloch Anderson of Edinburgh are tailors and kilt makers to The Queen, The Duke of Edinburgh and The Prince of Wales. They are also keepers of The Queen's private and personal tartan, the Balmoral, which was originally designed for Queen Victoria by Prince Albert.

The whole question of kilts and tartan, as explained by Harry Lindley, a director of the firm, is one mind-numbing complexity into which it would be foolish for a Sassenach to delve too deeply. It is, as everyone knows, a symbol of Scottishness and every clan has its own. Several can be traced back to 1715, and the Macrae of Conchra is even older, but the whole business is muddied by the blank years when tartan and the kilt were outlawed by act of parliament after Bonnie Prince Charlie was defeated at Culloden. Not until almost forty years later, in 1782, was the act repealed, and in the interim many clan records and patterns were lost for ever.

Kinloch Anderson stock over 350 authentic tartans as well as 'district checks' and 'modern checks'. They will produce a new tartan for anyone who applies, though proper tartans are as closely regulated by the Lyon King of Arms and his men as any coat of arms south of the border. On the other hand two-thirds of the company's market lies overseas and that means Japan as well as the great Scottish communities in the Antipodes and North America. With this in mind Kinloch Anderson sell such accessories as 'Sporran Hand Bags' in Dewar's Highlander Clan, in association with Dewar's whisky. They even sell a ceremonial skean dhu with the suggestion that if you do not wish to wear it in the traditional fashion, in your stocking, you 'may prefer to use this imported 7″ version as a letter opener, desk top accessory or conversation piece'.

It would be a brave Englishman who accused such a company of Scottish solecism and Kinloch Anderson are astonishingly erudite. Certainly the true kilt is a remarkable garment. At Kinloch Anderson they talk of 'building' them, rather than making them, and the real McCoy requires a full nine yards of tartan.

Occasionally Royal events take place under canvas – the Royal garden party is the most obvious example, although since the Field of the Cloth of Gold, if not before, Royalty has been associated with billowing canvas and swirling banners. Nowadays – the ritual teas apart – they may be seen annually at such events as the Braemar Gathering or the Badminton Horse Trials. Tents and flags come from Black and Edgington, who, as plain Edgingtons, earned the Warrant from Queen Victoria in 1863. Both are perennial Royal necessities, the one for reasons of pageantry, the other for the purpose of entertainment. You simply cannot, in the British Isles, even contemplate a garden party without providing a tent. The Benjamin Edgington who revived Victoria's accolade supplied Florence Nightingale with hospital tents for the Crimea and also military tents for the troops. He must have been a God-fearing man because at his own expense he provided a Bible to be placed in a special pocket sewn into all military tents.

His greatest achievement, however, was the provision of 'a monster pavilion' for the Coronation of Czar Alexander II in 1856. Edgington was specifically asked to go to eloquent chronicler of the most interesting event of the present century.

North of the border the tents for the Holyroodhouse garden parties are provided by Clyde Canvas, who also claim the record for the world's largest tent. This measures 130 metres by 95 metres and covers 12,000 square metres. It is twenty-five metres high and is built to withstand winds up to 87.24 mph. It belongs to an international missionary organisation in Zimbabwe.

The Monarchy is seldom more majestic than when in a horse-drawn procession, riding in one of the great state carriages with outriders and postilions and an escort of the Household Cavalry. This is fairy-tale stuff, but in the twentieth century carriages have to be held together by functional nuts and bolts. For example, it is not practical to drive, say, the Irish State Coach all the way from the Royal Mews at the back of Buckingham Palace to Edinburgh for a procession down the Royal Mile. If the coach has to be transported that far, the Mews would get on to Walter E. Sturgess and Sons of Almond Road, Leicester. Sturgess hold the Warrant as 'Suppliers of Horse and Carriage Conveyances'. Their main business is motor cars and they are Jaguar and Daimler dealers. But when required, they will move the Royal carriages wherever they have to go.

It is unlikely that many people, watching the Royal procession clatter down the Mall on the way to the State Opening of Parliament, pause to wonder about the coachmen's whips. In fact they come from Swaine, Adeney, Brigg & Sons Ltd in Piccadilly and they have done ever since King George III's coachmen purchased them from Swaine, Adeney in 1780. During the Second World War, the company acquired Thomas Brigg and Son, the umbrella manufacturers. They now make The Queen Mother's umbrellas. The present managing director, Robert Adeney, is descended from William Adeney's son and William Swaine's daughter, who married in 1802.

The carriages themselves are the responsibility of the Royal Mews but when major renovation and refurbishment are needed the work is carried out by the first Co-operative Society in Britain to be able to display the Royal coat of arms. The Scottish Midland Co-operative Society of Edinburgh, formerly St Cuthbert's, were granted the Warrant as coach painters in 1964.

Historically, of course, all Co-ops used horse-drawn transport but St Cuthbert's were unusual in that they persevered longer than most people and kept the horses on. (They do hire out limousines now as well.) In 1940 they

Royalty camped under Edgington canvas as far back as 1873

Russia by the Queen herself – an olive branch to celebrate the end of the Crimean War, perhaps. The occasion prompted a particularly lush report in the *Morning Post*.

The name of Benjamin Edgington has been associated with the most imposing fêtes which have taken place in Great Britain for a very long time past. No scion of a noble house has been ushered into manhood without calling in Mr Edgington's assistance to provide a monster pavilion for dispensing the family hospitalities; but it has remained for the Coronation of the Emperor Alexander of All the Russias to give to this famous contractor the widest renown as a British tradesman.

It will scarcely be credited, but it is not less true, that the magnificent addition to the Graziani Palace, was designed and planned in London, sent out to Moscow in charge of Benjamin Edgington's own artificers, and by them completed in a manner which, while it cannot fail to extend the world-wide celebrity of their employer, has entitled him to the well-deserved encomiums of the

*Floreat Moyses Stevens – a riot of colour and scent in the Bruton Street showrooms of
The Queen Mother's florist*

Robert Adeney under a Swaine Adeney Brigg umbrella, as supplied to The Queen Mother

acquired the first of their historic horse-drawn vehicles – a Victorian governess's car. And in 1948 the present collection of historic vehicles was begun in earnest. They now have thirty or so and are happy to hire out an elegant barouche for a wedding.

Their first Royal commission was to supply landaus for the 1953 Royal visit to Scotland, and they also mounted a section of the Royal Scots Greys. All the horses used to pull the state vehicles were veterans of the city milk rounds! There is a constant flow of Royal coaches between the Mews and Scotmid, as they are now called, and they also repair coaches for such dignitaries as the Lord Mayor of Newcastle. They refurbished the Glass Coach for Prince Charles's wedding and more recently carried out a major renovation of Queen Alexandra's State Coach.

There is paint and then there is paint. In 1800, when Joseph Mason, a Derby landscape gardener, trained his two sons as varnish makers, there was no such thing as paint in the sense that we understand it. The painters mixed it themselves. A typical superior coach would be painted to a specification which looked something like this:

> 4 coats of lead
> 7 coats of rough-stuff
> 1 coat of lead
> putty and face
> one coat of lead and sandpaper
> 3 coats of colour
> one coat of glazing
> 4 coats of hard-drying varnish
> one coat of best wearing body

Today the company are just as painstaking and take particular pride in the durability of their product, constantly testing in their laboratories for resistance to everything from automatic car-washers to salt-water spray. Their paint coats Rolls Royces, the vehicles of the National Bus Co., and the Orient Express.

No matter how resplendent a livery or a uniform, it needs a bit of twist or trim to give it just that extra something to distinguish it from the one next door. For over 300 years this has been done by Toye, Kenning and Spencer, whose Chairman, Bryan Toye, is a direct descendant of Guillaume Henri Toyé, a Huguenot weaver who fled from France in 1685. It was the year of the Revocation of the Edict of Nantes, which led to a wholesale emigration of French Protestants. As anyone who looks at the history of the Royal Warrant Holding companies will quickly realise, this was greatly to Britain's advantage. The year the first Toye, disguised as a cattle dealer, arrived in London was the year Monmouth was beheaded, the year Bach, Handel and Scarlatti were all born, and the year the first settlers arrived in Texas. To be able to trace your family back that far under any circumstances is an achievement; to be running the same business still is extraordinary.

The first Toye, like so many Huguenots, was a weaver. His speciality was gold and silver lace, and as military uniforms of the day were a mass of frogging and braid and other ornate embellishments, his business in Bethnal Green flourished from the first. In 1793 Guillaume's great-grandson William built a new factory in Camden.

The introduction of the rifle in the late nineteenth century could have destroyed the firm. Suddenly bright and garish uniforms became dangerously vulnerable and khaki and camouflage were the order of the day. William's eldest son countered this trend by moving into the production of banners, sashes and other regalia for friendly societies and the newly emerging trades unions. (Anyone who thinks the trades unions are averse to marching bands and heraldic banners has never been to the Durham Miners' Gala). They also took on metalwork, particularly sporting cups and trophies.

By doing this the company stayed alive through the Depression and they went on to acquire many other companies, including, eventually, George Kenning and Spencer, makers of ceremonial insignia, in 1956. They had been founded in 1801 and held George VI's Warrant.

However, the Toyes never abandoned Guillaume's original craft and today's Warrant is for 'Gold and Silver Laces, Insignia and Embroidery'. They were particularly involved with the Coronations of King George VI and Queen Elizabeth in 1937 and of Queen Elizabeth II in 1953. It was after the last Coronation that they were granted the Warrant.

The present range of products and contracts is positively bewildering. Apart from their traditional work they make Salvation Army hat-bands woven in scores of different languages, including Chinese, and they stock almost 9,000 designs for a variety of 'corporate' ties and badges. The thread, a gold and silver one in their case, which runs through these 300 years from Guillaume to Bryan is, they say, 'Identity'. That was what Guillaume's ribbons and laces gave. They marked the wearer out from other men in uniform.

For Royalty Toye, Kenning today provides the gilt on the gingerbread just as Guillaume Toyé did when he first arrived in England all those years ago.

Urn with wings – more precision porcelain painting, this time at Royal Worcester

Car-care – Susan White uses some of her car polish on a 1936 Rolls-Royce

THE OFFICE OF STATE

'There is always work. And tools to work withal'
(Lowell)

Like any large business – and 'the family firm' is an epithet the Royal Family coined for itself – the Monarchy operates a diverse fleet of motor cars, ranging from ceremonial state cars to racier, more 'private' cars and such utilitarian vehicles as the Renault 4 which was presented by General de Gaulle and was much favoured by Buckingham Palace staff as a London runabout.

The Royal romance with the motor car began in Victorian times but not with Victoria. The pioneer in all this, as in so many modern Royal customs, was the cavalier Prince of Wales. He may or may not have gone for a quick spin from Warwick Castle in a six-horsepower Daimler during June 1898, and he may have tried one out at the 1896 motor exhibition in South Kensington. He certainly went for a drive with the present Lord Montagu of Beaulieu's father in the New Forest in August 1899. The Prince was staying at Highcliffe Castle near Christchurch

when John Scott Montagu came to lunch driving his Daimler. After the meal Montagu suggested The Prince might care to be his passenger and the two, with two ladies in the back, drove seven or eight miles up the Lyndhurst-Southampton road and back. The Prince remarked jovially to the ladies that motoring would certainly change the fashion for wide-brimmed hats and quizzed his driver about what car would be most suitable for Royalty. A few weeks later Montagu and the Daimler were summoned to Marlborough House, where the car remained for a week of trial. At the end of it The Prince placed an order for the first in a long line of Royal Daimlers. Not that Daimlers were the only early Royal car. When Prince Philip's parents married in Darmstadt in 1903 the Czar gave them a Wolseley. King Alfonso XIII of Spain drove a Hispano-Suiza and even had a model named 'the Alfonso' in his honour; and the first car ever advertised as a 'sports car'

LEFT Hon. C.S. Rolls driving The Duchess of York in an 1899 Panhard and RIGHT Edward VII makes his motoring debut in John Scott-Montagu's Daimler

was named 'The Prince Henry' after the Kaiser's brother Henry of Prussia.

Despite variations – Queen Mary photographed with a Panhard in 1903, The Prince of Wales and Prince Albert outside a hotel in Newquay with a white Thorneycroft, Prince Philip in a Dodge in Delhi – the Daimler was the principal Royal car until the first Rolls Royce Phantom IV was delivered in 1950. The earlier ones are now being pensioned off to the Royal Motor Museum at Sandringham. One inch short of twenty feet, unnumbered, painted in a special Royal claret so dark it could almost be renamed Blue Blood, the Rolls Royce Phantom with the Royal Standard fluttering from the bonnet (it can be retracted for high-speed travel), has become synonymous with Royalty. Seeing The Queen in anything else is rather like seeing her without a crown: one can't help feeling, however unreasonably, a little let down.

One of today's most distinctive Royal cars is the Aston Martin DB6 owned by The Prince of Wales and given to him as a birthday present by Her Majesty The Queen. It has a silver Welsh dragon on the bonnet. This model was introduced by the company as an interim successor to the DB5, of which the most famous was probably the one driven by Sean Connery in the James Bond films *Goldfinger* and *Thunderball*. The Bond car had machine guns, a passenger ejector seat and hydraulic overrider rams, but The Prince's is conventional by comparison.

The original 1913 cars made by Lionel Martin were designed for 'the discerning owner-driver with fast touring in mind' and the specification holds good today, even though the modern cars are barely recognisable from the Aston Martin 'Bunny' which broke the world record at Brooklands in 1922 with an average of 76.20mph recorded in a run of sixteen and a half hours.

Although designed as a temporary version, the DB6 was produced from 1965 to 1971. The Volante convertible was the first European car with a power-operated hood. Although the company has undergone innumerable ownership changes, it still operates from Newport Pagnell in Buckinghamshire, where it is on the original site of

Edward VIII at Dagenham in a Ford V8, 1934

Two crated Bedford trucks in a dhow en route for Mecca

The Queen in an open Land Rover, Aden 1953

Salmons, Coachmakers of the Nobility, who started business in 1820. In 1986 the company unveiled a model called the Aston Martin Vantage Zagato, limited to an edition of only fifty and retailing at £95,000. In independent tests it has been proved to have a top speed of 185.5 mph and it accelerates to 60 mph in 4.8 seconds.

Daimler no longer exist as a separate enterprise. They are now part of Jaguar, who now hold the Warrant. Jaguar say that although Daimlers are similarly proportioned, unlike their Jaguar sisters they are not built on a production line but are constructed in a special Daimler Limousine shop in Browns Lane, Coventry, on a 'Unit Build' system. This means that the same small group is responsible for the same car 'from unpainted body shell to final despatch'. Thanks to this method it is possible to build in any number of personal options depending on the customer's whim. The Ford Motor Company also holds the Warrant – three, in fact. Ford has been producing cars in Britain since 1911, when a workforce of sixty assembled the first Model T made in this country, and they have been producing cars longer here than in any other country outside North America. The Royal Mews favour Granada Estates.

Austin Rover, Land Rover and Vauxhall also hold Warrants and the Royal Land Rover is a familiar sight outside London.

It is not just the cars themselves which qualify for the Warrant. When it comes to buffing up those superglossy vehicular surfaces a chamois leather from Eastern Counties Leather of Sawston near Cambridge will be the tool of the trade. Esso have the Warrant as 'Purveyors of Motor Spirit'. Oil features prominently in the Warrant portfolio – Mobil, Shell and BP also hold Warrants. Champion Sparking Plugs hold it and Godfrey Davis Europcar, the car hire firm, were granted it in 1982. In fact, the Davis association with Royalty goes back at least as far as King Edward VIII's abdication. On the night that the ex-King and Mrs Simpson went into exile, a daily newspaper rang Godfrey Davis and asked for a large Humber, specifying that it be driven by Driver Marlow, 'whose dash had impressed them on previous occasions'. As Marlow set off with a crowd of journalists and photographers on board, he was told to 'follow that car'. He soon realised that not only was he following The Duke and Duchess of Windsor but that his Humber was practically indistinguishable from the two in front of him. At Portsmouth Dockyard

OPPOSITE *Whispering Giants – a row of engines at the Rolls Royce factory in Crewe*

ABOVE *Hands on the wheel – a wheelwright at Croford Ltd., Coachbuilders to The Queen,
applies some finishing touches*

Castrol and Esso both have Warrants for lubricating and fuelling the Royal motor cars

the credentials of the leading car were examined and the two Humbers behind – Marlow's included – went through without being checked on the assumption that they were both part of the Royal party. As The Duke and Duchess disembarked at the quayside, the newspapermen leapt out and began firing off questions and flashbulbs. At last the authorities realised what had happened. The journalists were arrested and spent the night in the cells.

The company has always had a wide variety of clients. In 1932 just after the first speed limit was introduced, the police often had too few cars and had to hire from Davis. They would flag down lawbreakers by pulling alongside, ringing a handbell and holding out a wooden board on a handle with a message saying 'Police Car. Stop!'

It might be unexpected to find a car hire company among the Warrant Holders but it is even more so to discover that Edwardes of Camberwell have the Warrant for supplying Her Majesty with mopeds. This is not because we have a Monarchy given to hurtling about the streets on two wheels, but because those who have the Warrant do not supply just members of the Royal Family but the servants of the Royal Household too.

Perhaps this is the way of the future. In his book *Royalty on the Road*, Lord Montagu of Beaulieu, our leading authority on the motor car, wrote slightly gloomily that 'motoring as we have known it in the past is unlikely to continue, and the days of Royalty – or indeed any of us – on the road may well be numbered.' He wrote that in 1980 but, despite the creeping congestion of the M25, there seems little sign of the Royal Family abandoning the motor car.

Geography is perhaps the most essential subject for a monarch to master, even when the pink on the globe is in ever shorter supply. If Royalty needs to get from A to B, or simply contemplate the vestiges of an Empire on which the sun used never to set, then it is a Bartholomew globe or a Bartholomew map that they will consult. When The Queen was a child, her governess, Miss Crawford, once sent a curriculum to Queen Mary. More geography was Queen Mary's advice. Bartholomew's in Edinburgh still treasure the first rough work sheets of their founder, John Bartholomew, who in 1826 delivered the following

A rare early SSI model Jaguar

in 1760, only ten years after their foundation. In 1909 King George V, then Prince of Wales, spoke at the Festival of the Printers' Pension, Almshouse and Orphan Asylum Corporation and paid a handsome and much appreciated tribute to Harrisons and its then boss, James William Harrison. 'Until the Licence Act was abolished in 1695,' said The Prince, 'there was only one newspaper in these islands – the *London Gazette*. [Laughter] Its total circulation was 8,000 copies, much less than one to each parish in the kingdom, and no political intelligence was allowed to be published in it without The King's licence. Since 1760 the *London Gazette* has been printed by the House of Harrison. [Cheers] The head of that firm is present here tonight – [Cheers] – and he is the fourth direct descendant of the original founders of the business.'

The earliest reference to Royal service in this company's history is in an obituary to Thomas Harrison, who died in 1896 and was said to have been descended from an Alice Harrison, née Ward, who was 'cooferer' to Queen Elizabeth I. After over 100 years of printing the *London Gazette*,

An early brochure from the Royal mapmakers

invoice for the Royal account:

Reducing part of Persia, twice . . . 12s 6d
Finishing off North Germany . . . £7 5s 0d
Reducing Ancient Rome . . . £1 10s 0d

Today the company's elegant porticoed façade in Edinburgh conceals a wealth of sophisticated modern map-making equipment capable of everything from a full-colour map of the Scottish clans to over a million road atlases for motorists for serialisation in one of the Sunday colour magazines. They have held a Royal Warrant since the time of Queen Victoria but have never taken it for granted. When it lapsed in 1962 because of a later John Bartholomew's death, the new Chairman did not reapply for over a decade. 'We decided,' he said, 'that the Royal Warrant was something we ought to make ourselves worthy of before we accepted it again.'

Bartholomew's print maps. Different printing, different printers. Greenaway-Harrison hold three Warrants. They are traditionally the printers of the *London Gazette*, the official government newspaper, which they were printing

Instant Dates – Charles Bennet stealing a look at his 'At-a-Glance' calendars, as supplied to Royalty

No longer as pink as in the days of Queen Victoria, but maps from John Bartholomew and Son of Edinburgh still rule the world

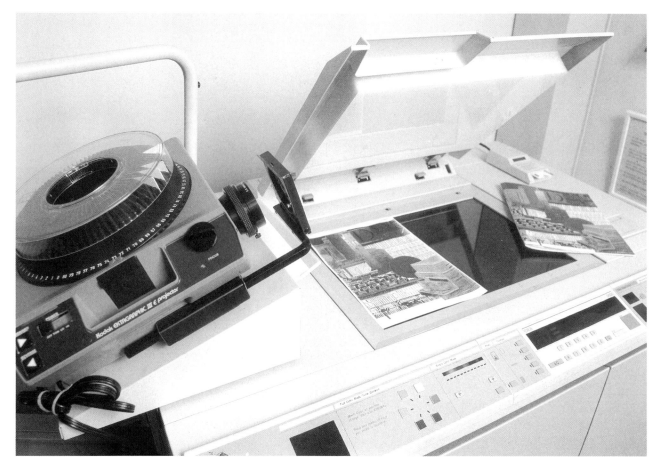

Clean copy – Rank Xerox hold The Queen's Warrant as 'Manufacturers and Suppliers of Xerographic Copying Equipment and Materials'

Harrisons were awarded the Warrant to Queen Victoria as 'Printers in Ordinary'. The designation 'in ordinary' became a matter of some dispute and when King George VI's Warrants were awarded in 1936 they had to revert to being plain 'printers'.

They still print the *London Gazette*, they still print the nation's postage stamps and they still do the printing on state occasions.

Many years ago Harrisons – they became Greenaway-Harrison only in 1982 – recorded with pride the work they had done at coronations, weddings, and the funerals of Disraeli, Palmerston and Queen Victoria. 'To record history,' they said, 'is the province of the printer, but his services are also required in the making of history.'

A different sort of printing is carried out by Norprint International Limited, whose slightly forbidding name disguises a descent from a traveller in buckram cloth, one John Fisher, who invented an untearable cloth tag in 1850. He and George Clark, a bookbinder's son, set up shop in Boston, Lincolnshire, where Fisher had fallen for a nubile

local widow who later became his wife. Early customers included Queen Victoria, Prince Albert, and The Prince of Wales. The early labels were quite primitive but did provide 'a durable card of direction, easily fastened to the traveller's trunk or Christmas hamper'.

The fortunes of the company fluctuated but by the Second World War they were considered sufficiently important to be moved away from Boston – vulnerable to enemy bombs – and over to four disused silk mills in Macclesfield. Here they were involved with government work, including the production of propaganda discs for dropping behind the German lines at Arnhem. These were headed 'Prisoners of Wars are also still soldiers' and reassured the enemy that in the event of capture they would keep their rank and medals, get the same food and medical care as the Allies, pay (guaranteed by the Geneva Convention), be allowed three letters and four postcards a month and be encouraged to learn a trade. 'Germany,' they concluded, 'will need skilled workers after the war.' It made a change from labels for Christmas hampers.

Royal Mail maybe, but Royalty's Express Parcels are handled by Securicor. This is their 'Sorting Out Centre'

Today's Norprint is a highly computerised operation producing 13 billion labels a year.

Lewis East Ltd, 'By Appointment Stationery Makers to The Queen', have been in envelopes since 1919, though their relationship with paper and ink could go back to 1531, when one of the first books in English was credited to a printer called Thomas East. Lewis's father, Walter, produced a penny stationery outfit of pen holder, nib, twelve sheets of paper, six envelopes and a blotter, which enjoyed a considerable vogue with the troops on the Western Front. In 1919 Lewis found a rusty, abandoned envelope-making machine in a scrap-metal merchant's yard in Peterborough. He had no idea whether it would work and, indeed, knew nothing about envelope machines, but he bought it for £100 and somehow got it going. When he died fifty years later his new machines were making 1 million envelopes and his was the most modern envelope-making plant in Europe.

Rexel Business Machines have the Royal Warrant for security shredders. Documents are regularly shredded at all the Royal Palaces and on the Royal Yacht and the company also supply shredders for Royal tours.

Before shredding, however, Royal documents and other parcels and packages are sped about the country by Securicor Ltd. This company began life as a sort of private 'Dad's Army' in 1935. It was originally called 'Night Watch Services' and was launched by the Rt Hon. Edward Shortt, KC, who had been Home Secretary in Lloyd George's last administration. Most of the employees were ex-cavalrymen made redundant by the advent of the tank and armoured car. They were given bicycles and told to protect wealthy clients' houses in Mayfair, Hampstead and St John's Wood. Despite its essentially amateur character, the organisation attracted a degree of opprobrium, and one MP said in the Commons that 'they represent the first halting steps down a road to Fascism'.

It was in the early fifties that one of its founding fathers, Colonel Sherbrooke-Walker, dreamt up the name Securicor while having a bath. A decade or so later, the company acquired an armoured-car company and by 1962

A fountain is the appropriate symbol of Royal Soapmakers Bronnley and Co. at their new factory

Taking his own medicine like a man. John Ainsworth pops a homoeopathic pill at the dispensary
where he produces homoeopathic medicines for Royalty

they had 200 vehicles. In the early seventies Peter Smith, the present Managing Director, took over and immediately set about expanding the company's parcel service. Since 1972 it has carried radio-active materials and more than 600 live kidneys for transplant operations. By 1985 the parcel fleet had grown to 2,500 vehicles and that year it was granted The Queen's Warrant. 'Securicor cares' runs the legend on the side of the company's vehicles, alongside the Royal coat of arms. The *Punch* cartoon response was a similar armoured truck with the slogan 'Burglars don't give a monkey's', which Peter Smith, a past President of the Warrant Holders' Association, thinks is quite a good joke.

Verbal communications are conducted by telephone from Telephone Rentals PLC – 'Dictograph Telephones' in the case of The Queen and The Queen Mother; 'Loud-speaking Telephones' in the case of The Prince of Wales. This company has been in business since 1902, when it first started renting out basic communications systems to businesses. They now supply 30,000 companies in Britain alone, including half in the top 100. Most of their business used to be providing 'internal' systems, but with the relaxation of the Post Office monopoly on 'external' phones that is changing rapidly.

The Royal Family have not been slouches when it comes to investing in new technology. Trivector Systems International of Sandy in Bedfordshire, who were described as 'the first British company to exploit microprocessors', once held a Warrant as 'Computer Suppliers' to the Duke of Edinburgh; and he currently gets his software from BOS Software Ltd of Saffron Hill, London. Stothers and Hardy of Henley and Unisys both have The Queen's Warrant and IBM supply electronic typewriters to The Queen and The Prince of Wales.

The Royal medicine cupboards are stocked from a variety of sources though the most recognisable one is almost certainly Boots the Chemists, launched with an amazing advertising campaign in the Nottingham *Daily Express* in 1877. Jesse Boot's original advertisement listed 128 items from Allen's Hair Restorer to Woodward's Gripe Water and it increased his weekly income from £20 to £100 a week. That same year Boot introduced his company's first ever 'own-brand' product – 'Boot's Lobelia Pills', prepared by his sister Jessica in the back room of their original shop in Goose Gate, Nottingham, with the slogan 'Health for a Shilling'.

His wife, Florence, was almost as instrumental in the company's early success as Jesse. It was she who

Boots, Royal Chemists, advertising in the Daily Mail, *1907*

pioneered the diversification into fashion, beauty and stationery, as well as making sure every Boots employee got a mug of cocoa before work, a silk scroll with an improving verse at Christmas and a Bible when they got married.

In 1931, two years after Jesse died, Florence opened the 1,000th Boots shop, and today the company has grown to such a size that the turnover is more than £2,000 million. When the company produced a full list of 'own brands' to celebrate its centenary, there were eight close-packed pages of small type. It is reassuring to find such hardy perennials as Friar's Balsam, Gee's Linctus and Syrup of Figs among them; and to realise that among the 50,000 or so items regularly stocked by Boots there are still bars of soap – the company manufactures 40 million a year.

Wallace Cameron of Glasgow supply 'Ultraplast' first-aid dressings and their sister-company, Cromessol, supply detergents and air sprays. A particular speciality of theirs is a range of industrial first-aid kits, including special ones for sports clubs, drivers and factories – these are designed to comply with health and safety regulations. There is even a kit 'for the individual worker travelling away from the office or place of work'.

When Queen Victoria succeeded to the throne in 1837 there were no bathrooms in Buckingham Palace, even though Louis XIV had been installing them at Versailles in 1667. A concerned parliament voted Victoria £5,000 a year for 'her toilette and clothes'. Today The Queen's soaps come from six different sources, including one of the rare foreign Warrant Holders, Roger & Gallet of Paris, whose eau de cologne was a great favourite of the Emperor Napoleon. He used to sponge some into his bathwater and emptied the rest unadulterated over his neck and shoulders. The cologne was devised by Jean-Marie Farina in Santa Maria Maggiore in 1806. Fifteen years later he set up shop in the Rue Saint-Honoré in Paris and eventually sold the business to a French family, two of whose members were Armand Roger and Charles Gallet. It was they who launched the famous soaps in 1889. Today the company uses a computer to monitor the blending of Extra-Vieille Eau de Cologne but the recipe is still Jean-Marie Farina's and it still incorporates eighty-seven oils based on such exotic natural ingredients as Sicilian limes, Portuguese oranges, Bulgarian roses and Grasse jasmin.

One of the more bashful Warrant Holders, in its early days at least, was Bronnley Soaps, whose founder, Jimmy Bronnley, was invited to greet Queen Mary when she came to open the YWCA in Acton, where the Bronnley soap

Lever Brothers still have a Royal Warrant for soap

factory was. Jimmy, who had started the company in 1883, was too shy to accept. Today the company is still private and run by his descendants. Soaps also come from Lever Brothers, Morny, Procter and Gamble, and Yardley.

Antiseptics are provided by the pharmaceutical division of Reckitt and Colman, whose activities, like those of some other Warrant Holders, are so diverse that they crop up in a number of different guises. As Colman's of mustard fame they feature under commissariat; Airwick does Airwick; and their household products division does air fresheners, polishes and cleaners. Each one has its own individual Royal Warrant.

It all seems a far cry from the mid-nineteenth century, when Isaac Reckitt and his sons produced their first washing blue and blacklead for polishing grates, and Jeremiah Colman and his nephew built their first mustard mill. Over the years Reckitt and Colman have introduced a number of products which have become so popular that they have slipped into the national vocabulary: Brasso arrived in 1905; Cherry Blossom boot polish a year later; and Dettol in 1933.

Their older Royal Warrants tended to be for 'Mustard, Starch and Blue', though it was not, alas, one of their starches that was described in a Victorian newspaper advertisement as 'used in the Royal Laundry and pronounced by Her Majesty's Laundress to be the Finest Starch she ever used'. On the other hand, Sir James Reckitt did beard the person in charge of Napoleon III's laundry in Paris and get them to promise to give his starch a trial.

Although the Royal medicine cupboard is well stocked with conventional products, the Royal Family has long been associated with homoeopathy. Here a crucial Warrant is held by Ainsworths homoeopathic pharmacy in New Cavendish Street, London. Even the homoeo-pathic remedies for the common cold by Ainsworths make fascinating reading: Aconite and Arsenic Alb; Belladonna and Bryonia, Phosphorus and Pulsatilla. 'If possible,' they advise, 'establish a link with a homoeo-pathic doctor', adding with practical good sense, 'In any case, keep in touch with your NHS doctor – you may need help when least expected.'

Mercifully, the Royal Family has not had much use for invalid carriages or wheelchairs since the late King George VI had to use a Carters Electric Carriage. Queen Elizabeth The Queen Mother did once have to launch a ship from one after spraining an ankle, which explains why Carters hold her Warrant.

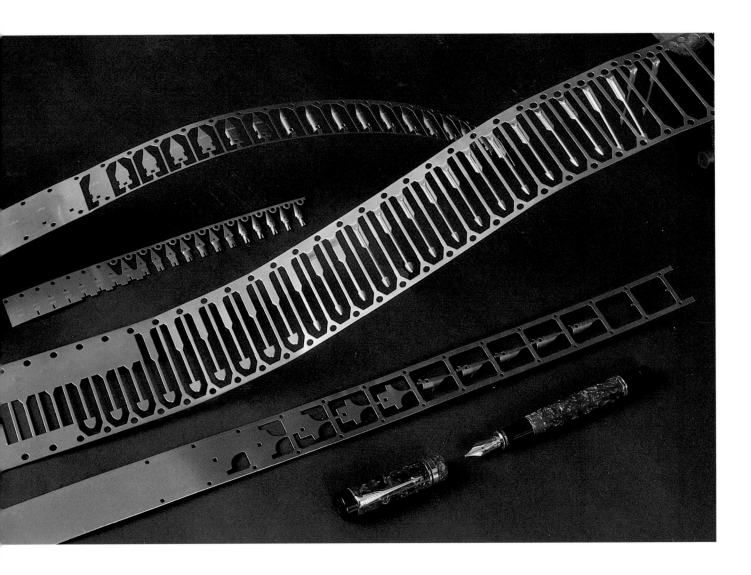

ABOVE Nibs and distinctive arrow-shaped clips from Parker Pens of Newhaven, Sussex, who supply Her Majesty The Queen with pens, pencils and ink

OPPOSITE A Royal Flush. Grantee and former Warrant Holders' President Victor Watson of Waddington Ltd. looking out from between the company's playing cards

Another unusual Warrant in this area is the one granted to James North and Sons for supplying safety footwear. When North began in 1868 in Colne, Lancashire, he was in chamois dressing. From that he and his three sons moved into gloves. They made the gauntlets for Shackleton's expedition to the Antarctic, and Sir Ernest said they were the finest gloves he had ever seen. Up until the outbreak of the Second World War the firm was mainly concerned with fashion, but between 1939 and 1945 Norths specialised in anti-gas mittens and webbing for the forces.

Afterwards the company pioneered work in plastics and PVC, patenting the first plastic glove in 1947, but this, alas, proved to be ahead of its time. In desperation the company donated the surplus plastic gloves to industry as 'samples'. Mercifully, this was a success and the gloves were subsequently marketed under the trade name 'Glovelies'. Thus encouraged, Norths began to concentrate on safety garments for industry. Safety footwear was first introduced in 1963. In 1972 the company was absorbed into the Siebe Group and they say that now their special skills and developments 'are in a different field from that for which we were honoured with the Royal Warrant'.

Since 1761, when John Dollond was appointed optician to King George III, Dollonds, or their present-day successors Hamblin, have been opticians to every King or Queen with the exception of Edward VII. The Dollonds were originally Huguenot silk weavers in Spitalfields but by 1752 they were firmly established in the optical trade, operating from a shop near the Strand at the sign of the Golden Spectacles and Sea Quadrant.

As well as succeeding his father as optician to George III, John's son Peter was a master maker of optical instruments, particularly telescopes. Frederick the Great bought two of these in 1776 and the East India Company bought three for the Emperor Ch'ien-lung in 1793. In the Napoleonic Wars the telescopes were so popular that they were generally known as 'Dollonds'. It was almost certainly a Dollond that Nelson clapped to his blind eye during the Battle of Trafalgar.

In the mid-nineteenth century Dollonds fitted the Royal Yacht with optical instruments, but the last Dollond left the business in 1871 and two new families, the Aitchisons and the Hamblins, joined the company. Today all three names are preserved and the present Warrant Holder, and therefore successor to George III's optician, is the Chairman of Hamblin the Opticians, who are now

A presentation pair of Aitchison binoculars dated 1900. For use in the Boer War

part of the Dollond and Aitchison Group.

Denis Vere Collings of New Barnet is The Queen's calligrapher, but members of the Royal Household clearly do some of their own writing too. Pens, pencils and ink are supplied by Parker, who, together with Berol of King's Lynn, are the only company with Warrants for writing implements. Parker's is one of those cheering stories where a management team 'bought out' their company from a parent and transformed it. The Parker buy-out happened in 1986 after the American company had experienced five years of poor results, partly through trying to compete with the cheap end of the market. It cost the team $100 million, but since they bought it the company, based in Newhaven, Sussex, has been transformed.

The original Parker, George, was a Wisconsin schoolteacher who sold pens to his pupils in order to supplement his income. In 1894 he patented the 'Lucky Curve', which was his revolutionary way of feeding ink to the nib. In 1898 he patented the first slip-on pencap. In 1899 a jointless pen was introduced to eliminate leakage and in 1904 the company invented a rubber sac and pressure bar. Before that fountain pens had been filled from a container much like an eye dropper.

Other Parker innovations have included the capillary filling system (1956) and Super Quink (1931), the first ink which incorporated its own pen-cleaning formula.

Today Parker is emphatically back at the top end of the non-disposable pen market, where it is the world's brand-leader. In their first year of independent British ownership they exceeded all financial targets. The Queen has been writing with a Parker filled with Parker ink since 1962.

The Queen's and The Queen Mother's Christmas card and calendar suppliers are Valentines of Dundee. The company began in 1825, when John Valentine set up as an engraver of wood blocks for linen printing. His son James joined and designed a series of illustrated envelopes, which were the forerunners of the picture postcard. After studying photography in Paris he began printing well-known scenes, and by 1890, the year the Forth Bridge was opened, Valentines had 30,000 views catalogued.

Postcards were still a government monopoly, but in 1897 Valentines got permission to write on the other side of them. This concession, coupled with their pioneering of 'collotype' printing, brought them a worldwide reputation for picture postcards.

Despite the two world wars and the Depression, business flourished until, in 1963, Valentines became a wholly-owned subsidiary of another Royal Warrant Holder, John Waddington of Leeds. Sadly, at the same time Valentines withdrew from the long-standing postcard business and the views which had made them famous and went into gift paper, matching tags and ribbons instead. In 1980 Waddington sold the company to Hallmark of Kansas City, USA.

The company's first Warrant was as photographer to Queen Victoria. From 1945 until 1970 they were fine art publishers to Queen Elizabeth, first as Queen, then as Queen Mother. Then, in the early seventies, this became a Christmas Card Warrant, though they were only granted The Queen's Warrant in 1985.

Her Majesty The Queen's plastic-bag suppliers are R and L of London, who have mushroomed in less than a decade from a three-person family company to a concern

The sex appeal of the early fountain pen

with an annual turnover of millions and a capacity for turning out every conceivable sort of polythene bag. It is perhaps not surprising to find the Laurier family describing themselves as 'the Bags to Riches Company'.

But the final word, as far as the Royal Family's office work goes, surely belongs to Medway Packaging of Larkfield, near Medway. Every day some forty lorryloads of sacks, mainly of paper, leave Medway for any number of destinations. Those for Her Majesty Queen Elizabeth II, however, represent the end of the line. They are for domestic refuse.

Alan Woolner of the Fen Ditching Company at the helm of one of his ditch-digging machines near Wisbech, Cambridgeshire

FARMING AND THE LAND

'This other Eden demi-Paradise'
(Shakespeare: *Richard II*)

It is easy to forget that the Royal Family are considerable farmers. The great estates at Sandringham and Balmoral are not just holiday houses but the focal point of large modern farms. Any uncertainty on this point is quickly dispelled by seeing how many agricultural companies hold Royal Warrants. Many of these are, to the layman at least, quite unexpected if not actually bizarre.

The Royal estates use a great deal of agricultural machinery, including what is possibly the largest harvester in modern agriculture and one which is exported to twenty-six other countries. This is the great pea harvester, introduced by the FMC Corporation in the early 1960s. It is manufactured at Fakenham, Norfolk, only a dozen miles from Sandringham. The pea harvest usually takes place over six weeks between late June and early August and during that time the harvesters work day and night. The latest machines can cope with 1,000 acres a season and have a special patented method of getting the peas out of the pod without damaging them – a definite improvement on human endeavour. Each machine can harvest enough peas for more than a million individual helpings every working day.

There is a lot of Royal grass to be cut. Atco of Derby make motor mowers for The Queen and The Prince of Wales. Ransomes of Ipswich have The Queen's Warrant for the more indeterminate 'Agricultural and Horticultural Machinery', a reflection in part on the fact that they tend to refer to 'grass-cutting machinery' instead of lawn mowers for professional users – local government authorities, golf courses, playing fields and the larger ornamental gardens.

Robert Ransome started the business at Norwich when he took out a patent for tempering cast-iron plough shares and moved to Saint Margaret's Ditches, Ipswich, four years later. At first he specialised in ploughs, but he soon diversified into farm machinery of every kind. In 1832 the firm started making lawn mowers. One of these was presented to Queen Victoria at the Royal Windsor Show in 1889. She already owned a Ransome thrasher but was so pleased with the mower that she promptly ordered a second. In 1902 Ransomes produced the world's first petrol-powered mower and later demonstrated it to King Edward VII at Buckingham Palace. W. G. Grace was a fervent admirer of the new machine, which damaged the wicket so much less than the old-fashioned horse-drawn contraptions. During the First World War Ransomes converted to munitions and produced 790 aeroplanes and 3 million shell and fuse components. The first plane ever produced by them, an FE2B, shot down a German Zeppelin at Theberton.

Today the company is the biggest manufacturer of grass-cutting machinery in Europe, though they are also well known for their ploughs. In addition they make potato planters and harvesters, sugar and fodder beet harvesters, straw choppers, powered rotary harrows, grain drills and fertiliser distributors.

Edwin Budding of Stroud invented the lawn mower in 1830, and Ransomes sold it. Today's Ransome Express has an electric start and is self-propelled. 'Country gentlemen', ran the 1830 specification, 'may find in using a machine themselves an amusing, useful and healthy exercise.' *Plus ça change!* At least, up to a point.

It is not the grass, however, but the soil itself which is a problem in a country like Norfolk, where the Fen Ditching Company and the Lincolnshire Drainage Company have The Queen's Warrant for 'Drainage and Irrigation'.

Milking machines for the Royal cattle are from

Sledgehammers for nuts – massive FMC pea harvesters, as used on the Royal estate at Sandringham

Gascoigne-Melotte, whose installations can be found in more than sixty countries around the world, including such unlikely ones as Egypt, Saudi Arabia and Libya. They were in the innovative van in the 1880s, when they developed the 'Melotte Cream Separator', and today they are still pioneers, with new developments on the farm involving micro-processors.

The Royal cattle-feed is provided by BOCM Silcock, the biggest animal-feed manufacturer in Britain, who produce almost 2 million tonnes of feed for cattle, sheep, pigs and poultry. They employ 1,700 people, have twenty-one feed mills all over the country and invest more than £2 million a year on research and development. Their nutritional development farm in Cheshire has eighty dairy cows, forty followers, 300 beef animals and 1,200 purchased calves. There are 150 breeding ewes and 150 sows

producing 3,000 pigs a year, and the poultry trials involve 9,000 layers, 4,500 pullets and more than 20,000 broilers. They are the main company in what they describe as 'Unilever's world-wide Agribusiness Co-ordination' and statistics such as these, not to mention the annual turnover of more than £400 million, are a potent reminder that farming today really is an industry.

Experimental herds – one of Poll Hereford cattle and another of Dorset sheep – also play a key role in the work of Chapman and Frearson and their subsidiary, Equiform of Grimsby. They have Warrants for animal food additives (technically 'protein balancers, mineral supplements, vitamin feed supplements and feed additives').

Nine different companies hold the Warrant under the generic heading of agricultural chemicals and fertilisers. This is perhaps not surprising given the claim of Reg

Anthony Bamford, Chairman of the family firm, at the controls of a 'JCB'

'Royal dairymaids phased out'. Thanks to Warrant Holding Gascoigne milking equipment this Kent farmer can milk all two hundred cows on his own

*'I am His Highness' Dog at Kew – pray tell me, sir, whose dog are you?' Dalton Supplies Ltd. make
identity tags for Royal animals*

Royal rubbish – BACO-Compak (Norfolk) Ltd. hold The Queen's Warrant for waste disposal

Norman, Managing Director of the Warrant-Holding Ciba-Geigy Agrochemicals, that, 'In Britain the agrochemicals industry's success in protecting food production from the losses caused by the competition of weed, pest and disease has been one of the main factors in the achievement by the UK of its near self-sufficiency in food needs.' Mr Norman cites four of his products – Dicurane, Ridomil, TopClip Sheep Dip and Nuvan Top – as examples of major breakthroughs in weed, pest and disease control which have gone on to become best-selling brands taken for granted by today's farmers. Dicurane cures black-grass; TopClip deals with blowfly strike and sheep scab; another product, Tilt, was the first 'broad spectrum material to control Net Blotch' in cereals.

Their British company at Whittlesford, Cambridge, is a subsidiary of the vast Swiss concern and most original research is carried out in Basle. Subsequent trials, however, take place in this country in more than 500 farms, and testing never really ceases because farmers continue to report back on products as long as they are in use.

ICI also hold a Warrant for fertilisers and they too have a product range of stunning complexity and sophistication. It is salutary for those who think agriculture is as simple as Richard Briers and Felicity Kendal made it look in the TV series *The Good Life* to

realise quite what has happened in recent years. In 1986, for example, ICI reported that the collapse in oil prices had led to rapid falls in the price of ammonia, methanol and urea. Because of this we imported a lot of cheap East European urea. As a result sales of catalysts to methanol producers declined. Meanwhile, in North America fertiliser prices fell by 30 per cent and Canadian gas costs failed to keep pace with American ones, as a result of which . . . It all seems a far cry from *The Archers*.

Scottish Agricultural Industries, who have the Warrant for seed and fertiliser, are now a wholly owned subsidiary of ICI. Another Warrant Holder, Kemira of Lincoln, claims to be the oldest fertiliser company in the country, with roots going back to 1835.

Some of the Royal farm buildings come from Frank Dale Ltd of Leominster in Herefordshire, a company begun in 1932 with capital of £100. With no money to spare the original terms of business were noticeably fierce. 'Prices have been fixed on a VERY LOW BASIS,' said an early prospectus, 'and are to meet the CASH BUYER ONLY. To save delay it is respectfully requested to send CASH WITH ORDER.' Poultry sheds were the first speciality, but the firm could do anything from wheelbarrows to pigsties, provided they were made from timber.

By the fifties they had expanded to the point of

'Woodman, woodman ...' William Matthews of Southern Tree Surgeons, Tree Surgeons to The Queen, supervises a minor arboreal operation

OPPOSITE *Roger Taylor, of O.A. Taylor and Sons, Royal bulb growers, stands among some new-style lily hybrids in Spalding, Lincs*

ABOVE *Mending wall. Robin Callander of Finzean, Aberdeenshire is the Royal Drystane Dyker, building and restoring walls in time-honoured Scots fashion*

Willem den-Hartog of the Lincolnshire Drainage Company puts the pipes into the ditches dug by his friends and neighbours at Fen Ditching

employing 250 men and making hop-kiln units, farm cottages and even a pectin-loading bay for another local Warrant Holder – Bulmers, the Hereford cider makers. Frank Dale was granted The Queen's Warrant for work on the Balmoral estate and though he died before his company's fiftieth anniversary, it is still very much a Dale company with his two sons at the helm.

'The magnificent lawns at Sandringham', as Bryan Hall of Eastern Counties Farmers Ltd describes them, owe some of their magnificence to the herbage seed provided by his company in the early sixties. Since then ECF have supplied a wide range of products to the estate, mainly large purchases of grain and peas. ECF is a farmers' co-operative started in 1904 by seven perceptive farmers and expanding to its present membership of more than 6,000. Its original aims – virtually unchanged today – were 'to provide a continuing independent force, strong enough to exert an influence on the market for the benefit of, and

within the control of, its trading farmer members'. Or, as Ken Doughty of White Hart Farm at Thorney near Peterborough puts it, 'Only co-operatives can stand up to the multi-nationals and save the family farms as we know them.'

There are forty-five miles of private roads at Balmoral alone and in 1982 the Leicester engineering firm of E. C. Hallam was granted a Warrant for providing Hallam Graders to build and maintain them. Hallam Graders are used for road construction and maintenance all over the world, from the West Indies to the Solomon Islands. In the mid-seventies they branched out into aviation tractors and in 1985 sold twenty-seven to the Ministry of Defence. Their association with the Royal Family has been enhanced by this because one of them is now at RAF Benson, headquarters of The Queen's Flight.

Some of the produce of the Royal gardens at Windsor is sold by J. and E. Page (Sales) Ltd, who have been in flowers for over 100 years. Like the rest of the industry they have now decamped from Covent Garden to the new market at Nine Elms, south of the Thames. Although they were founded in the last century, there was a change of emphasis in the twenties, when Carlo Naef, grandfather of Patrick Hackett, the present Managing Director, joined the Pages. It was then that an enduring relationship with the Spalding Bulb Company commenced and Pages began to concentrate more on selling than growing. Pages now sell flowers to Buckingham Palace and Windsor Castle and have a team of thirty-two specialist salesmen. They sell all sorts of flowers, though most of their people were, as they put it, 'brought up on a diet of daffodils and tulips'.

The Queen's trees are cared for by Southern Tree Surgeons of Crawley Down in Sussex, who have held the Warrant since 1983. They have been specialists in tree care for more than thirty years and are the largest organisation of their kind in Europe. W. E. Matthews, their Managing Director, says that their work at Sandringham is 'entirely concerned with amenity trees – planting the right ones in the right place at the right time'. Then they have to go on making sure that they survive in a healthy condition.

On their first visit to Sandringham a theory had just been published that the normal broad-leaved tree grew at the rate of one inch circumference every year. As all the Sandringham trees have plaques giving the exact day they were planted, it was an obvious place to test the theory. Unfortunately, however, they had not brought a long-enough tape measure. They therefore measured everyone's 'arm-spread' and then linked arms around the tree to arrive at the total. Others present that day must have assumed that they were observing some ancient Druidic rite. Most tree owners assume that any accident involving their trees is automatically an act of God, but this is evidently not so. Under the law tree owners are required to examine all their trees at least once a year to check for signs of trouble. Southern Tree Surgeons say that if this were done by an expert, nearly all tree accidents could be prevented.

Forestry equipment is the province of Stanton Hope, a small company based in Basildon, Essex, which only employs about half a dozen people but turns over £½ million a year selling mole traps, respirators for forestry spraying, heavy-duty Irish slashers with rings and bolts, debarking knives, Forestry Commission-style carrying frogs with stones and edge-tool gauges, Fussel fagging

hooks, climbing irons, creosote thermometers and all the other alarming tools of the forester's trade.

Perhaps the most surprising of all Warrants are the ones held by Semex of Tunnoch Park, Dalrymple, in Ayrshire. Semex (UK Sales Ltd) have The Queen's and The Queen Mother's Warrants for cattle-breeding services. It is a Canadian company which exports Canadian bulls' semen to fifty countries all over the world. They now produce more than a million 'doses' a year. By using artificial insemination a single prolific bull can sire tens of thousands of daughters.

When Semex began their British initiative in 1974 they encountered strong resistance to the idea of Canadian strains being introduced into the country. This has now been largely overcome because the Canadians apparently have one of the most effective 'Sire Proving' programmes in the world. Every year these involve mating more than 180,000 officially identified cows with 300 promising sires under strict government supervision. The Canadians are now so expert that they can offer specifications on their bulls which are as detailed as those in the average car manual.

In 1984, the centenary of the Canadian Holstein Breeders' Association, they produced a long-term strategy. At the moment the average Canadian cow has five calves and milks for five years with an average annual production of 1,475 gallons. The Canadians are now aiming for six calves a lifetime and an annual milk yield increasing by 1 per cent a year.

After their matings the young bulls are sent into retirement to await results. So stringent are the Canadian rules that only one in seven is returned to service. A typical bull specification runs as follows:

Thunder is one of this generation's truly elite sires. He has an impressive conformation proof and at the same time is a significant improver of milk and butterfat. Thunder sires tall dairy cows that have good capacity. Thunder daughters have high, wide rear attachments with strong suspensory ligaments. He can be used to best advantage on cows with good depth of heel and some straightness in their legs. Thunder is being used by many organisations as a planned mating sire.

At moments like this agriculture seems to move almost into the world of science fiction. Advice from some of the specialised seedsmen, for example, sometimes beggars belief. 'Contamination by less than 5% of a feed wheat variety in a quality wheat can halve the hagberg falling number. For example, a Norman contamination in Mercia

OPPOSITE *Fred Newman and family of Abbey Rose Gardens, Rose Growers to Royalty, at home in Buckinghamshire with selected blooms*

ABOVE *One of Royal florist Edward Goodyear's vans displaying that enviable distinction – a full set of all four Warrants*

The Old Flower Seed Order Room at Sutton's in Reading. They now supply seeds from Torquay, Devon

could reduce the Hagberg from 280 to 140, changing the sample from bread making to feed.' That is from Sinclair McGill of Boston, Lincolnshire, Seedsmen to The Queen. They have just introduced 'electrophoretic varietal finger printing' into their quality-control system.

The Royal gardens are fertilised by 'horticultural chemicals' from four different sources. Bentley of Barrow-on-Humber have been established over 100 years and have held the Warrant continuously since 1909. Their sulphate of ammonia is particularly recommended for cabbage, spinach and rhubarb; their mercurised lawn sand destroys moss; their sulphate of potash is good for tomatoes and apples; and their gruesomely named 'Hoof and Horn' and 'Blood, Fish and Bone' are both totally organic.

The Royal seedsmen, nurserymen, plant specialists and their ilk tend to congregate near the Royal country houses, but in a nation of gardeners it is hardly surprising to find them cropping up everywhere, all with different antecedents, all with different strengths. One, Dobbie & Co., the Edinburgh nursery and garden centre company, was started by a Victorian Chief Constable, James Dobbie, whose first great success was leek seed, packeted under the name 'Dobbie's Champion'. At the 1988 Glasgow Garden Festival, Dobbie's shared a garden with the National Trust for Scotland. Fargro of West Sussex are horticultural sundriesmen, offering an almost bewildering variety of products in their latest 128-page catalogue. They are a 600-strong co-operative, supplying peat, fertilisers,

chemicals, polythene, packaging and any number of other products to the Royal parks in Windsor and London. Their Managing Director, J. C. Gilford, is on his second Warrant because, in a previous incarnation, he supplied the Royal parks with chrysanthemum cuttings.

Sandringham sugar beet seed comes from Booker Seeds of Sleaford, Lincolnshire, a subsidiary of Booker PLC, which has an immensely complicated business history that can, by a tortuous route, claim descent from a Mr Field and a Mr Child, who were selling seeds in Pudding Lane in the City of London in 1560. The modern company also supplies flower and vegetable seeds for Balmoral, where the head gardener has a notably knotty problem in supplying fresh produce for a Royal visit which always takes place so late in the season. Balmoral has also been used by Bookers as a test bed for new pelargonium hybrids which originate from the unlikely source of the German Democratic Republic! Other seedsmen such as Suttons and Hilliers – both with two Warrants – provide horticultural as opposed to agricultural seeds.

Perhaps the most symbolic of all the Royal plants is the rose. All the Royal gardens contain a predictable variety of different blooms, but two rose growers hold The Queen's Warrant, Cocker and Sons, at Lang Stracht on the outskirts of Aberdeen, and the Abbey Rose Gardens at Burham – the first conveniently placed for Balmoral, the second for Windsor. Both are family businesses, with Mrs Cocker (whose late husband was responsible for breeding the world famous Silver Jubilee rose) running the Scottish and Fred Newman the English. The Royal connection leaps out from every page of their catalogues. Duke of Windsor has 'vermilion blooms and bush habit'; Royal William was 1987's Rose of the Year and is a 'strong healthy grower', deep red and fragrant with good foliage. There is Silver Jubilee itself, another named Elizabeth of Glamis and a miniature bush of carmine pink known as Royal Salute. And then there is Mountbatten, 'vigorous and upright with trusses of mimosa yellow flowers', which was Rose of the Year in 1982, and naturally, Queen Elizabeth, 'extra tall with hybrid-tea-type flowers of purest pink'.

'What's in a name?' asks Juliet of Romeo. 'That which we call a rose/by any other name would smell as sweet.' Royal roses might smell as sweet by another name, but it wouldn't be the same.

The Queen Mother visits Hilliers

Simone Mirman came to Britain from Paris in 1947 with a working capital of just £1. She has made hats for The Queen since 1965

STYLE AND RADIANCE

'The appearance of Your majesty, as of the Sun in his strength'
(Introduction to the Authorised version of the Bible)

Superlatives are invidious but few living Warrant Holders can have had more effect on the Royal image than Sir Hardy Amies, as he described in his autobiography, *Still Here*. 'I think it was one of the biggest surprises in my life as a dress designer,' he says, 'when I saw the gold coach coming out from under the arches of Buckingham Palace and we suddenly caught a glimpse of The Queen wearing a bright-pink silk dress. "Goodness me!" we all cried. "It's our dress from Montreal."' This was the Royal Jubilee and the dress in question was the one that Sir Hardy had designed for the Montreal Olympics.

Throughout much of his working life Sir Hardy has been present for numerous ceremonial occasions when Her Majesty The Queen has been clothed in his own designs. He has been making clothes for her since 1950, when as Princess Elizabeth she first called at the Amies's headquarters in – of course – Savile Row and installed in the dressmaker 'a deep feeling of chivalry which has never subsided'. Born in 1909, the dapper, witty Sir Hardy was still, at the time of writing, going strong and was very much in charge of the famous fashion house he started himself just after the Second World War.

Despite taking a proper pride in having contributed what he refers to as 'one tiny spot to the superb panorama of her successful reign', he is meticulous about not scooping all the credit for himself. He is one of four dressmaking Warrant Holders; other hands are responsible for parts of the outfits – the hats, the belts and the handbags, for instance. And perhaps most important, in the beginning, was the late Sir Norman Hartnell.

'I am not giving to praising my colleagues,' Amies wrote in his autobiography, when he recalled the Coronation, 'but I do think that Norman Hartnell had done an absolutely superb job and I can think of no one who could

have done it better. I have to this day a clear picture of the dress as being very pearly in appearance, made up of muted pale colours, each blending into the other, giving an effect of immense iridescence. What I also admired when I saw pictures of the service later on television was the cut of the skirt which moved so gracefully as The Queen walked in her procession.'

Although Hartnell himself is dead his company survives and still holds the Warrant. He first began making The Queen's clothes in 1935. His was the Coronation dress and his the wedding dress. After the wedding in 1947 James Laver, the historian of dress and costume, declared Hartnell 'no mean poet' for his 'design based on delicate Botticelli curves' with its 'ivory satin garlands of white York roses carried out in raised pearls, entwined with ears of corn minutely embroidered in crystal'. Laver added: 'By the device of reversed embroidery he has alternated star flowers and orange blossom, now tulle on satin and now satin on tulle, the whole encrusted with pearls and crystals.'

For many years the design of The Queen's special outfits was a matter of intense speculation. Eventually an arrangement was worked out whereby newspapers could publish sketches on the morning of the ceremony concerned. Much the best of these were the ones in the *Daily Express* by Robb, the paper's resident illustrator, also famous for his illustrations of the James Bond books. After every assignment Hartnell would reward Robb with a square of satin with a sample of the exquisite embroidery by which he had made the House of Hartnell famous. Robb had them framed and when Hartnell first saw them he commented: 'Amongst them, for Canada, was the maple leaf in green velvet and emeralds on pale green; for Australia the yellow mimosa (or wattle); for

Norman Parkinson's 80th birthday tribute to The Queen Mother shows her, The Queen and Princess Margaret all in blue satin capelets by Royal dressmaker, Sir Hardy Amies

France the fleurs des champs – gold with Napoleon's busy bee in brown chenille; for the Vatican jet and diamonds on black lace with a veil for an audience with the Pope; for Pakistan emerald beads and diamonds and for Japan a mist of pink cherry-blossom cascading down a backcloth of azure chiffon. And in another all the emblems of Great Britain and the Commonwealth clustered together upon the dress I designed for Her Majesty's Coronation.'

Obviously there is more to royal dressmaking than meets the eye, though few Warrant Holders' work meets the eye so obviously as that of the dressmakers. These mementos, continued Hartnell, 'hang there not as a memoir of ephemeral fashion but as a reminder of the historic significance of all the great State visits, so dutifully undertaken by our beloved monarch Her Majesty The Queen'.

The Queen's various accessories, as Sir Hardy Amies is quick to point out, are made elsewhere. Gloves are from Cornelia James of Brighton, who also make scarves and various institutional or club ties. The company has made the Royal gloves since the end of the last war, and also does film and TV work. They made Worzel Gummidge's gloves and gloves for the film *Star Wars*. No order is too eccentric for them. They once supplied 400 white scarves with a female face printed on them. It was imperative that this order be met in four days. When they asked why they were told that they were to be handed out to the mourners at a funeral in Nigeria. The face belonged to the deceased. On another occasion they finally asked why, for eighteen years, they had been supplying one customer with an annual order for one left- and fifty-two right-

The Queen's wedding dress by Norman Hartnell

for over forty years. It was said, in tribute to his footwear, that when The Queen was in public she invariably appeared 'to be walking on air'. Sir Edward's company is no longer in family ownership. The Queen's handbags are by S. Launer and Co., who also manufacture handbags to match the shoes of Russell and Bromley. They tend to use German leather and Italian fittings and all their bags are handmade. The Queen's belts are made by Rony, whose Polish-born grantee, Bronislaw Lubowicki, works by hand in what must be one of the smallest workshops in London, tucked away at 8 Avery Row, in the West End of London just behind Bond Street.

Much of the Royal Family's cashmere and other woollen sweaters will come from the little Scottish border town of Hawick, long famous for its rugby football and its knitwear. Thanks to the woollen industry the town has one of the most enviable unemployment records in Britain. Lyle and Scott, now part of Courtaulds, hold Prince Philip's Warrant and Pringle hold The Queen's and the Queen Mother's. Both companies have a huge export trade and both sponsor world-class golfers to promote their wares. The surge in that game's world-wide popularity and the trendiness of golfing clothes has made such a difference to the knitwear industry that some estimates suggest that golfing woollens account for almost half the world market. Tony Jacklin is a Lyle and Scott man; Nick Faldo a Pringle.

Mirman milliners making millinery

handed gentleman's white dress glove. Simple. This elegant person always wore the left glove but carried the right. As he reckoned to lose one right-hand glove a week this order matched his requirements to perfection.

Two milliners have The Queen's Warrant: Simone Mirman, makes the hats which traditionally go with The Queen's Hartnell outfits, and Freddie Fox, makes those which go with the Amies ones. The third dressmaker, Ian Thomas, makes his hats 'in-house'. Mme Mirman, whose daughter Sophie has had an even more sensational success with her Sock Shop chain, trained at Schiaparelli, eloped shortly after the war and started with virtually no capital in 1947. Mr Fox is an Australian who arrived here from Sydney in 1947 and made his first regal hats for The Queen's visit to Mexico.

Sir Edward Rayne had The Queen's Warrant for shoes

*The Queen's gloves come from Cornelia James in Brighton, seen here (OPPOSITE) with her son
Peter, the present grantee, and daughter Genevieve. The scarves also come from Cornelia James.
But not the daffodil (ABOVE)*

The Investiture of The Prince of Wales in Caernarvon Castle. The Queen's hat is by Simone Mirman and the umbrella was restored by her

Lyle and Scott started in 1874, making resolutely functional 'unshrinkable hose and underwear' from the wool of the local sheep. Sadly, that wool is inappropriate for the more luxurious garments they now make and wool is imported – cashmere from Mongolia and merino from Australia. Cashmere is an extraordinary story of its own. In an attempt to destroy the Chinese stranglehold on the market and its sky-rocketing price, there have been efforts to set up cashmere goat farms in Australia, New Zealand and Scotland itself. But so far nothing has seriously damaged Chinese supremacy. All Lyle and Scott's sheep's wool is Australian.

Their friendly rivals across the road, 'Pringle of Scotland', were founded in 1815 by Robert Pringle in the romantically named Whisky House Mill in Cross Wynd. They too started in stockings and underwear but have gradually shifted to more glamorous outer garments, often easily identifiable, just like Lyle and Scott's, by the modern 'designer' custom of wearing the trademark on the outside, almost as part of the design. Pringle is one of

those words which is seen as a desirable piece of self-advertisement.

Pringle now employ around 1,500 people, in a factory studded with sophisticated computers which have accomplished the extraordinary feat of translating the most complicated knitting patterns into full-colour screen diagrams which can be altered at the press of a button. At the same time there are other parts of the process which are still done by hand, much as they have been done for the last 150 years, so that alongside the clinical precision of modern technology you will find sweaters being individually stretched on a Paris press in the scouring house and then squirted with a shot of steam to take out any redundant creases.

They have had The Queen Mother's Warrant since 1948 and The Queen's since 1956, but they have also supplied many other members of the Royal Family, including The Princess of Wales, The Duchess of York, Princess Margaret, The Princess Royal, The Duchess of Kent and Princess Alexandra. They have certainly come a long way since they produced 'Gentlemen's Combinations' in 1927, advertised by a perfectly splendid gentleman posing with one hand resting on his hip while the other clasps a smoking cigarette.

Wolsey, like Lyle and Scott part of Courtaulds, have The Queen's and The Queen Mother's Warrants for 'Hosiery and Knitwear'. The original business from which this world-famous company derives was founded as a cottage industry in Leicester in 1755. The original motto, once the company had been translated from cottage to factory, was 'Weave Truth and Trust'. The name was

"TOO PROUD TO DRESS"

Wolsey underwear in seaside vein

chosen to commemorate Cardinal Wolsey, who is buried at Leicester Abbey, only a few hundred yards from one of the Wolsey factories. Another woollen Warrant Holder with an unusual name is the Corgi Hosiery Company of Ammanford, one of the few Welsh Warrant Holders. Appropriately, they hold The Prince of Wales's Warrant and their name is doubly appropriate – first because it celebrates a famous Crufts victory for a famous Welsh dog, in 1948, and secondly because the dog is also such a well-known Royal favourite. This is a real craft concern. For instance, the hand-finishing of Corgi's cashmere is still the prerogative of just two experts, both female.

A less expected Warrant Holder among the knitwear producers is Remploy Ltd, a company which began in 1945 as 'The Disabled Persons Employment Corporation Ltd'. Its philosophy is that 'severely disabled people can, with just a little bit of help, do real jobs in the real world just like anyone else'. The original initiative came from a committee set up by Ernest Bevin when he was Minister of Labour and National Service during the war. Today

there are Remploy factories all over Britain producing an extraordinary variety of goods: footwear and surgical appliances in Aberdare, cartons and boxes in Aintree; wheelchairs in Ashington; ring binders in Aycliffe; and so on through Brynammon and Cowdenbeath, Hartlepool, Huddersfield, Lydney, Merthyr Tydfil, Penzance, Pontefract, Spennymoor and Wisbech and on through the alphabet to Ystradgynlais.

As they say at Remploy, 'When you have produced furniture, clothes, packet food and washing materials, assembled car and television parts, made leather goods and slippers, printed books and advertising leaflets, produced luxury goods for some of London's top stores, supplied library shelving and made choc-ices, there cannot be many members of the population who have escaped your grasp.' They have had the knitwear Warrant since 1977, but perhaps the most unusual Royal task ever assigned to the company was the manufacture of all 4,600 gold and vermilion chairs for the Investiture of The Prince of Wales in Caernarvon Castle in 1969.

Another organisation which gives work to the disabled and has a Royal Warrant is Papworth Industries, who make travel goods for The Queen and trunks and cabinets for The Queen Mother. These are based on two village settlements, both registered charities. One is at Papworth near Cambridge and the other at Enham near Andover.

Evolution is sometimes so complete that it totally disguises the origin of the species. Aquascutum, for instance, who now offer a wide range of clothing for both sexes in their Regent Street store, hold The Queen Mother's Warrant for weatherproof garments. The firm began simply by manufacturing waterproofs, as its name suggests (*aqua scutum* means water shield in Latin for those who have forgotten their Kennedy's *Latin Primer*!). Invented by two Englishmen in 1851, the original Aquascutum coats were worn by many officers in the Crimean War and were even responsible for saving the lives of a Captain Goodlake and his sergeant. These two were cut off from their comrades but to their amazement the Russians paid them absolutely no attention. The reason was that their coats were – in appearance though not, of course, quality – indistinguishable from those of their enemies. The captain and the sergeant formed up alongside the Russians, marched with them until they were in reach of their own lines and then made a successful dash for cover. Goodlake's lifesaving Aquascutum is now on display at Newstead Abbey in Nottinghamshire, ancestral home of Lord Byron.

A man and his clothes. Sir Hardy Amies, The Queen's dressmaker, together with his fine collection of oriental art. Sir Hardy also designs men's clothes, including his own

Mr and Mrs Bronislaw Lubowicki, who as 'Rony' make belts for The Queen in this tiny workshop just off London's Bond Street

LEFT Edward VII in his famous Aquascutum coat and RIGHT Three military coats from Burberrys as supplied to generations of Royalty

In the First World War Aquascutum said that any officer who complained about one of their coats letting in water would be supplied with a replacement 'free of all charge and argument'.

The hyper-masculine Aquascutum trench coat had epaulettes for binoculars, brass rings on the belt for hand grenades and a gun flap on the right shoulder for extra protection. It was further popularised on cinema screens by Humphrey Bogart, Robert Mitchum and, perhaps less plausibly, by Peter Sellers as Inspector Clouseau.

The first Royal wearer of Aquascutum was King Edward VII, who admired a friend's coat and told his tailor to make one like it. When the tailor tried to buy the Aquascutum cloth he was told loftily that only Aquascutum made Aquascutum coats. Once he had become a customer The King appeared to wear his Aquascutum incessantly, particularly on his European travels, persuading a number of other crowned heads to buy similar coats.

Burberrys, just around the corner in the Haymarket, are another Warrant Holder whose name was originally synonymous with a waterproof coat. Thomas Burberry, a non-smoking teetotaller who never read novels, opened his draper's shop in Basingstoke in 1856 and invented a cloth called 'gaberdine' which was 'untearable and completely weather-proof'. The name 'gaberdine' or 'Gaberdinee' remained until Edward VII changed it by calling repeatedly, 'Give me my Burberry.' Scott, Shackleton and Amundsen all wore Burberry clothing and in the First World War they, like Aquascutum, supplied countless military trench coats. They also provided 'The King of Weatherproofs', a 'Regulation Greatcoat for Officers of the King's Household and Guards'. This was advertised with a paragraph which took breathtaking commercial advantage of the Royal favour, saying:

The fact that two Kings of England, both for the adornment and protection of a splendid *entourage*, and for the familiar uses of themselves in every pursuit dear to the traditions of their august line, should have adopted Burberry, sets a seal on Burberry's Commercial Patent of Precedence which no Committee of Privileges can ever question nor Act of Parliament annul.

G. B. Kent and Sons, who used to make King William IV's toothbrushes, hold the Warrant for brushes and are now probably best known for their hand-made hairbrushes, though they are still in the toothbrush market too. Kents were founded by William Kent of Barnard Castle in 1777. Until the beginning of this century they made their brushes in London, but for the last eighty years or so they have been out at Apsley near Hemel Hempstead, where they now have modern premises. Much of the manufacture, though, is carried on by hand and the smell of the woodshavings and is much, one suspects, as it was in 1777.

In the earliest days William Kent produced brushes for boot-tops, bitts, hair, cloth, hat and flesh, and exhibited no false modesty in promoting his wares. 'These brushes, which are entirely different to any hitherto offered to the public,' said their first advertisement on the front page of *The Times* (those were the days before the Thunderer sank to the vulgar indignity of allowing news on the front page), 'are so decidedly superior in principle as to convince at first sight the most incredulous. By their peculiar arrangement they at one action remove the dirt or dandruff and polish the surface, at the same time leaving the most beautiful gloss on the coat that can be imagined.'

'Observe, none are genuine that are not stamped on the back of the brush, "Kent's Patent Improved Union".'

G. B. Kent, from whom the company takes its name, held Queen Victoria's Warrant and ran the business from 1854 to 1900, presiding over a massive expansion in the range of products and the number sold. By the end of the century Kent's were making so many bone-handled toothbrushes that they were using the leg bones of 600 bullocks a week.

Alan Cosby, the present Chairman and Managing Director, says that the company is keen to retain 'all the skills and expertise of this traditional art' and they are one of the few companies able to repair ancient family brushes, very often ones made by Kents themselves, even when it means 'hand drawing' – literally sewing in each new bristle tuft by hand. Not for the first time it is fascinating to see how much craftsmanship and how many exotic ingredients are needed for even the most seemingly workaday Warrant Holder's product.

An early visitor to the Kent factory observed: 'bristles from Russia, Siberia, China and India; badger hair from Germany and the Balkans; whalebone from the Antarctic; fibres from Mexico, Brazil and Africa; beech, cherry, birch and sycamore from the English countryside and tropical timbers, ebony and satinwood from the forests of Ceylon, the West Indies, South American and Indonesia'. There have been some marginal changes since then, but you do see why, in the fine tradition of their original advertisement, Kent still claim to be 'The World's Finest Brushmaker'.

Like The Queen's clothes, Royal jewellery is, as already suggested, an unusual amalgam of the personal and the public. The Crown Jewels themselves are a public statement – symbolic heirlooms handed on from one generation to another, in no real sense a reflection of personal taste. Yet all Royal jewellery has an element of public ceremony about it since one of the burdens of Royalty is that no member of the Royal Family, least of all those leading members who grant Warrants, is ever really wholly off duty or away from popular appraisal.

Several jewellers hold Warrants and their history is

Asprey's famous dressing cases won prizes at the Crystal Palace Great Exhibition in 1851. Today they hold three Warrants

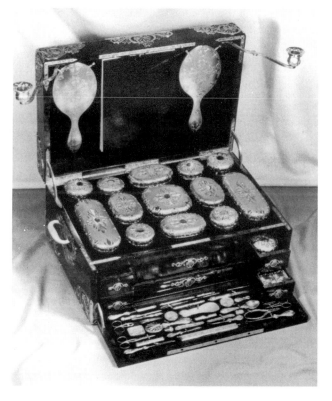

A close shave – Alan Cosby of G.B. Kent and Sons, Royal brushmakers, with staff and traditional badger shaving brushes

A Pringle sweater being checked for dropped stitches at the factory in Hawick

dotted with Royal points of reference – some more public than others. Several remain relatively private despite efforts to make them more public. For example, when Asprey's made Edward VII a cigarette case they put a Royal monogram on it which so delighted him that he suggested to Austen Chamberlain, Mr Balfour's Postmaster-General, that the device, an elided ER with a Roman VII let into the bottom of the R, should be incorporated into the new pillar-box design. The suggestion was rejected.

More recently Asprey's have gone further afield for Royal custom. Haile Selassie, the former Emperor of Ethiopia, became an Asprey's fan when he was exiled to England during the Second World War. When he first came to Asprey's the Emperor was a somewhat neglected guest and said, diffidently, that if his purchases could be sent to Brown's Hotel he would pay cash on delivery. 'Nothing of the kind,' said Asprey's Mr Hubbard. 'If you care to take them, you may do so, and the account will follow in due course.' The gesture paid off. Reinstated on the imperial throne, he invited Mr Hubbard out for a visit and greeted him with the words: 'I shall never forget how you treated me when I was more or less an outcast.'

Another foreign Royal was King Olaf of Norway, who used to visit Asprey's when he and his father, King Haakon, were also exiled in London during the war. King Olaf still drops in during the annual meeting of the Royal Yacht Squadron and on his annual Christmas shopping excursion, when he also tries to take in a football game at Upton Park, home of his favourite team, West Ham United.

Like other West End Warrant Holding jewellers, Asprey's still have workshops high above the shop floor. In these antiquated attics craftsmanship continues much as it has for hundreds of years, though the expertise is often deployed in curious ways. Asprey craftsmen spent 2,000 hours making a silver and silver-gilt replica of a Harrier jump-jet and only a little less time on a silver model of the *QE2*. One Texan oil millionaire even has a silver three-decker bacon and egg sandwich modelled from real toast and fry-up, cooked in the workshops above Bond Street.

Sometimes Warrant Holders lapse, only to make a welcome return. One such case is Skinner's, the jewellers, a family firm founded in 1880 who have held the Warrants of Queen Victoria, King George V, the late Prince of Wales and Queen Mary. They were granted The Queen's Warrant in 1988.

Cartier are long-standing Warrant Holders, who con-tinue to hold the Warrant of Queen Elizabeth The Queen Mother, for whom they made a diamond tiara in 1953. Cartier also made the diamond necklace and rose-blossom tiara which the fabulously wealthy Nizam of Hyderabad gave the Queen when she married Prince Philip. The Queen also has the tiara made for the Grand Duchess Vladimir, one of the company's most important customers. At the time of the Russian Revolution the Grand Duchess fled across the Caucasus in her own private railway. She died in 1920, leaving her jewels, which had been smuggled out of Russia by an English friend, to her children and other members of the Royal Family. The Grand Duke André got the rubies; Grand Duke Cyril the pearls; and Grand Duke Boris the emeralds. The diamond bow-knot tiara with drop pearls which she gave to Queen Mary of England and which is now The Queen's was apparently The Grand Duchess Vladimir's most treasured possession.

Cartier have another more obvious Royal connection in their annual sponsorship of the International Polo Day

The Grand Duchess Vladimir. One of the greatest of many Royal Cartier Customers

Diamond collar from Cartier, 1912

every summer on Smith's Lawn at Windsor, but the Romanovs provide perhaps their most historic Royal patronage and certainly their most poignant. Today the crown Cartier made for the Russian Royal Family can be found in the Merryweather Post Collection in Hillwood near Washington.

Some time earlier there was a moving occasion in New York when Prince Christophe of Greece called on Pierre Cartier at his office. Suddenly Cartier 'took a velvet case from his private safe, laid it on the table and opened it. Within lay a diamond crown with six arches rising from the circlet and surrounded by a cross. "Do you recognise it?" he asked me. I nodded wordlessly, seized by a sense of melancholy that rose from the depths of my memory. It was the crown of the Romanovs. My mother had worn it and her mother before her; it had adorned all the princesses of the imperial house on their wedding days. All at once, it seemed to me the room was filled with shades of long-dead brides.'

As well as his elegant contributions to the Royal ladies' attire, Sir Hardy Amies also designs menswear, though he does not have the Warrant for the male members of the Royal Family. When I saw him he said that he had recently been visited by some gentlemen from Japan who were extremely interested to know how an English gentleman would dress. Amies is very successful in Japan and his office has some of his Japanese advertisements on the wall, featuring models who look curiously occidental for orientals. A certain sort of Japanese dresser is anxious to emulate the classic English look. Sir Hardy Amies duly talked his visitors through an English gentleman's wardrobe from top to toe, finally remarking with a wry smile: 'And definitely nothing Italian.'

Just as The Queen has been, *inter alia*, the most effective model imaginable for the British fashion industry, so the Royal men dress as an English gentleman would be expected to dress. Their Warrants are awarded only to the very best of British. Starting, like Sir Hardy Amies, at the bottom, Royal shoes will probably come from Mr Lobb, who occupies one of that little group of shops around the bottom of St James's Street which still exude the unchanging authentic air of London before the Industrial Revolution. Mr Lobb is not, however, the oldest shoemaker in Britain. Nor is he likely to make the first

Royal children start right with 'Start-Rite' shoes.
Here uppers and soles are being pressed
together at the company's factory in Norwich

OPPOSITE *Shoes fit for a Prince or Princess*

ABOVE *Putting on a good front. Paul Cuss of Turnbull and Asser, shirtmakers to The Prince*
of Wales, framed and flanked in his Jermyn Street shop

Soles being applied at Kendal, Cumbria, home of 'K Shoes', bootmakers to The Queen and The Queen Mother

Royal shoes. Both honours belong to Start-Rite of Norwich, who descend from a Norwich leather seller called James Smith who was, in 1792, the first man to start making shoes from standard lasts. Their children's shoes were a relatively late idea, however, and were introduced only in the 1920s.

When it comes to shoes for the adult male, though, we are probably looking at Lobb's. Like others of the older Warrant Holding shops, the premises of John Lobb Ltd, Bootmaker, give the faintly alarming impression of being a private house or club, but the most extraordinary feature of the place is the great collection of wooden lasts. Here, piled one above the other, alphabetically labelled, is a *Who's Who* of more than 20,000 life-sized replicas of top people's feet. It is a pediform equivalent of Debrett, with faintly macabre overtones. Half of you can't help feeling that there is something eerily human about these disembodied limbs entombed below St James's.

Lasts are, of course, absolutely essential for making the perfect boot or shoe, contoured to every last corn and bunion. It takes six separate craftsmen between four months and a year to turn out a pair of Lobb shoes or boots, so it is small wonder that the finished articles cost hundreds of pounds, and that the company have the Warrant as bootmakers to The Queen, The Duke of Edinburgh and Prince Charles.

The original John Lobb was a Cornishman, born in Fowey in 1829. A childhood accident left him with a bad limp and precluded the agricultural career that had been intended. Instead he learned the cobbler's trade, walked, in boots made by himself, to London to seek his fortune, failed and went to Australia, where he invented a clever gold prospector's boot with a cavity for gold nuggets hidden in the heel. The profits enabled him to set up shop in Sydney, from where he sent an entry to the shoe section of the Great Exhibition of 1862 and won a gold medal for 'Good Work and First Class materials'. Thus encouraged, he made a beautiful pair of riding boots and sent them off to The Prince of Wales, quite unsolicited, together with a note asking that he be made The Prince's bootmaker. The effrontery and the craftsmanship paid off. His Warrant is dated 12 October 1863 and can be seen today in the St James's Street shop.

Business prospered through Edward VII's reign, but the thirties were disastrous and the firm nearly went into liquidation. The present Mr Lobb, Eric, born in 1907, joined the company in 1939, kept the business going through the war and saw it prosper afterwards. The Warrant had lapsed with the death of Edward VII, but in 1956 he was granted The Duke of Edinburgh's and in 1963 The Queen's. The Duke is a notably loyal customer. When Eric Lobb congratulated him on his fiftieth birthday he replied: 'One of the reasons I am going so well must be that I have always been well shod.'

The bootmakers Maxwell, now an associated company of Huntsman, the Savile Row tailors, also hold The Queen's Warrant and have been in existence longer than Mr Lobb. They were started by Henry Maxwell, a Worcester spur maker, in 1750 and moved to Piccadilly in 1820. K Shoes also pre-date Lobb and were started in Kendal, Cumbria, by a Scottish leather merchant, Robert Miller Somervell. His son, also Robert, introduced the K trademark – it stood for Kendal – but left the company to be a schoolmaster at Harrow. There his job was to teach English to the stupidest boys, including Winston Churchill, who said of him, 'a most delightful man, to whom my debt is great – he knew how to do it. He taught it as no one else has ever taught it.' Another men's footwear manufacturer – though they hold The Queen's Warrant – is John White Footwear, started by John White in 1918 and now producing about 20,000 pairs of men's shoes from their quiet corner of Northamptonshire. No mean achievement when one reflects that Mr White himself began work in the 1890s, inserting eyelets in two gross pairs a day – for 18d a week!

Prince Philip's socks are from Stephens Bros., a subsidiary of Austin Reed of Regent Street, whose Chairman, Barry Reed, is to be the President of the Royal Warrant Holders' Association during their sesquicentennial. Stephens's most distinctive contribution to the Royal wardrobe is the Tenova sock, first worn by King Edward VIII, later Duke of Windsor, when he was Prince of Wales.

Like his grandfather, Edward VII, he was a leader of fashion, to the point of seeming positively dandified. In

The modern face of knitwear – spindles and computers at Lyle and Scott's state of the art factory in the Scottish border where they make knitwear for Prince Philip

sartorial matters these two were always fascinated by anything new and unusual. Until the 1920s the male sock was kept up by suspenders. These had none of the sexual allure and exoticism of their female counterparts but were simply the only known way to stop socks or stockings from drooping round the ankles. They were a bit of a bore.

In 1924 two brothers named Stephens set up a partnership as hosiers. One of them, Arthur, conscious that the suspender should be phased out, invented 'an amazing sock'. It was three-quarters length with an elasticated top and a cut-out in the calf for comfort.

The Prince ordered them in the Fair Isle and Argyle patterns he was fond of and in 1934 rewarded the Stephens brothers with his Warrant. His friend Lord Mountbatten also took to the socks and communicated the

*Sable, ermine and other exotic furs have ancient and symbolic Royal connections. Here are two
more contemporary examples from Calman Links, Furriers to The Queen and The Queen Mother*

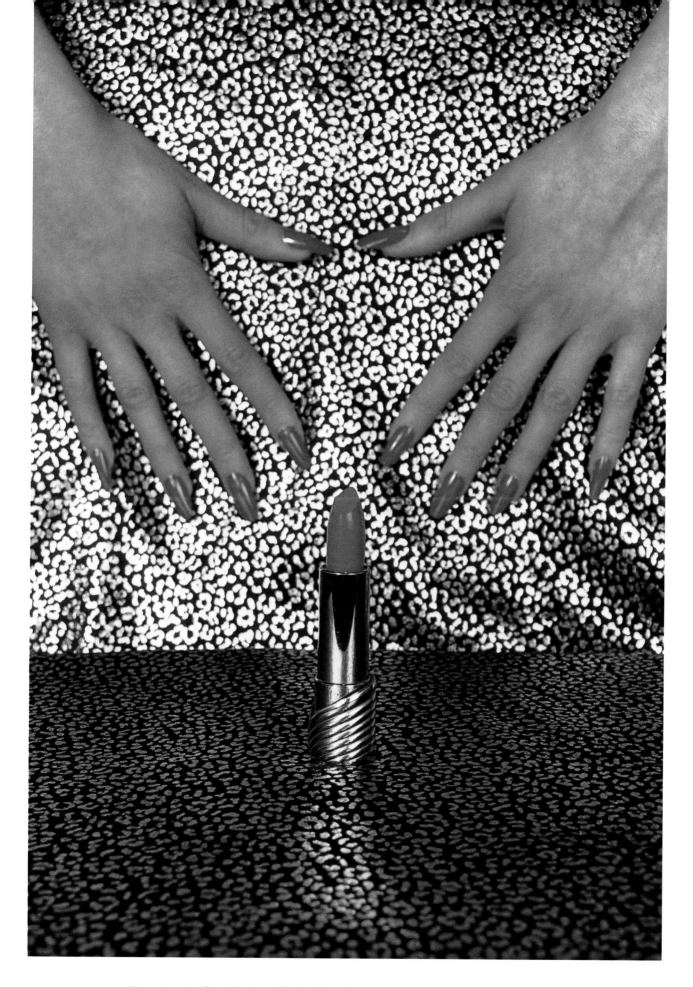

Prize winning lipstick from Elizabeth Arden, cosmetic manufacturers to Royalty

of fashion, supplied Thanets and tricorns, Blenheims and Kevenhullers, Aylesburys and Angleseys, Cokes and introduction of the all-elastic-topped ankle sock ruined the market for these rather Heath Robinsonish garments, but the Royal Family has remained loyal. Today Tenova socks are still produced in limited numbers for the use of Prince Philip, Prince Charles (who has also granted them his Warrant) and Barry Reed himself.

Some of Prince Philip's shirts come from Stephens, of Tenova sock fame, but the oldest shirt makers appear to be Thresher and Glenny of the Strand, who claim to be the 'holders of the oldest Royal Warrant in the hands of a private trader'. This is the one granted by King George III in 1783. It appointed Richard Thresher to be 'one of the Hosiers of His Majesty in Ordinary'. Today Thresher and Glenny shirts are woven in Lancashire and Switzerland and made up in Chard, Somerset.

Royalty apart, they used to make Garibaldi's shirts, Nelson's stockings and David Livingstone's mosquito nets. Garibaldi's famous shirt, bright red and much darned, the great symbol of Italian liberation, can be found on display at the Museo de Risorgimento in Milan. The name Thresher and Glenny is clearly visible on the inside of the collar. When Nelson, who lived next door, lost his arm in 1797 Mr Thresher expressed his regret, but Nelson was having none of it. 'Tut, tut, man!' he said. 'Lucky for you it wasn't my leg. I want another dozen pairs of silk stockings!'

Turnbull and Asser have The Prince of Wales's Warrant, thanks largely to Earl Mountbatten of Burma, who, like Sir Winston Churchill, also favoured their shirts.

Van Heusen also has The Queen's Warrant for shirts, which have in their time been endorsed by no less than Denis Compton, who said that he had 'no clothing worries' when wearing one for cricket, and by Ronald Reagan, who in pre-presidential days described them as 'the neatest Christmas gift of all'.

Simpson of Piccadilly hold three Warrants as outfitters and Georgina, daughter of the famous Doctor Simpson who established the wartime officers' club on their fifth floor, maintains a family tradition established by Simeon Simpson in 1894.

The top of the Royal male head is traditionally covered by Mr Lobb's neighbour in St James's Street, Mr Lock, whose hatter's shop was 'established not later than 1676 to wait upon the Court at St James's'. Over the centuries Mr Lock and his successors have, according to the whims

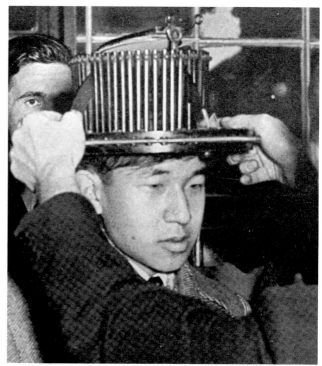

Crown Prince Akihoto, now Emperor of Japan, being measured by the 'Confirmateur' for a hat at Lock's while in Britain for The Queen's Coronation in 1953

enthusiasm to his nephew, Prince Philip, who gave Stephens his Warrant in 1956. Unfortunately, the Cambridges, and Anthony Edens, along with a whole host of more conventional pieces of headgear.

Their association with members of the Royal Family has not always been as successful as they would have wished. There was a lamentable failure in the last century when that restless innovator, Prince Albert, designed a special hat for the infantry in 1843. His perfectly sound reasoning was that the existing hat was too stuffy and a hot head made a poor soldier. His hat had a revolutionary side ventilation system and it was, naturally, made to his designs by Mr Lock. The War Office, not, one suspects, without some relish, turned it down out of hand and the news was leaked to *Punch*, who wrote,

> Come away to the Palace! and look at the show
> Of elegant garments by Albert and Co . . .
> And look at the beautiful infantry hat –
> Did aught ever bear a resemblance to that?
> With its side ventilation, intended 'tis said,
> To keep all the soldiers quite cool in the head.

Hardly Swiftian, but then, *Punch* never really was.

After the war Prince Philip earned marks for wearing a bowler at the Ideal Home Exhibition in 1949, thus helping to re-establish, however briefly, a dying fashion. Like his predecessor as Prince Consort, he was also involved in a revolutionary new hat, this time for polo players. It was made of fibreglass and, unlike Albert's experiment, was a great success. It has entered the sartorial vocabulary as 'Polo Cap, HRH Pattern', but despite hopes that it might prove a big export earner, the foreign market has proved limited.

Lock's are essentially gentlemen's hatters, but on one vital occasion they aided The Queen. When she succeeded her father in 1952 the Imperial State Crown had to be altered to fit her. This was done by Garrard, the Crown Jeweller, but it was also decided that a special fitment should be added to make it more comfortable. This was devised and fitted by Lock's.

There are a number of Royal tailors, though not all dress the Royal Family itself. Redmayne of Wigton in Cumbria, for instance, have The Queen's Warrant because they are responsible for clothing the outdoor staff at Sandringham. Their particular speciality is copying. Send them any garment you like and they will make an exact replica in any fabric you care to choose.

All these Royal clothes have, of course, to be cleaned, and there are Warrant Holders for that as for everything else. The British laundry industry went through a disastrous decline in the fifties and sixties. At the end of the last war there were about 4,000 firms, but by 1970 fewer than 400 remained. The Sycamore Laundry of Clapham Old Town, which holds all four Warrants, was founded by the present Managing Director's great-grandmother in 1865. She began in a very modest way by taking in the washing of the local gentry. Now the fifth generation of the Leman family is working in the company and they have a substantial two-storey dry-cleaning factory.

Another of the Royal dry cleaners, Lilliman and Cox of Berkeley Square and St John's Wood High Street, was founded in 1944. As befits a Warrant Holder their brochures quote – in Royal purple print – prices for ladies' silk dresses and evening gowns and gentlemen's 'Pink Hunting Coats' and smoking jackets. Not to mention that half-forgotten relic of a more formal age, the stiff collar. They will even increase your waistband for a fee of not less than £10.50.

The Sandringham launderers and cleaners have since 1978 been Donovan Fry's Fenland Laundries of Skegness, with their distinctive brown and orange livery. Although still active as a laundry, this company has coped with the declining market by branching out into providing clean clothes for the pharmaceutical, aerospace and micro-electronic industries, and this accounts for two-thirds of the modern business.

Penhaligon's in Covent Garden were originally, in the person of William Henry Penhaligon, Queen Victoria's court barbers. They still have The Duke of Edinburgh's Warrant for 'Toilet requisites'. Their 'Hammam Bouquet' is the oldest blend and mingles rose, jasmine and English lavender. It is advertised as 'only for the most sophisticated English gentlemen'. The Prince of Wales's Warrant for 'Toilet preparations' has gone to Floris, who also supply perfumes to The Queen and have been in business since the early eighteenth century. They were supplying The Prince of Wales with combs in 1800.

Omnia Omnibus Ubique is the Harrods motto. It can be loosely translated as meaning that whoever you are, wherever you are, Harrods will get you whatever you want. They even provided a baby elephant for Ronald Reagan in 1975 when he was Governor of California. This

The Tenova Sock is still manufactured in small quantities and supplied to Prince Charles and Prince Philip by Stephens Bros, a subsidiary of Austin Reed

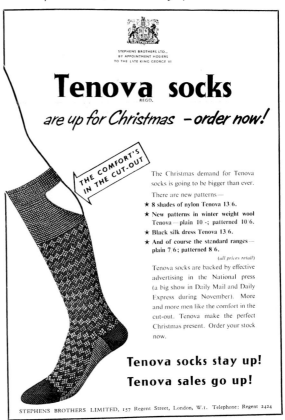

STEPHENS BROTHERS LTD.,
BY APPOINTMENT HOSIERS
TO THE LATE KING GEORGE VI

Tenova socks
REGD.

are up for Christmas – order now!

THE COMFORT'S
IN THE CUT-OUT

The Christmas demand for Tenova socks is going to be bigger than ever.

There are new patterns –
★ 8 shades of nylon Tenova 13 6.
★ New patterns in winter weight wool Tenova – plain 10 -; patterned 10 6.
★ Black silk dress Tenova 13 6.
★ And of course the standard ranges – plain 7 6; patterned 8 6.

(all prices retail)

Tenova socks are backed by effective advertising in the National press (a big show in Daily Mail and Daily Express during November). More and more men like the comfort in the cut-out. Tenova make the perfect Christmas present. Order your stock now.

Tenova socks stay up!
Tenova sales go up!

STEPHENS BROTHERS LIMITED, 157 Regent Street, London, W.1. Telephone: Regent 2424

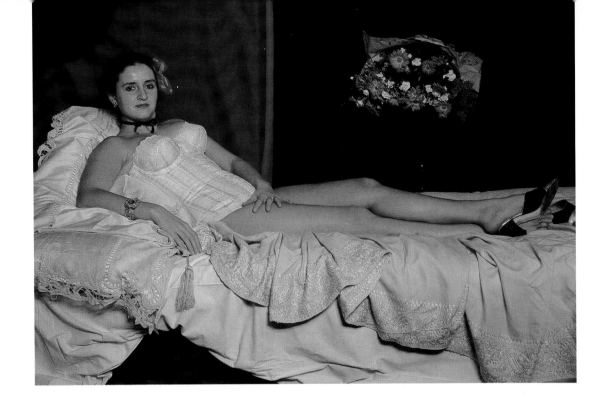

*ABOVE Manet provided the inspiration for the top picture, and Velasquez for the bottom one.
Rigby and Peller, the Royal Corsetières, provided the corsets for both*

*OPPOSITE Part Pasha – David Part of the General Trading Company in Sloane Street among
some of the 'Fancy goods' which he supplies to all four Royal Grantors*

*Getting the name taped is what J. and J. Cash have done for generations of schoolchildren and for
the Monarchy. Here a veritable gazeteer of name tapes are inspected at their Coventry factory*

ubiquity makes them impossible to categorise. They could
perfectly well be included under food and drink or office
supplies or gardening or anything at all. But as a certain
style is what Harrods lays claim to, it seems only proper
to include them here.

The great Knightsbridge store began as a small shop in
1849 and its enlargement to the present four-and-a-half-
acre island was a process of gradual encroachment, viewed
at times with special Royal interest. In 1903, when new
drapery and fashion rooms were first opened, they were
greeted with a special encomium from Queen Alexandra.

'The New Buildings,' she opined, 'are certainly unique
of their kind. The decorations are really beautiful, the
richest materials being lavishly used. The attentions of
the Firm have not, however, by any means been confined
to beauty alone; they have studied the convenience and

comfort of their customers in the most thorough fashion.'

To commemorate the completion of the present
Harrods building in 1911, and also to mark the
Coronation of George V, the store planned a grand 200-
foot-tall clock tower, but the idea was abandoned. A
plaque in the delivery area records this forlorn endeavour.

Queen Mary was a regular visitor and Harrods held
Warrants for her and for George V. Indeed, their fortunes
seemed at times to be quite peculiarly entangled. In 1928,
when The King was dangerously ill, Harrods' trade took a
disastrous nosedive. In January, when his doctor, Lord
Dawson of Penn, pronounced him on the road to recovery
the reaction among customers was so euphoric that the
store had to take on 2,000 extra staff to deal with the rush.

More recently, The Princess Royal opened the
renovated Food Halls, The Duchess of Kent opened Hong

Kong promotions in 1984 and 1987, and Princess Michael of Kent was guest of honour at a special Spanish promotion in the store. For some years Harrods have sponsored the International Driving Grand Prix at the Windsor Horse Show. Prince Philip is a regular competitor and The Queen presents the prizes.

Today Harrods has all four Warrants. Every day fresh supplies from the Food Halls are delivered to the cooks at Buckingham and Kensington Palaces; The Queen Mother has granted her Warrant to the China and Glass departments; Prince Philip and Prince Charles to the Man's Shop. Harrods specialises in polo gear and has its own master saddler, Colin Missenden, which is why they hold Prince Charles's Warrant for saddlery.

The store not only contributes to the style of the Royal Family but it also has style itself. This is particularly true of two other sartorial Warrant Holders. The Speaker of the House of Commons, the Rt Hon. Bernard Weatherill, is no longer able to take an active part in the affairs of Bernard Weatherill Ltd, who hold three Warrants as Livery Tailors. But his appearance in the House of Commons, ever immaculate in the traditional Speaker's outfit with wig, buckled shoe and breeches, is a daily advertisement for the best tailoring. And J. G. Links, who holds The Queen's Warrant as Furrier, is not only a master furrier, a former Director of the Hudson's Bay Company with a compendious knowledge of the fur trade; he also wrote, with Dennis Wheatley, several stupendously successful and original murder mysteries and is the author of the best walking guide to Venice, the aptly named *Venice for Pleasure*.

The General Trading Company in Sloane Street is another of the relatively rare companies with all four Warrants. It is widely recognised as an ideal home for the discerning bride's list of desirable wedding presents (an accolade shared with another Warrant Holder, Peter Jones, just round the corner in Sloane Square). It is not just because of his geographical location that David Part, the grantee and an ex-president of the RWHA, is universally known as 'Mr Sloane'!

The best Warrant Holders are themselves persons of style, consequence and parts!

Bernard Weatherill, Royal tailors, where the grantee is the Speaker of the House of Commons

Thomas Joy, former grantee and now grand old man of Hatchards of Piccadilly, the Royal booksellers, with the present grantee, P.W. Giddy, coming down the stairs behind him

THE SPORTS OF QUEENS
(AND PRINCES)

'In our play we reveal what kind of people we are'
(Ovid: *The Art of Love*)

It has been said of Her Majesty The Queen that 'she is an outdoor person' and of the Royal Family that 'they are country folk'. There is a strong sense that in their time off they are happiest out of doors – not necessarily in good weather! Nevertheless, as the list of Warrant Holders demonstrates, they do have indoor pleasures too. Every year, in a loyal gesture, the National Book League makes up a reading list for the Balmoral holidays. Not only does Prince Charles read books, he has had one published too. And other loyal subjects, like the Crime Writers' Association, occasionally send unsolicited gifts of their Dagger-winning books – a consignment arrived in 1988 at Sandringham just in time for Christmas.

There are six Royal booksellers. Hatchards, with its expanding chain of high street stores and its great flagship in Piccadilly, supply all four Grantors. Maggs Brothers, an extraordinary warren of rare and ancient leatherbound volumes in Berkeley Square – more like a ducal library than a shop – is the antiquarian bookseller. Menzies of Edinburgh have The Queen Mother's Warrant. And there are two small shops, Alden and Blackwell, the Eton College bookshop, and the Petersfield Bookshop in Hampshire, which though it *is* a bookshop actually holds its Warrant for framing pictures and supplying art materials. The one remaining bookseller is perhaps the least expected.

Just behind Buckingham Palace, within a furlong or so of the Royal Mews, is one of the true curiosities among Warrant Holders. Since 1926 the Horseman's Bookshop has been run by J. A. Allen, and since 1926 very little seems to have changed. From his eyrie at the top of his thin, tall house Mr Allen, now in his eighties, conducts

business with the personal touch that has characterised his life so far.

A telephone call comes through from Paris. Mr Allen listens attentively, he is at ease with foreigners. 60 per cent of his business is abroad. There is a letter from Buenos Aires lying on a table, beginning, *'Estimados Señores'*. Nearby there are two volumes entitled *Essai de Bibliographie Hippique*. The caller from Paris wishes to pay by credit card and Mr Allen takes down the number, carefully jotting it on a piece of paper. Much of his filing is done, as he is keen to point out, in old laundry bags. His office has a Dickensian air, yet despite the lack of high tech it is quite clear that the system works. When the transaction is complete the customer has a question. Mr Allen listens attentively. 'It's only the equine quadrupeds I do, I'm afraid, though I make an exception for hounds.' A pause. He shakes his head and seems sad. 'No, I'm sorry. Not Labradors.'

He came to horses through his father, who published a racing paper called *Sporting Luck*. An equine educational trip to Ireland proved only that he 'had no affinity with horses' in the flesh, but he did become interested in the horse in print. Then when his father died he found himself, only in his late teens, with his considerable library of second-hand horse books and very little cash. A bookshop was the obvious answer.

His early customers tended to be people who had known his father – the sporting aristocracy, epitomised by men like Lord Wavertree. There were not very many of them, however, and business was slow. Nor did his extreme youth help. He even invented an imaginary, older partner to give the firm credibility.

Hatchards bookshop in Queen Victoria's reign

During the Second World War he served in the Sudan and North Africa with the Royal Field Artillery and the Ordnance Corps. When he returned he found the world was changing. 'More people had more time and more money,' he says, 'and riding began to be very popular among what one might call the general people. The girl on the petrol pump would be a member of the pony club. That wouldn't have been possible in the thirties. Then it was all children of members of the hunt.'

Business boomed. The little bookshop attracted customers. As his reputation grew, so more and more equine bibliophiles around the world began to come to him with their needs. Publishers consulted him over which horse book should be reissued, which new ones written. In time he started his own publishing house, now a thriving and effectively autonomous organisation based in Stowmarket and using all the new technology so conspicuously absent from the little shop in London SW1. He has published *Arabian Horses* by Prince Sherbatoff and Count Strogonoff, *The Art of Driving* by Max Pape, with a Foreword by The Duke of Edinburgh, and the classic *An Introduction to Polo* by Marco. Marco was Earl Mountbatten's pseudonym and the Foreword to the sixth

edition is by that other keen polo-playing member of the Royal Family, The Prince of Wales.

Mr Allen has never been taken over, never merged, never even borrowed from the bank. Nor has there ever been a partner, unless you count the fictitious elderly gent of the early years. He has a small cottage near Westerham, where he spends a now marginally prolonged weekend. During the week he lives, literally, over the shop. The only extravagance he admits to is the occasional lunch.

'I have no *folie de grandeur*,' he says, 'though I must be the last individual tradesman round here with his own name on the facia. It's been hard work but it's very pleasurable and enjoyable. And it's kept me young and active.'

Equestrian literature is, of course, a highly specialised field, but in view of the monarchy's long-standing love affair with the horse it is hardly surprising to find Earl Mountbatten, Prince Philip and Prince Charles all making their contribution. Horse racing is, after all, the sport of kings. The royal racing stables go back to the reign of King James I, and although some Kings and Queens have been less than passionate about it (William IV was said

164

Frank Westwood of the Petersfield Bookshop in Hampshire whose Warrant is actually for picture framing and the supply of 'Art Materials'

John Maggs of Maggs Bros Ltd., with his head in one of the many rare books at his famous antiquarian bookshop in Berkeley Square

J.A. Allen, Equine and Equestrian bookseller to The Queen and Prince Philip, at home above his shop just behind the Royal Mews

to be 'bored to death at Ascot' and King George VI was noticeably lukewarm), Queen Elizabeth II is an acknowledged enthusiast and expert.

Personal enthusiasm apart, there is a sense in which patronage of the equine scene could be considered a sort of Royal obligation. For, as the less than horsy William IV once declared:

I consider this to be a national sport – the manly and noble sport of a free people, and I deeply feel the pride of being able to encourage these pastimes, so intimately connected with the habits and feelings of this free country . . . we are here to enjoy these liberties and sports which I will, with my utmost power, ever protect and foster, and in so doing, never lose sight of the welfare and enjoyment of every class of my people, from the highest to the lowest.

This protecting and fostering continues today and is exemplified by the large number of horse-related Warrant Holders. The Royal Stud at Sandringham was founded by King Edward VII and has bred, as James McCulloch points out, 'some of the greatest winners the racecourse has ever seen'. Mr McCulloch is the grantee at Equiform Nutrition Ltd, who hold The Queen's Warrant for 'Equine Vitamin Supplements and Feed Additives'. His roll of honour would include Eclipse, Persimmon, Aureole and Dunfermline, who won the Oaks and St Leger for The Queen in her Jubilee year. He adds that the stallions Bustino and Shirley Heights have produced some top-class progeny, notably Height of Fashion, Head for Heights and Slip Anchor.

James McCulloch's father, Max, was responsible for a big expansion in the number of products on offer. One of these, called Codolette Crumbs, is particularly popular at the Royal Stud, where the Stud Manager, Michael Oswald, and the Stud Groom, Jimmy Scanlan, have a considerable reputation for preparing The Queen's horses: whether they are on the track, in the sale ring or at stud they are always in peak condition. Mr McCulloch wouldn't claim all the credit, but he does think his products help! He adds that he likes to employ experts and that one of his longest-serving representatives is Johnny Bullock, who won the 1951 Grand National on Nickel Coin. It was the year they dubbed it the 'Grand Crashional', when a third of the field fell before they had covered half a mile!

The horse feed which Equiform supplements comes from Mark Westaway and Son, of Love Lane Farm near Torbay. It is called HorseHage and marketed under the slogan 'All the goodness of natural grass – sealed in a bag'. HorseHage, for the technically minded, is made like hay but is baled when the grass is half-dry, which may mean in less than two days. The bales are then treated to eliminate harmful heating and compressed to less than half-size. The great benefit in feeding HorseHage is that it is dust-free and therefore reduces the chance of respiratory diseases in horses, which are growing at an alarming rate. Pioneered in the early seventies, the forage is so successful that it has been used by British Olympic Equestrian teams abroad and endorsed by such famous riders as Virginia Leng and David Broome.

The Royal Family's passion for the shoot is a matter of history. Indeed, the location of both Balmoral and Sandringham has at least something to do with their being prime spots for game – grouse and deer in the case of Scotland, pheasant, partridge and such like at Sandringham. The family have traditionally been fine shots and it was said that George V was one of the five best of his day – the others were Prince Duleep Singh, Lord Huntingfield, Lord Walsingham and Lord Ripon. (George V's father, Edward VII, was said by the super-marksman the Marquess of Ripon to be 'variable'.)

Royal sportsmen have always been particular about their guns and of all gunmakers none can have secured quite so much Royal patronage as Purdey and Sons of

Purdey craftsmen still 'build' their shot guns by hand as they have always done

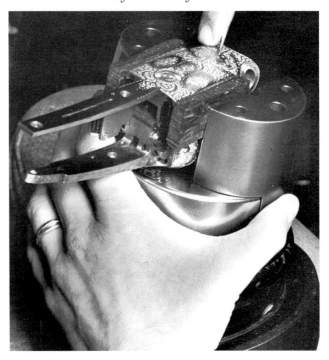

Richard Woodhouse of the Sandicliffe Garage with son and favourite Argentinian pony. He holds
The Queen's and The Prince of Wales's Warrants for supplying Motor Horse Boxes

Michael Gidden, saddler to The Queen, astride the wooden horse at his company, W. and H. Gidden Ltd.

*Brian Hatson of Culford Fencing which makes 'specialist fencing' for The Queen.
The 'stallion fencing' shown here at stables near Newmarket is all his own work*

London. After the funeral of Edward VII (who, it should be said, also owned guns from Purdey's rivals and fellow Warrant Holders, Holland and Holland), nine Kings posed for a photograph. Purdey's had built ('built', not 'made') guns for each one. They were King Haakon VII of Norway, King Ferdinand of Bulgaria, King Manuel II of Portugal, Emperor William II of Germany, King George I of Greece, King Albert of Belgium, King Alfonso XIII of Spain, King George V of England and King Frederick VIII of Denmark.

Queen Victoria was the first member of the Royal House to buy from Purdey's when she paid £73 10s for a brace of pistols for the Imam of Muscat. She had consulted her Prime Minister, Melbourne, about what would be most suitable for the Imam and he had promised to ask Lord Palmerston, the Foreign Secretary, to go out and buy pistols. They were numbered, like all Purdey's guns, and came in a rosewood case inlaid with buhl and lined with crimson velvet. Arms were engraved on the centre of the case and a crown and cipher on the stocks. In considering the guns from the Royal Warrant Holders it is almost as if one were considering jewellery, so lavish and intricate are the embellishments. But they are none the less deadly for that.

This trend-setting purchase was made in 1838, almost a quarter of a century after James Purdey opened his first shop, building flintlocks and duelling pistols off London's Leicester Square. That autumn Her Majesty bought a gold-mounted double gun and a gold-mounted rifle. The following year she acquired a pair of flintlock pistols and a year later Prince Albert ordered a 'best double gun', No. 3309, a sixteen-bore with thirty-inch barrels inlaid with gold. He also took a small rifle, No. 3259, for £36 15s.

The Prince of Wales granted Purdey's his Warrant in 1857, though his first Purdey guns were not purchased until ten years later, when his wife bought him a pair of twelve-bore breech-loaders for his birthday, as well as a pair of double-barrelled pistols with Prince of Wales feathers. In 1878 The Prince started his son, later George V, off with a Purdey sixteen-bore. The boy was fifteen years old and grew up to have a very special relationship with Purdey's. To mark this, Purdey's presented him with a pair of shotguns. The King had been particularly pleased with the miniatures provided for Queen Mary's doll's house, but this time the Purdey, one-sixth the size of The King's real guns, had one important difference. Cartridges, containing 1·62 grains of EC and 2·02 grains of dust-shot, were made up by ICI in Birmingham and the tiny thirteen-dram guns were capable of firing them. They were packed in a case specially made by another Warrant Holder, the Crown Jewellers, Garrard, and presented at the Palace by Tom Purdey in person. A third gun was made and retained by Purdey.

Edward VIII was given his first Purdey at only five years old; George VI received his in 1910, and thirty-seven years later ordered a pair for his son-in-law Prince Philip as a wedding present. The Royal tradition is now preserved with the granting of The Prince of Wales's Warrant. It is symptomatic of Purdeys' style that on the occasion of Prince Charles's wedding they held a celebration dinner. All employees who had been with the firm more than forty years qualified for an invitation and that made sixteen, of whom only two were unable to attend. It represented 910 years of service, and as Richard Beaumont, the Chairman, points out, between the beginning – a year before Bonaparte was defeated – and that moment – a year before the Falklands – Purdey's have continued to build guns. By 1983 there were still only 28,600 – an average of 170 each year over 168 years.

Holland and Holland, who have had The Duke of Edinburgh's Warrant as rifle makers since 1963, also have a tradition going back to the early nineteenth-century, when it seems that the original Holland, who started out as a wholesale tobacconist, must have shot with the first Purdey – James – when both were members of the Old Red House and Hornsey Wood, two famous pigeon-shooting clubs of the day. Holland and Holland too are famous for an almost incredible attention to detail. When they presented a set of guns to mark The Queen's Silver Jubilee they were engraved on the lock plates and actions with scenes from the twenty-five years of The Queen's reign, beginning on the lock of the No. 1 gun with Westminster Abbey just after the crowning. All around these engravings were the floral emblems of Britain and on the trigger guards were shields with the crosses of St George, St Andrew, St Patrick and the Red Dragon of Wales.

When Holland and Holland celebrated their centenary in 1935, the congratulatory telegram from Purdey's said succinctly, 'You have made a hundred runs in best cricket.' A fine English sentiment to applaud fine English craftsmanship, and what appears to be an exemplary relationship between rivals!

There are many paradoxes in country life, the equation between culling and conservation being the most fundamental. It is perhaps an extension of this to find

Armitage's of Nottingham are, by appointment, petfood manufacturers to The Queen. This means Good Boy dog chocs for corgis

Gilbertson and Page Ltd of Welwyn Garden City holding the Warrant for the manufacture of both dog and game foods. The firm used to make Queen Victoria's pheasant food and were granted a Warrant from her and The Prince of Wales in 1884, just over a decade after a Hertford grocer, Henry Gilbertson, formed a partnership with his manager, Alfred Page. Page had previously managed a game-feed producer in Norwich and between them the two were so successful that they quickly won contracts for the Royal estates at Windsor, Sandringham and Osborne, as well as with the Dukes of Wellington and Edinburgh and the Marquis of Salisbury.

Shooting was probably at its most popular in the years leading up to the First World War, and at the height of the fashion Gilbertson and Page were sending out twenty railway wagons of game feed every day in May and June. The war meant change, however. In the first they were reduced to baking 'Submarine Biscuits' and in the second

something even more horrific-sounding – Dehydro Sausage Rusks!

The company has had its share of trauma: a disastrous fire in 1918; a German landmine in the Second World War; and – sign of the times – an arson attack on behalf of animal rights. But perhaps the most intriguing was what is still referred to as 'The Great Egg Scandal', when as the result of some unknown wrongdoing, the Gamekeepers' Association, established by Gilbertson and Page, upped sticks and went off to become independent. A legacy remains in *Dog and Country*, still run by the company, but the precise details of the Great Egg Scandal still remain a tantalising mystery.

The Queen and her family have always been a fine example to a nation of dog lovers. Few informal Royal photographs are complete without one or two corgis or a Labrador, and this interest is reflected in the list of Warrants.

Hon. Richard Beaumont, Chairman, and Laurence Salter, the Grantee, at Purdey's. The company make guns and cartidges for The Queen, The Duke of Edinburgh and The Prince of Wales

Roger Mitchell of Holland and Holland, rifle makers to The Duke of Edinburgh, with one of the firm's classic 'Fourten Rococo Guns'

A.J. Stevenson of Shirras Laing, Royal ironmongers, enjoys a picnic with items from his shop near the premises in Aberdeen

Armitage's Pet Products have been going – a shade improbably – since 1775, but have held The Queen's Warrant as pet food manufacturers only since 1976. The founder, Samuel Fox, was a Nottingham grocer whose nephew, Samuel Fox Armitage, started a wholesale business to supply him. His descendants have run the company ever since, though it has undergone a bewildering number of changes encompassing the Mikado and Oriental cafés, the bombing of their Victoria Stores in 1940 and the recent acquisition of Happy Pet Products and Binzo, who manufacture Binzo dog bones. The pet food connection began in 1901, when they started producing chicken feed. As Warrant Holders they supply, among other things, Good Boy Choc Drops. Pedigree Petfoods also have The Queen's Warrant, which in their case is specifically for canned dog food. Their Pedigree Chum is the leading brand of dog food in Britain, Whiskas is the biggest-selling pet food in Europe, and their Melton Mowbray cannery is the largest in Europe. As they say, 'We must be getting something right.'

Many people's introduction to 'play' and 'leisure' has come through Hamleys of Regent Street, who describe themselves as 'The Finest Toyshop in the World' and have held a Royal Warrant since being granted Queen Mary's in 1938. Hamleys, started by William Hamley of Bodmin in 1760, has moved through several ownerships and sites. They provided toys for the young Princesses Elizabeth and Margaret as well as for Prince Charles and Princess Anne. If it hadn't been for Hamleys we might never have heard of ping pong, for the game was launched exclusively through them under the name 'Gossima'. Ping pong was the popular slang for it and it was not officially christened table tennis until 1921.

The Royal Family has owned pianos or harpsichords at least since the early eighteenth century and the modern Royal houses are still full of them. Indeed, the importance of the Royal piano is such that when The Queen and Prince Philip made their first overseas tour, the liner SS *Gothic* was provided with special pianos for the occasion. When the Royal Yacht, *Britannia*, was fitted out in 1954, special pianos were again part of the requirements.

The Royal piano makers, or more correctly pianoforte manufacturers, are John Broadwood and Sons, who have been making keyboard instruments for English monarchs

*Geoffrey Simon of John Broadwood and Sons, the world's oldest piano makers, at the keyboard of
a restored Broadwood grand. There are even Broadwood pianos on the Royal Yacht*

Richard Roberts, of Roberts Radios, with early TV, radio and gramophone. Mr Roberts is a former
President of the Warrant Holders and The Queen, The Queen Mother and The Prince of Wales all
listen to his radios

James Mackie, of Wilson and Sons, piano and harpsichord tuners to The Queen, at work on a piano in his Edinburgh workshop

A Victorian musical Warrant Holder – now no more

since George II and claim to have held Royal Warrants for longer than anyone else. Superlatives are dangerous but the claim seems well founded in this case. They are certainly much older than Steinway (also Warrant Holders), Bechstein and Bluthner, all of whom started business, by a bizarre coincidence, in 1853. The original founder was a Swiss émigré, Burkat Shudi, who set up shop in Soho as a maker of harpsichords. The first Broadwood was a Scots cabinet maker who became an assistant to Shudi and married his daughter, thus establishing a dynasty. Apart from this continuous service to the Monarchy, there is almost more romance in the fact that in 1740 Shudi made a harpsichord specially for that accomplished composer Frederick, Prince of Wales, and then 241 years later Broadwood's made a grand piano for his successor Charles, Prince of Wales, also a genuine musician (though more usually associated with the cello) and, incidentally, a passionate admirer of Frederick.

Handel – a friend of Shudi's – played one of their harpsichords. Mozart played another when, at nine years old, he performed at Hickford's Room, the most fashionable small concert room in London. Mozart was accompanied by his fourteen-year-old sister. 'Both,' said the *Europaeische Zeitung*, 'perform wonders.' Haydn, Beethoven, Chopin, Mendelssohn and Elgar all owned Broadwoods. Beethoven's, a six-octave grand made in 1817, was later passed on to Liszt and can now be seen in the National Museum of Hungary in Budapest. The *Vienna Gazette of Arts* described it as 'the most perfect Grand Piano Forte perhaps ever constructed'. There is a wonderfully melancholy description of the composer, already half-deaf, enthusing about the piano – a gift to which several friends and admirers subscribed – but unconsciously striking the wrong notes when seeking to demonstrate its beautiful tone: 'The greatest musician on earth did not perceive the discord.'

King George VI and Queen Elizabeth listening to a Roberts radio

On a slightly less exalted note a sixteen-year-old Sir Arthur Sullivan once played the bass drum in the Broadwood factory band and later composed the Gilbert and Sullivan operas on a Broadwood. Today they turn out 600 a year from their factories in Buckinghamshire and Yorkshire. For about £2,000 you can buy a Broadwood upright; a grand would be about five times as much. And you would be owning a piece of musical history as well as an artefact with as long a Royal association as any other available to the man in the street.

Three companies have the Warrant in organ building and tuning. William Hill and Son and Norman and Beard's Warrants can be traced back in unbroken line to 13 October 1835, which was the day that the original William Hill was sworn in and admitted to the palace as 'Organ Builder Extraordinary to His Majesty'. J. W. Walker and Sons of Brandon were started in 1828 but now pride themselves on their 'progressive outlook in Organ

design and technology'. Apart from their work for the monarchy, Walker organs can be found in endless different sizes and settings, from the modest 254-pipe instrument at St James-without-the-Priory-Gate at Southwick, Hampshire, to the great 3,339-pipe behemoth in Bolton Town Hall.

The Queen, The Queen Mother and The Prince of Wales all listen to Roberts Radios and have done so since before the last war, when The Queen Mother bought one as a birthday present for Princess Elizabeth at the Army and Navy Stores in 1939. A year later a friend of Harry Roberts, founder of the company, wrote from Harrods to say that he personally had had the pleasure of selling Her Majesty The Queen 'one of your Model M4D for her personal use'. Members of the Royal Family have several times been photographed and filmed listening to their Robertses. In the film *Heir to the Throne* Princess Elizabeth was shown on her eighteenth birth-

181

Patrick Robbins of Holme Park Hatcheries with young pheasant chicks. His company supplies The Queen with 'Stock Game'

*James Hardy, of the House of Hardy, who make The Prince of Wales' fishing tackle, making a cast
with a Hardy rod near his headquarters in Alnwick, Northumberland*

183

Tuning a reed stop after 'voicing' at J.M. Walker's of Brandon, Suffolk – organ tuners and builders to The Queen

day switching on her Roberts portable – massively cumbersome compared with today's tiny transistorised versions – to listen to an item about herself. And in 1948 the *Illustrated London News* carried a picture of The King and Queen with their Roberts perched a little precariously on a coffee table, above the caption: 'A distraction which their Majesties enjoy as greatly as the majority of their subjects: The King turns on the wireless.'

The company was started by Harry Roberts in 1932 and is now run by his son Richard. In a market dominated by foreign competition they are the only remaining British manufacturer. The firm's philosophy has been the same from the very beginning: 'Make a top-quality product and sell it to top-quality customers.'

Their speciality was always the portable radio, though the early ones were almost a foot square. 'Ideal for the

Home, the Car, picnics, holidays, nursing homes', ran the advertisements of the thirties, but they were not the sort of machines you could walk around with. The first of these came after the war when the company produced a 'Junior' weighing only ten and a half pounds. It came with a weatherproof carrying bag and before long it was a status symbol.

By 1947 Harry Roberts knew that at least half a dozen of his wirelesses had been supplied to the Royal Family, but his first request for a Royal Warrant was turned down. It was not until 1955, after the firm had supplied a specially adapted model for The Queen's 1953–4 Royal tour, that the Warrant was finally granted. Two years later Richard was summoned to Buckingham Palace to demonstrate his latest models to Prince Charles and Princess Anne.

The first, prototype, Roberts transistor was presented to The Queen in 1958 as a present from the Radio Industry Council, who had originally commissioned it. It went into production a few months later. Later still Roberts took over the Dynatron company, who specialised in upmarket TV sets. They still have The Queen's Warrant for televisions and 'Radiogramophones'.

Richard Roberts, who has been President of the Royal Warrant Holders' Association, maintains a museum of old portables at his factory in West Molesey, Surrey, which he reckons is the best in the country. It is a marvellous evocation of social change over the last fifty years. Then you could run an advertisement showing a couple contemplating their car and their 'portable' wireless with the words 'Shall we take the car or the wireless set? We can't take both.' Now Roberts produce a truly portable machine with a synthesiser, pre-set digital tuning and a level of electronic sophistication which must have been inconceivable when most radios had to be connected to an outside aerial or a three-foot-square 'frame' one, and had external batteries and separate loudspeakers.

Fishing is nearly always bracketed with shooting, and in the case of the Royal Family the association is appropriate. Prince Charles, a notably keen fisherman both in Scotland and on well-publicised salmon-seeking forays to Iceland, has granted his Warrant to Farlow of Pall Mall, London's oldest and, since 1984, largest fishing tackle shop. The shop was started by Charles Farlow, whose aim, in 1840, was to supply 'The Angling Brotherhood of the nobility, gentry and public at large'. The Prince's Warrant for the manufacture of fishing tackle is granted to the House of Hardy in Alnwick,

Hammering out horses' bits at Matthew Harvey's of Walsall, the Royal bitmakers

Small customer with furry friends – shopping at Hamleys of Regent Street who have The Queen's Warrant for toys and sports

Crowned heads worth rather more than the paper they are stamped on – Penny Blacks at Stanley Gibbons Ltd., the Royal philatelists

A 57lb Manseer caught in the Ganges with Farlow fishing tackle as used by Royalty

Northumberland, where they now have a museum, opened in July 1987 by The Prince's aunt, Princess Margaret, which boasts 'the finest collection of quality fishing tackle in the world'. The House of Hardy has been diversifying in recent years. They make canoe paddles and violin bows, and in 1986 even landed a £½ million contract to produce vital components for 7,000 Barra Sonobuoys being made by Plessey. But it is as 'the premier fishing tackle manufacturer in the world' that they most like to be known. Founded in 1872, the House of Hardy prides itself on a happy combination of revolutionary high tech alongside individual skills passed down by craftsmen from generation to generation. It was this fusion of ancient and modern, they claim, which led to such breakthroughs as the revolutionary 'Zane Grey Big Game Reel', which helped create a world record by landing a Blue Marlin weighing 1,656 lb.

All these outdoor pastimes and pleasures necessitate dressing for the notorious British climate. (Should this prove too inclement even for the Royal Family, they might choose to stay indoors and play whist or bridge with cards from John Waddington, who make special Royal packs.) There is clearly something cyclical about British inventiveness in the field of weatherproof garments. In the last quarter of this century the ultimate chic for a day in the country has been the distinctive Barbour raincoat in olive green with brown corduroy collar, poacher's pockets and serviceable zips, and the green wellington boot or wellie. In fact Barbour, where

Mrs Margaret Barbour is the grantee, have been in business since 1890 so their current trendiness and their modern factory on Tyneside are mildly deceptive. But both Barbour and the Gates Rubber Company of Dumfries have the Warrant – Barbour for Barbours and Gates for green wellies. Aquascutum, Burberry, Barbour and others are well versed in protecting their customers from wind and rain, but there are even more specialised companies. One of these is Haythornthwaite and Sons of Burnley, which makes Grenfell garments, first produced for Sir Wilfred Grenfell by Walter Haythornthwaite, a Lancashire mill-owner, in 1923. Grenfell, famous for his medical missionary work in Labrador, was invited to give a lecture by Haythornthwaite and in the course of it drew attention to the difficulty of finding adequate protective clothing. Haythornthwaite rose to the challenge and within a year had produced an experimental sample. Grenfell was delighted: 'It really has been a boon to us all and I think the public should know of it. They will be grateful, I know.' The secret lies, apparently, in the best cotton, the best craftsmen and an exceptionally tight weave – 600 single threads to the square inch. Since then Grenfell garments and tents have frequently been to the Himalayas and other mountain ranges. When Admiral Byrd flew over the South Pole he wore Grenfell cloth, which, he said, 'was the finest for our particular purpose'. Amelia Earhart wore Grenfell; so did Sir Malcolm Campbell and his son Donald while breaking their land and water world records. For years Stirling Moss drove in it and still the International Grenfell Association, which carries on the work of Sir Wilfred, uses it all over Labrador and northern Newfoundland.

The Royal Family's recreational enthusiasms are not quite as ruthlessly masochistic as their patronage of Grenfell garments might suggest. Stanley Gibbons still have the Warrant as The Queen's philatelists and the great stamp collection established by George V is still very much alive and growing. Stamps, incidentally, are printed by the Royal printers, Greenaway-Harrison, who hold three Warrants.

Royal interests encompass the library and the music room too. As far as the Warrant Holders are concerned the various crafts and trades in this part of Royal life read very much like a trade register of services for the landed gentry. The shooting, the fishing, the stables, the library and the grand piano are all, in their different ways, symbols of the very traditional country life of the English stately home and the Scottish baronial castle.

Margaret Barbour, of J. Barbour and Sons, who holds three Royal Warrants for supplying the eponymous waterproofs, at the factory in South Shields on the Tyne

Dorothy Ewers of D. and G. Ewers Pet Supplies in Windsor. Mrs Ewers holds the Royal Warrant for supplying The Queen's birdseed. The shi-tsu is her own and not for sale

VILLAGE SHOPS

'Where smiling spring its earliest visit paid'
(Goldsmith: *The Deserted Village*)

For eighty-seven miles from Ben Braeriach in the west to the great granite city of Aberdeen in the east, the River Dee flows through country known not just as 'Deeside' but 'Royal Deeside'. The British Royal Family has had a home here for almost 150 years.

On 8 September 1848 Victoria and Albert stayed at Balmoral Castle for the first time. That afternoon they walked out and strolled to the top of the hill. 'It was so calm, and so solitary,' wrote The Queen, 'it did one good as one gazed around; and the pure mountain air was most refreshing. All seemed to breathe freedom and peace, and to make one forget the world and its turmoils.'

Ever since then the Royal Family has been coming back to the castle at Balmoral, designed by Prince Albert to replace the earlier, much smaller one belonging to the Earl of Aberdeen. The mountain air is still pure and refreshing, and although the single policeman who used to 'walk about the grounds to keep off impertinent intruders' has now made way for a large and sophisticated security presence, it is still, relatively speaking, a place where there is freedom and peace and a chance to forget the world and its turmoils. At Balmoral itself and the nearby and smaller Birkhall, the Royal Family now traditionally holds a late summer and early autumn court away from the hurly-burly of England and the south.

In the nineteenth century Queen Victoria seems to have used her Scottish excursions to throw off the trappings and pomp of majesty in order to behave as simply as possible. She mixed with the local people and was famous for her charity and good works. On more than one occasion she recorded that she 'walked out with the two girls and Lady Churchill, stopped at the shop and made some purchases for poor people and others'.

Today the local shop which serves the Balmoral estate is still there, a massive Royal coat of arms overpowering the modest shop front of what is, in reality, little more than a Highland cottage built in the foursquare granite style needed to withstand the Highland winter. 'George Strachan,' says the legend above the window, 'General Merchant'. And inside you find a well-stocked village store and post office with nothing particular to single it out from any other such shop in the British Isles apart from its remarkable location a few yards from the Balmoral gates and hard by the Royal Lochnagar Whisky Distillery's visitors' centre.

Even in this Royal shop so far from the tourist centres of London and Windsor there are reminders of what the Royal Family has become. There is a set of colour photographs mounted on one wall which shows HRH The Prince of Wales touring a fudge factory. The postcards include pictures of the castle itself and many more of the family. There are even – or were on my visit – copies of the *Sun* Souvenir Royal Album.

It is unlikely that you will find George Strachan himself at the Balmoral shop, for Mr Strachan is not just the local sub-postmaster. He is a veritable Fortnum or Mason of Royal Deeside, with three other shops in the valley bearing his name, not to mention others in Braemar which trade under a different name and another company dealing in gambling machines. Not, he admits dourly, one that is likely to gain the Royal Warrant.

Standing in the office at the parent shop in Aboyne, a rambling treasure trove with everything from clan tartan ties to a miniature arcade of game machines, Mr Strachan said that he first came to Deeside when he was six; he is sixty-seven now. He has spent a lifetime as a 'General

George Strachan, General Merchant to the Royal Family on Deeside, minds the store. Mrs Strachan is at the till

Colonel Jefferies MBE, Field Sports Outfitter to The Queen, in the doorway of his shop in Ballater

Merchant' and is intensely proud of his Royal Warrant. And discreet with it.

However, what emerges in listening to Mr Strachan is something which seems to be common to most of the Warrant Holders in this part of the world, in marked contrast to the attitude one finds in supposedly more sophisticated metropolitan areas. It is not that the Deeside Warrant Holders take the Royal Family for granted. They are as loyal as the best and, like other holders, they regard holding the Warrant as an honour. But on Deeside, it seemed to me, there was much less of the almost crippling deference and painful tact that characterises some people who serve the Crown.

One Warrant Holder said that his young son and some friends had been out walking in the woods on the Balmoral estate when they had happened on The Queen out riding. 'Hello, boys!' she said. 'What are you up to?' It was exactly the same sort of encounter you would have expected from any little group of village boys meeting the lady from the big house. Perhaps that is what makes the difference. Most Warrant Holders deal with the Palace and sense the whole unwieldy apparatus of the court

bureaucracy in their dealings. Up in Aberdeenshire the Warrant Holders deal with the factor or the housekeeper or the cook – a name which has a face and a presence and a local identity. Once a year they are invited to a party up at the big house and they may manage a little chat with Prince Charles or a dance with The Queen Mother. The Royal Family on Deeside seem more like Highland lairds than Monarchs of the realm, and the relationship between them and their servants is correspondingly closer. At least something of that relaxed escape which appealed to Queen Victoria still lives on.

George Strachan's little shop on the South Deeside Road, a few hundred yards from the austere and world-famous Crathie Church, is an isolated outpost, but just down the valley at Ballater, a village of some 2,000 inhabitants, the Royal coat of arms is everywhere.

Colonel Jefferies of Countrywear, for instance, has two shops on the main street and is The Queen's Field Sports Outfitter. One shop tends to specialise in high-class woollies and the other, more predatory, branch goes in for guns and rods. They stock books on salmon fishing and gundog training; they sell dog discs, Royal Scot travel

Mr Sheridan, the Ballater butcher, displays a right Royal haggis made to his own personal recipe

rugs and elbow patches from Wilson's of Pitlochry; and most evocative of all, fishing flies with wonderful names like Logie and Dunkeld, Stoats' Tail, Munro Killer and the euphemistic General Practitioner.

At Mr Sheridan's, the butchers, you can buy rolled venison and home-made venison sausages, Scotch pies and, of course, haggis. When the Royal Warrant Holders' Association had a Scottish President, the annual dinner became a traditional Scottish banquet and it was Mr Sheridan's haggis – some 130 lb of it – that was supplied to the Grosvenor House kitchens. It is made to his own special recipe and is, he says, a drier haggis than most. Mr Sheridan started out on his own with a mobile butchers after National Service in the Royal Signals and has since traded up to his present spacious premises, where he can be found either serving behind the counter or on the phone in his minute office. His beef, naturally, comes from the Aberdeen Angus Society.

Over the road John McBeth Murray has been the Ballater chemist since he and wife, Doris, also a qualified

TOP Robert Pringle and staff outside the garage where they service Royal cars from Balmoral
ABOVE William Murdoch, of G. Leith and Son of Ballater who bake for Balmoral

pharmacist, moved to Ballater from Elgin in 1970. He is a keen fisherman and it was this, as much as anything, that brought him to the area. There is a great deal more than the average chemist's to the Murrays's shop. He has a popular line in binoculars, especially with his 'Deeside Hiker', and he has also taken on the 'Emollient Skin Cream' made by a predecessor, Mrs Ironside. 'Matchless for the complexion,' says the label, and Mr Murray will produce a great sheaf of letters from enthusiastic users all round the globe to endorse this claim. At peak production

he, his wife and their assistants can churn out five gallons a week. He also produces Highland Fern aftershave and Dee Heather perfume.

But it is not this entrepreneurial flair which impresses one most. Nor the racks of homoeopathic medicines – a good touch in view of the pioneering homoeopathic tendencies of the Royal Family. What strikes one is the rapport and sense of community. 'My God, Janet,' he exclaims, as an elderly customer opening the door almost knocks him over. 'And how are *you* doing?' he asks

Alastair Cassie at his shop in Station Square, Ballater, from which he supplies and services the televisions at Balmoral

another, before pausing for a muffled confidence with the postman, who has not brought the parcel of drugs for which he was hoping.

On being asked if he knows everybody in Ballater, he shrugs and says that he supposes he does.

This is a pervasive sense in the village. We are not in the anonymous city supermarket or the even newer hypermarkets. People come to the Ballater shops as part of the ritual of life. They expect to recognise and be recognised; to be called by name; to gossip and be gossiped about; to meet their friends. This is old-fashioned neighbourhood shopping in old-fashioned neighbourhood shops. When Alastair Cassie, who supplies and maintains the Balmoral television sets, talks about the intricately wired distribution system there, he is talking about a system he installed with his own hands. And by the same token you sense that he could talk with similar first-hand expertise about any television set in town. Like Colonel Jefferies, he has two shops, dealing not only in TV sets but such esoteric items as 'walking stick ends'. If the shop in Bridge Street, Ballater's main

thoroughfare, is closed, a sign in the door advises: 'Contact Alastair Cassie: Station Square next to Clydesdale Bank'.

At George Leith and Son, the bakers, Mr and Mrs William Murdoch, holders of The Queen's, The Queen Mother's and The Prince of Wales's Warrants, preside over a real Scottish bakery. Daily bread: 'Can't get enough in summer,' says Mrs Murdoch; 'more of a problem getting rid of it in winter.' They bake their own oatcakes – plain and cheese. And butter puffs. And they have a special whisky cake, baked to a traditional recipe and sold in a pack with a miniature of the local Lochnagar malt. It's a traditional rich fruit cake with marzipan and icing plus the essential extra ingredient of Highland malt whisky.

On my way out of the village I was picked up at the Riverside Garage by an unmarked police car which had spotted my rented car loitering in the vicinity of the Royal residences and their tradesmen. It was reassuring to find the Royal security operating unobtrusively and efficiently and it also prompted the thought that during the Royal

John Murray, of J. and D. Murray, the Royal Deeside chemist also in Ballater

TOP Heather Gale of Caleys, the department store, with Windsor Castle reflected in the window
ABOVE Mr Patel of the Castle Pharmacy, who supply medicines to the Castle in Windsor

Norman Wisker of H. Hodgkiss and Son, reaches for a pheasant at his shop in St Leonard's Road, Windsor. He supplies fish to the Castle

presence on Deeside there is a vast influx of high-powered motor cars. The Metropolitan Police bring their own, of course, and so do the members of the family. Mr Beaton of the Riverside Garage, an ex-security man who used to work in East Africa and Asia, still displays a large Royal coat of arms and holds the Warrant, but he concedes that his Royal service is 'fairly modest nowadays'.

The man who actually looks after the police and the Royal vehicles is Robert Pringle, whose father held the Warrant before him. Mr Pringle is the sort of garage proprietor who is most often to be found under a vehicle, with thick black grease up to his armpits. His father, John, Rolls-Royce trained, died in 1985 and his son has kept his name above the garage because he was both fond and proud of him. It was his father who taught him his trade. 'We can only do the smaller type of repairs,' he says modestly. 'The sort of thing that can happen to any car.' He would not be fazed by a failed Royal windscreen wiper or a faulty exhaust but there would be a moment, he concedes, when he would have to suggest that it might be a case for Rolls themselves. Not that he need be over-modest. Quite apart from the Royal Family he numbers two Rolls-Royce owners among his regular clients.

Like other Warrant Holders, discretion is sometimes at odds with pride. He was very nervous when I saw him that an impending TV interview might trap him into talking about The Queen's clothing or what she said at her annual party, but at the same time he wanted to convey something of his enthusiasm for the very special job he did. The Queen Mother's Daimler had recently been in and his eyes really sparkled as he remembered it. 'I've never seen paint finish like it,' he enthused. 'I don't know who does the painting, but it's wonderful. They're lovely, lovely vehicles.' And echoing all the Warrant Holders on Deeside he says, 'It's an honour, there's no doubt about that.'

What strikes one most, however, about these relatively small tradesmen of the Scottish Highlands is that the honour is so peculiarly personal. These are not the chairmen of great public companies, nor are they people who send their orders to an anonymous official in the post. These lucky few may actually see their Royal customers on their premises and can expect to be known by them as individuals. For them The Queen is not only The Queen of the United Kingdom; she is also, in a very real sense, the local laird.

The Royal Family's Scottish homes are the most remote from London but that sense of community,

strengthened by a hard core of small, usually family businesses, is also evident in other parts of the kingdom. If you were to stick a flag representing each Warrant Holder into a map of Britain you would, inevitably, find the greatest concentration in the London area, but you would also discover significant thickets around Sandringham in Norfolk and Windsor in Berkshire. There are also smaller pockets around The Prince of Wales's home in the Cotswolds and The Queen Mother's Castle of Mey in Caithness.

A good way of sensing the spirit of these provincial communities of Warrant Holders is to attend one of their occasional get-togethers. Every year, for instance, the Sandringham Association holds its Annual General Meeting at Jesus College, Cambridge. Coffee in the minstrels' gallery; formal business in a conference room which neatly accommodates up to about 100; sherry in the cloisters; luncheon in hall. All jolly civilised.

The overwhelming impression was of dark suits. Even the solitary woman, Pam Johnson of Eldernell Vehicles, was in a smart charcoal pin-stripe. Her company started by supplying cross-country vehicles, trailers, pumps, mowers and various small pieces of machinery to stables, studs and market gardens. Later it came to concentrate on hot and cold pressure washers. Like other female Warrant Holders, she took over her company after the sudden death of her husband. He, Major Sam Johnson, died in 1985, having founded the company in 1968.

In the conference room the top table was covered in green baize. Mr Donovan Fry of the Fenland Laundries presided. In front of him was an enormous silver cup called the Bishop Aubrey Memorial Trophy. It should have been presented to the winners of the cricket match on the day of the Sandringham Flower Show, but this, in accordance with English tradition, had been abandoned without a ball being bowled on account of rain.

The tone was light. President Fry welcomed the National President and the Secretary of the Association. Apologies were noted from a past president who was on organ-playing duty in his local church, from one company playing golf at Turnberry, one which was entertaining thirty foreign visitors, a third which had a board meeting, a fourth which was budgeting and a fifth which had just been taken over. This seemed a neat summary of the national business life on any given day and the minutes were taken as read.

A cautious treasurer's report occasioned some discussion on fund-raising. One member light-heartedly suggested there should be a levy on those members not wearing the Association tie. Another raised the question of how the produce should be priced at the Flower Show. Someone else wondered whether the Secretary had sent out enough books of raffle tickets. As the raffle had raised £1,650 for the Sail Training Association there was a general feeling that the Secretary had done all right. The previous chaplain, the Vicar of Sandringham, had been sent to the Falklands as Chaplain to the Forces and, as it was felt he could not continue with his duties at such a distance, he had been presented with a glass rose bowl and the Bishop of Lynn had agreed to succeed him.

The President made one of his characteristically effervescent speeches with a promise of more to come after lunch. The Secretary announced the next Golfing Day and Donovan Fry handed over the Presidential chain of office to his successor, Doug Walker of John Deere tractors. There was then a brief discussion about future meetings and, finally, there being no further business, the company adjourned for sherry.

It was a good party. College servants circulated. The enormously tall figure of Julian Loyd, Her Majesty's Land Agent at Sandringham, circulated among a catholic assortment of timber merchants, fence makers, builders, lift manufacturers, cidermakers and shopkeepers of almost every description. As the man who runs the Sandringham estate for the Royal Family, he was obviously a key figure in this gathering. Then the college butler rang a bell and everyone followed him into hall. Inside there were two long tables and no seating plan except for a high table on a slightly raised platform for officials and honoured guests.

The Sandringham Association Secretary, John Storrs – of Berol of King's Lynn, manufacturers of writing instruments – banged his gavel and the President said a simple 'For what we are about to receive' grace. Before people started on the fruit compote he read a gracious message from Her Majesty. It is not every Annual General Meeting that starts lunch with a few words from The Queen. The words were genuinely warm and friendly and produced an almost visible glow among the members. It is moments like this which make an outsider sense something of the real personal pride involved in holding the Warrant.

After an excellent luncheon the loyal toast was drunk with a more obvious sincerity than usual on such occasions. The National President revealed himself as a man not afraid of telling rambunctious jokes about Scotsmen, Irishmen and Englishmen marooned on desert islands. He further endeared himself to the assembled company by saying that they were a 'couthy' collection of people – a good old Scots word which apparently means amiable, gregarious and good to be with.

The cheque for £1,650 was then presented to the Sail Training Association and a generous and informative response was made by their representative, the only other woman present apart from Pam Johnson.

Finally, Donovan Fry presented a framed quotation from John Ruskin as his leaving present to the Association. It was a characteristic aphorism to the effect that anybody can cut costs by lowering standards; if you want the best you may have to pay more. It seemed a good motto for Warrant Holders, who are anything but cut-price.

It might be misleading to infer too much from a single gathering such as this, but the feeling that I got here was very much the same as I had sensed on Deeside. Of course, some of the Warrant Holders at Jesus, Cambridge – President Doug Walker of John Deere himself being the most obvious example – were the representatives of big international companies. But even they felt like parts of a small, almost feudal, society. The rose bowl for the departing vicar, the rained-out cricket match and the apologies from the organ-playing past president are not irrelevant details in a picture of the Royal Warrant Holders' Association of today. Men and women who hold the Warrant, particularly what I think of as the village-shop type of Warrant Holder, tend to be traditionalist, to have a sense of etiquette, of protocol and, perhaps above all, of attending to those little grace notes which distinguish special service from everyday take-it-or-leave-it.

Perhaps there is a danger of over-romanticising the small local shopkeepers among the holders of the Royal Warrant, but it is difficult not to warm to Alastair Munro and his sister, who run the Ship's Wheel at Thurso in Caithness and have had The Queen Mother's Warrant since 1977. The Queen Mother visits the shop at least once a year, usually with her lady-in-waiting, Lady Fermoy, who is almost as popular a local visitor as The Queen Mother herself. The Munros are particularly proud of their Warrant, because it is so personal and because, unlike so many Warrant Holders, they actually have regular visits from the Grantor. They are also models of discretion and never say what Her Majesty has purchased. They deal in what they describe as 'general antiques'. Alastair Munro amplifies this by saying that

Harold Cox, jeweller to The Queen and The Queen Mother, outside his shop in Market Street, Windsor

Anthony Tate, the village chemist shop conveniently situated in Grosvenor Gardens, just round the corner from Buckingham Palace

Paul Cockerton with family, staff, fruit, veg and van at the Wandsworth home of Hyams and Cockerton, Royal greengrocers

R.F. and J. Scoles, outside their butcher's shop in Dersingham near the Sandringham Estate.
J, alias Jean, Scoles is the grantee

Heather Waddilove, supplier of sausages to The Queen Mother

Lidstone's of Mayfair, one of the Royal butchers

this means 'furniture, china, glass, silver, old maps of the area and what I think are described as *objets d'art* but I prefer to think of as bonnie bitties'. It seems reasonably safe to assume that The Queen Mother has an eye for the Ship's Wheel's bonnier bitties.

Like other members of the family The Queen Mother can obviously inspire quite unremarkable-sounding Warrant Holders to extraordinary feats of ingenuity. Coombs of Guildford, for example, have a Warrant for supplying The Queen Mother with cars. They supplied and still service the Daimler V12 – unique because it has a Jaguar radiator – which fills Mr Pringle of Ballater with such enthusiasm. They are based on an estate on the Woking Road and switched allegiance from Jaguar-Daimler to BMW in 1980.

In 1970, thanks to a suggestion from the late Dick Wilkins, senior partner at Wedd Durlacher and a friend of The Queen Mother, they demonstrated and later sold a Royal Claret Daimler as a replacement for an earlier Rolls Royce. Shortly after delivery, Michael MacDowel, now Managing Director of the company, had a call from Her Majesty's senior chauffeur of the day, Don Redwood. The 'sill line' was a little high and Her Majesty was experiencing some difficulty getting in and out.

Mr MacDowel borrowed a car from Vanden Plas which had 'pull out' steps for the rear doors and drove it round to Royal Lodge, Windsor Great Park, for a demonstration. The Queen Mother was pruning roses but put Mr MacDowel at his ease, tried the steps, got a couple of corgis to try them too and then asked, in what Mr MacDowel describes as 'her special way', 'Mr MacDowel, do you think they could be electrically operated?'

As far as he knew, no one in the world had ever installed a set of electrically operated steps in the rear of a limousine. But despite the inner panic he immediately replied, 'Yes, Ma'am,' and went back to Guildford. Despite exhaustive enquiries he could find no one to help with the electrification, so he and his team had to design it from scratch. They used the electric motors from the central division window as a basis, devised a push-in fail-safe mechanism to prevent Her Majesty having to drive off from an official engagement with two unretracted steps mowing down dignitaries like the knives on Boudicca's chariot, and finally burned the midnight oil before devising an effective way of sealing the contraption off so as to prevent water getting in.

Two years later at a staff party Her Majesty remarked to Mr MacDowel that she had much enjoyed showing off her electric steps at Buckingham Palace. A fine example of the sort of special service provided by a Warrant Holder of, essentially, the village-shop variety who was prepared to take time out to provide something which he believes to be unique.

Most of the 'village' shops are, of course, outside London but one which embodies the essential virtues of villageness is Anthony Tate, the chemist's shop in Grosvenor Gardens. Mr Tadros, the grantee, is just round the corner from Buckingham Palace and therefore invaluable should anyone there suddenly run out of aspirins or sticking plaster.

It might be considered stretching a point to include Caleys of Windsor as a village shop. It is a large department store and, since it was acquired from the Selfridge Provincial Stores Group in 1940, a member of the John Lewis partnership. However, it belongs in this category partly as one of the flagship enterprises of the Windsor Association, whose members service the castle, and partly because in its origins it was very definitely a small family business in a small provincial town.

It was in 1778 that King George III and Queen Charlotte decided that Windsor would be a congenial place to live. For a time they were not actually in the castle but in the Queen's Lodge opposite the south front. Almost at once they galvanised the local tradesmen by what a guide book of the day described as 'the benevolent diffusion of their favours'. Thanks to the Royal purchasing power, Windsor's traders began to 'vie with each other in the improvement of their shops, and in the quality and cheapness of their various commodities so that most of

A Royal invoice from Caleys of Windsor, dated 1846

the necessaries with many of the superfluities of life, may be purchased here on as eligible terms as at the first shops in the metropolis'.

One of the earliest of these shops was the milliner's run by Mrs Caley, who after a couple of moves was established in the High Street on the same site that bears her name today.

It is all too easy to forget that while Royalty often requires and receives special luxury goods and services out of the reach of most of their subjects, they also have to have the ordinary and the day to day. So when The Princess of Wales gave birth prematurely in 1864, her lady-in-waiting, Lady Macclesfield, was sent into town to get together a hasty layette. This included two yards of coarse flannel and six yards of superfine flannel. These, we are told, were brought from 'Caleys, the draper of the town of Windsor'.

By around 1900, before the cataclysm of 1914–18 swept away so much of European Royalty, Caley and Sons, as they had become, claimed no less than twenty-two Royal Warrants: The Queen, The Empress of Russia, The Empress of Germany, The Empress Frederick, The Prince and Princess of Wales, The Grand Duchess of Saxe-Coburg and Gotha, Princess Christian of Schleswig-Holstein, The Duchess of Connaught, Princess Louise, Princess Henry of Battenberg, Princess Leiningen, The Duchess of York, The Duchess of Albany, The Crown Princess of Greece, Princess Henry of Prussia, Princess Louis of Battenberg, The Grand Duchess Serge of Russia, Princess Adolphus of Teck, Princess Victoria of Schleswig-Holstein, Princess Victor of Hohenlohe and The Princess of Saxe-Meiningen.

Today Caleys have the Warrant only for The Queen and The Queen Mother. This is no reflection on what has happened to the store over the last ninety or so years, but rather what has happened to Monarchy.

Today in Windsor 'the benevolent diffusion of their favours' still means that you can wander about the town and constantly be aware of the profusion of Royal coats of arms in and above shop fronts. Waitrose of Windsor no longer have the Warrant they did when the late Queen Mary came into the shop, unannounced, to purchase her favourite soap and caused the unprepared relief manager to disappear under the counter in a dead faint. But you will find plenty of Windsor Warrant Holders to replace them, not all of them conventional or likely.

In Alma Road, there are Berkshire Air and Hydraulics, who make hydraulic hose assemblies. Over the Thames at Eton is Alden and Blackwell's bookshop, where the Warrant Holder is a former Eton College 'beak' called Raymond Parry. Harold Cox, Windsor's representative among no less than sixteen Warrant Holding jewellers, is in Market Street, just behind the Guildhall. Umakant Patel, recently President of the Windsor Branch of the Royal Warrant Holders' Association, runs the Castle Pharmacy in Peascod Street. A. A. Clarke, Automobile Engineers, are in Arthur Street. Clarke the saddlers are in Eton High Street. Dorothy Ewers supplies The Queen with bird seed from her pet supplies shop at 10a Clarence Road. And so it goes on, through Hodgkiss, the fishmonger, and Pratt and Leslie Jones, who supply fancy goods at the Token House, right through to the Windsor Glass Company on the Vansittart trading estate. Not for nothing is the Royal Family the House of Windsor.

Anna Plowden and Peter Smith, aka Plowden and Smith Ltd, Restorers of Fine Art Objects to Her Majesty The Queen, pictured with some typically Restored Fine Art Objects in their Wandsworth workshop

BRICKS AND MORTAR, CURTAIN AND CARPET

'A man builds a fine house; and now he has a master,
and a task for life;
he is to furnish, watch, show it and keep it in repair
the rest of his days'
(Emerson: *Society and Solitude*)

The Royal Warrant confers glamour and prestige on those who hold it, but the Monarchy itself cannot function without a lot of hard and sometimes prosaic-sounding graft. Anyone reading these pages will already be aware that the institution is in many ways the equivalent of a government ministry or a considerable private company. Its smooth running demands an enormous range of services and products and some of these are very definitely not what one would expect from concepts of Monarchy conditioned by fairy stories, glossy magazines or even Walter Bagehot. Floors, for instance. Axminster and Wilton – yes, certainly. But it would be madness to run a modern business on priceless carpeting. It should, therefore, be no surprise, beginning at ground level, to discover that for more than ten years Gaskell Textiles Ltd of Lee Mill, Bacup, Lancashire, have been supplying carpet underlay. Their Home Sales Director points out that 'Once it is laid it is, under normal circumstances, never seen again.' That means that it's doing its job, but it is difficult to be lyrical about it, sturdy, dependable and necessary though it unquestionably is. Still at floor level, Armstrong World Industries hold The Queen's Warrant for 'Floor Coverage'. The British Armstrong Company is a wholly-owned subsidiary of an American Company, based in Uxbridge and manufacturing mainly in the north-east of England, where they employ about 1,300 people. 'We are the largest manufacturers of resilient floor coverings in the world,' says their Managing Director, Robin Kemp. British Nova

of Southall make The Queen's 'Floor Maintenance Products and Waxes'. Apart from all the more or less conventional products they even manufacture 'Novafrost', which is a chewing-gum remover.

While on the subject of floors, consider Kircaldy. The home of Raith Rovers Football Club on the east coast of Scotland used to be famous as the floor-covering capital of the world, and it had a pervasive smell of linseed and canvas to prove it. When Michael Nairn decided to make floorcloth in 1847 the locals called the factory 'Nairn's Folly'. Yet today Forbo-Nairn are still turning out acres of floor covering. They are still justifiably proud to hold the Royal Warrant.

Linoleum, from the Latin *linum* (flax) and *oleum* (oil), was invented in 1860. Since then it has been through some lean, unfashionable patches, but in an age which is looking increasingly 'green', its time may have come again. For as Forbo-Nairn are proud to claim, it is 'unique among modern floor coverings in that it is made from natural raw materials'. What's more, the lino-cut is a reviving form and lino's manufacturers are taking out and dusting down their old Victorian pattern books. In addition, a new generation of artists has been experimenting with laser-cutting lino. Marbled linoleum has been used as a flooring for a major exhibition of Sir Edwin Lutyens's work; for the stylish TV-am studios; and to re-create the company logo of other Royal Warrant Holders such as Jaguar Cars. As the Warrant suggests, it may be chic once more.

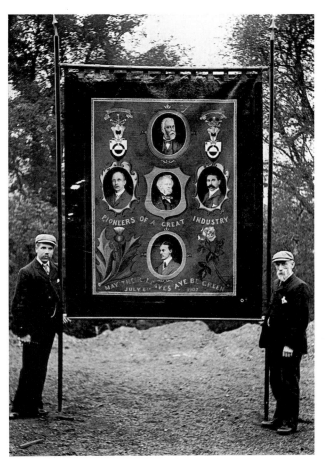

The great industry pioneered by Forbo-Nairn was linoleum

When it does come to Axminster and Wilton, they might well be from the looms of Hugh Mackay plc in Durham, where they have been making carpets since just after the end of the Boer War. In 1929 Edward, Prince of Wales, went to the north-east and wove the first few inches of a special rug later auctioned in aid of Durham Castle's restoration. This was a Yakcam – not an ancient Tibetan weave but simply the name Mackay spelt backwards! Today there are Yakcams or Mackays in the shops of many fellow Warrant Holders, including Boots, Harrods and Jenners of Edinburgh; in the Carlton at Cannes, the Savoy in London, the George V in Paris and any number of hotel chains. They can be found aboard Cunard and P & O ships and the Royal Yacht, *Britannia*; in the Royal Bank of Scotland, the House of Commons, the Happy Eater, the Royal Blackheath Golf Club and Trum Harrahs Casino, Atlantic City. And when it comes to the ultimate, which in this case must be the world's Royal palaces, you will tread on them not only at Sandringham, in Kensington Palace and Buckingham Palace but also in the Sultan's palace in Muscat, King Hussein's in Amman and the Royal Palace in Stockholm. But, of course, Wilton still comes from Wilton and the only one of the Warrant Holders who is entitled actually to use the adjective 'Royal' is the Wilton Royal Carpet Factory itself.

It was for carpets that Whytock and Reid first received the Royal Warrant in 1838. Now the company once described as 'one of the most eminent houses of business in Edinburgh' are 'Decorators and Furnishers to Her Majesty The Queen', though their beautiful showrooms bounded by the Water of Leith are still full of fine carpets and the adjoining workshops are still making traditional handcrafted furniture like the famous Cockpen Chair in the same way that they have been doing since the early nineteenth century.

Most of Whytock and Reid's work is done at Holyroodhouse. Further north another old family firm, Archibald's of Aberdeen, have the Warrant as cabinet-makers and upholsterers and service Balmoral. Their contracts department make a speciality of boardrooms – much in demand in the area after the oil boom!

The security of the Royal homes and their occupants is, of course, partly an official responsibility of the military and the police, but it also has to be provided by civilian contractors. 'Fire Protection Systems' are the province of BBC of Norwich, not *the* BBC but a young company founded in 1979 whose first three directors are Messrs Bushell, Burr and Copeman. Called in to provide some 'small services' in connection with the fire alarm system in 1981, they were awarded a maintenance contract for the fire alarm and the emergency lighting that same year.

Lady with Chubb Fire Extinguisher – from Minimax News, 1904

Although small – sixty people – the company operates nationally and in 1986 they went north of the border to install new fire alarms and emergency lighting at Balmoral and Birkhall. As a result of this they have also been employed by the Property Services Agency to do similar work on the official Royal residences, though Mr Copeman, the 'C' of the title, says they 'cannot always be described in detail due to their sensitive nature'. Like other Warrant Holders, particularly smaller companies, they are particularly appreciative of the 'acceptance and hospitality' they encounter when on Royal duties – an attitude which they feel sure 'emanates from "the top"'.

The Queen's 'Fire Engineers' are Merryweather and Sons who can trace their history back to the period just after the Great Fire of London when the only firefighting equipment was the 'brazen hand squirt' and the leather bucket.

Chubb Fire Security Ltd hold The Queen's Warrant for fire extinguishers, Chubb Alarms for 'intruder alarms' and Chubb & Son's Lock and Safe Co. for locks and safes. As a result of their merger with the Racal Group the company now claims to be 'probably the most powerful electronics communication and security group in Europe'. Chubbs are one of the more venerable Warrant Holders but the last Chubb to be actually in charge of Chubb's was Lord Hayter, the third Baron, who was Managing Director from 1941 to 1971 and Chairman for ten years after that. He was also President of the Royal Warrant Holders' Association in 1967.

It is a fairly commonplace observation that the Royal palaces must be murder to heat. Charringtons, now part of the Coalite Group, supply The Queen's fuel oil and have held a Royal Warrant since the reign of George IV. Cochrans of Annan in Dumfriesshire have supplied a number of boilers to the Royal Family over the years, although at the moment they have just two steam boilers in operation at Sandringham. As far as light is concerned, Crompton of Cliftonville, now part of Hawker Siddeley, have held a Warrant for supplying electric lamps since they restored the lighting in Sandringham Parish Church in 1949. The firm's founder, Colonel Crompton was at school with Lewis Carroll, came under fire in the Crimean War while only eleven, played football with Ellen Terry in her back garden and was in charge of mechanical transport in the Boer War. After pioneering work in the fledgling electrical industry, he installed the first electric lights at Buckingham Palace and Windsor under the personal supervision of Queen Victoria. After that, at the request

W.S. Lusher and Son, Royal builders, outside the octagonal meeting room of St Peter Mancroft in Norwich, which was built by the firm.

of the Emperor Franz Joseph of Austria, he put in electric light at the Vienna Opera House and introduced the Crown Prince Rudolf to Marie Vetsera while waltzing with the beautiful baroness. So perhaps Colonel Crompton could be held partially responsible for their tragic deaths at Meyerling in 1889. On a happier note he was certainly responsible for introducing electric light to the British Royal Family.

Electric cables come from BICC Pyrotenax of Tyne and Wear. They take such pride in the resilience of their cables that when their first factory was opened in 1937 they invited Viscount Ridley to smash some of it with a hammer. It took him forty-nine blows. Apart from the Royal palaces, their cables now wire St Paul's Cathedral, the Mersey Tunnel (28,000 metres), the Humber Bridge (2 km) and the Thames Barrier.

Her Majesty's cement manufacturers are Blue Circle Industries PLC, who are just one of the fifteen Warrant Holders listed under the general heading of 'Building Materials'. It is often difficult to be sure precisely what items some of these companies supply, though C. N. Brown, former manager of the King's Lynn branch of Crossley's, which used to be Dawber Townsley of King's

Samples from the 1920s – silks from the Gainsborough Silk Weaving Co. Ltd., who make furnishing fabrics for The Queen.

Tassels and trims – Two generations of G.J. Turner and Co, at the first floor workshop in Scrutton Street, London EC2 where they make furnishing trimmings for The Queen.

Graeme Wilson, celebrated amateur thespian and supplier of plumbing, electrical and building materials to The Queen, strikes an Alfred Hitchcock pose in a bathroom at his Aberdeen showroom.

Lynn, remembers helping Mr Lusher the builder, also a Warrant Holder, when Sandringham House had to be extensively refurbished. Mr Brown supplied Green Westmoreland Random Slates for the roof and cleverly managed to identify the ridge tiles from a very indistinct logo. He ran identical replacements to earth, almost literally, from the manufacturers' 'overgrown and weed-covered stockyard'. It is reassuring to find that kind of attention to detail in a company so large that it turns over £200 million a year.

A big builder's merchants like William Wilson and Co. of Aberdeen is an extraordinary Aladdin's cave of household essentials from pipe scaffolding to two-inch nails and lavatory seats and washing machines and any conceivable sort of appliance plus the means of fitting it, all scattered about 50,000 square feet of industrial estate on the outskirts of Aberdeen. When it was built, it was the largest single spa building north of Edinburgh.

Graeme Wilson, energetic amateur thespian, Baden-Powell aficionado and scout, and an exuberant recent President of the Royal Warrant Holders' Association, has been the Chairman of this family enterprise since 1972. It is still known to many in the area by the original familiar name of 'Willie Wilson's'. They were plumber's merchants at first, though the money to back the company came from the original Willie's brother, Alexander, who was in granite. Much of their business came from Orkney and Shetland via 'the North Boat'.

By 1933 they had diversified to such an extent that they took an advertisement to announce the fact to the trade. 'William Wilson and Co. (Aberdeen) Limited, Brass Moulders and Finishers, Electro-Platers in Copper, Silver, Tin, Nickel and Brass, Art Bronzers, Iron Merchants, Engineers, Factors, Template and Solder Agents, desire to inform the Trade generally that they have now been appointed Wholesale Electrical Factors of all standard Electric Lamps, Cables, Conduit Tubing, Switchgear etc.'

Graeme Wilson joined the company as a young man in the mid-fifties. 'I wasn't prepared to sit back,' he says. He opened branches in Inverness and Elgin, Fraserburgh and Kirkcaldy. He bought old rivals like Whiteheads. He moved south and bought Sellers of Leeds. And now a company which was turning over a mere £100,000 a year in the mid-fifties has an annual turnover of many millions. The original deliveries were made by a horse and cart on contract hire from their neighbours, Atlas Express of College Street. In the early twenties the horse driver transferred to a 25-cwt-truck. Now they have over twenty modern vehicles.

For years Graeme Wilson's father, was supplying plumbing materials for Balmoral. 'We'd send a parcel up on the bus,' says Mr Wilson, 'if there was a leaky tap or something. But it never entered our heads to apply for it.' They did, however, once Graeme became Managing Director, and in 1963 were awarded the Warrant. 'It's something very, very precious,' he says, managing to sound as if he is still amazed that such a thing should have happened to a family firm that was so recently and so literally in the era of the horse and cart.

Power tools come from Kango Wolf of Ealing, London, who have held the Warrant since 1959 and claim to be the only remaining British-owned company in their field. Their specialities are hammers, drills, grinders and saws. Pest control and timber preservation are done by Rentokil, now a vast company but one which began only in 1927 when a young man called Anker-Petersen came to England to market Danish rat poison. 'Ratin' was originally marketed with horror tactics worthy of Hammer films. The reps' printed card used to have a message saying: 'I have tried to tell you the facts about what has become a major menace, but I have not been able to tell you all the facts – they could not be printed – they are too alarming, too terrible for general publication.' This was supplemented with a book called *The Menace of the Death Rat*, its cover with a vast rat towering over a cowering family of four.

Quite apart from the bricks, the mortar and the basic fabric of the Royal homes and offices, there is a colossal range of Warrant Holders who supply what in a more everyday establishment we would class as 'household contents'. Ranged on the shelf, displayed in cabinets or placed at the dining table, we tend to take such artefacts for granted. Confronted with, let us say, a twelve-ounce Royal Brierley Crystal Braemar tumbler (Ref. No. c2148) few of us would pause to speculate on its ingredients. We would not know, and perhaps not care, that it is composed half of silica from Scotland and almost a third of red lead oxide from Australia. Nor that 19 per cent is potassium carbonate and nitrate from France and that a magic 1 per cent is a mix of secret clarity and lustre including ingredients known only to 'a handful of Royal Brierley craftsmen'.

A glass like this tumbler from which the average guest would so casually sip whisky, is fired in a pot which takes thirty-six hours to reach a temperature of 1,400 degrees. It is made in a 'glasshouse' around the sides of which are

Michael Latham of James Latham PLC, The Queen's wood merchant, at one of his company's timber yards

David Williams-Thomas of Royal Brierley Crystal, suppliers of crystal glassware to The Queen and The Prince of Wales, with an array of his glass

Mr and Mrs Swann of Heddon-on-the-Wall, near Newcastle-on-Tyne, working on one of their special numismatic cabinets for coins and medals, as suppliers to The Queen

small furnaces called 'glory-holes'. The men who make this glass work in teams called 'chairs'. Their boss is a 'gaffer'. His number two is a 'servitor'. They are assisted by a 'blower', a 'bit gatherer' and a 'taker in'.

They and their ancestors have been making crystal in the West Midlands since the Huguenots – Henzeys and Tyzacks and Titterys – first settled there in 1610. In 1740 John Pidcock, nephew of the last Henzey, married the daughter of Honeybourne the glass maker, who worked from the Moor Lane Glass House at 'Briar Lea Hill' in Pensnett Chase. Early in the next century that glass house was leased to Joseph Silvers, who begat Ellen Silvers, who married Samuel Cox Williams, and so on, until in the present day there are two of Joseph's great-great-great-grandsons at the helm of Royal Brierley Crystal.

All that and more can be prompted by a single tumbler. Today the company has The Queen's and The Prince of Wales's Warrants. At Royal marriages and jubilees they have become accustomed to presenting special crystal to those concerned and to producing souvenirs for the rest of us. They made a crown-shaped scent bottle for Queen Victoria's jubilee and a beer tumbler for Edward VII's Coronation. For Lord Kitchener's death they produced a 'Goblet flanged with hollow knop stem on welded foot. Engraved with coronet and monogram with date of birth and death in laurel wreath opposite an inscription: "His work was done ere we could thank him." Engraved and gilt.' Not to mention goblets for the King of Nepal with his Royal cypher and rhododendron, and a bucket-shaped goblet with 'flat cut flutes' for Grand Duke Nicholas of Russia, and sherry glasses for the Royal yacht of King Faroukh of Egypt.

Something to ponder next time you are lucky enough to be offered a glass from Royal Brierley.

The Royal cutler is Arthur Price of England, a patriotic name for a company founded in 1902 which now describes itself as 'Britain's First Family in Cutlery and Silverware'. Their manufacturing is done in those two traditional

220

centres, Sheffield and Birmingham, and company HQ is in Lichfield, conveniently situated in between. John Price, the Chairman, who joined the company in 1949 and changed the name to incorporate 'England', is passionate about his company and its roots. 'So many companies in many fields,' he says, 'have brand names that boast a heritage that bears no relation at all to their origins. Some are names that have been bought and some even are just famous names from the past that are fronts for cheap Far Eastern products. I am proud that Arthur Price of England is a real family company making superb cutlery and silverware.' Beware, in other words, of cheap imitations. Or, as he puts it, 'If it doesn't say "Made in Sheffield", then it isn't!'

Apart from Royal cutlery Mr Price's company designed and made all the cutlery for Concorde and, indeed, all British Airways planes. They are also expert in renovation and repair, and recently completed a massive job of refurbishing 100,000 pieces of silver-plated cutlery for the Crown Suppliers. It is difficult to think of any item of cutlery they can't provide, for their catalogue contains everything from asparagus racks and tongs, cocktail shakers and spoons, corn on the cob holders, crêpe Suzette pans, grape scissors, ice hammers, Parmesan cheese dishes, tooth pick holders to wine coasters, coolers, cradles, funnels and even wine-waiter keys and chains.

Since January 1912 the Royal matches have come from Bryant and May, the company founded in the early nineteenth-century by two Quaker businessmen who originally imported their 'lucifers', 'congreves', 'vestas' and 'tändstickor' from Lundströms of Jönköping in Sweden. For a while this was a cordial arrangement, with the Londoners' letters regularly signed, Quaker style, 'We are thy friends, Bryant and May'. Sales rose from just under a quarter of a million 'capsules and boxes' in 1850 to 27,922,788 ten years later. In 1852 Johan Lundström invented the first 'safety match', but he was never able to supply sufficient for Bryant and May's demands and correspondence became increasingly acrimonious, with such tetchy demands as 'Thou dost not allude to the Patent Match. How does the case stand in reference to that article?' Eventually Bryant and May decided that they must go their own way and manufacture their own. In 1861 they opened their first factory in the East End of London, manufacturing such exotic items as 'The only vesuvian that can be carried in the pocket with safety', 'palace flamers' and 'London Flaming Cigar Lights, warranted to light in wind and rain'. Today their

Carvers and Gilders, whose Royal Warrant is, as their name suggests, for carving and gilding.

HQ is in High Wycombe, but the boxes still look remarkably like their Victorian ancestors, with the gold medals they won in London and Dublin and the trademark of a Noah's Ark, emblazoned with the word 'security', which has been in use since 1872.

The Queen's candles are made by Price's Patent Candle Company in cavernous premises just south of the Thames in Battersea. At the time of writing the company was still planning a move to a more modern factory in Wandsworth. 'I think the night life of society a hundred years since was rather a dark affair,' wrote Thackeray in *The Virginians*, contemplating the stink of mutton-based tallow candles: 'Let us bless Mr Price and other Luciferous benefactors of mankind for banishing the abominable mutton of our youth.' They have been making candles since 1830 and now specialise in very superior ones characterised by an even burn, extreme longevity and sometimes exotic smells. They even produce a candle clock, modelled on those used in pre-clockwork monasteries when there wasn't enough sun to operate the sundial.

When Robert Lacey wrote his best-selling *Majesty* in 1977 he remarked that 'behind the baize door', the Royal apartments were not tremendously lavish or up to date and that 'an aged bar electric fire' was an 'unmistakable sign that one is in a Royal residence'. Whether this was a reference to Belling and Co., who hold the Warrant for electrical appliances, is unclear but it is true that when the company produced a book to celebrate its first fifty years they reprinted one letter from a Londoner which ran: 'I

David Wilkinson, of R. Wilkinson and Son, The Queen's glass restorers – note the EⅡR ciphers
engraved on the side of the glasses

Clive Swindle, The Queen's porcelain restorer in his workshop at the bottom of his garden near Westerham in Kent

A rat-killing sash from Rentokil who hold a Royal Warrant for 'pest control and timber preservation'

am writing to tell you of the wonderful service which I have had from one of your electric fires. When we came to this house in 1926, we took it over from the previous owner and paid ten shillings for it . . . it is still working very well.' As the writer came from SW11 and as the Warrant was only granted to Belling in 1962, it could not have anything to do with Lacey's observation except to emphasise the longevity of Belling's products. They are also versatile – one satisfied customer wrote to say how delighted she was with her Belling's clothes drying cabinet. She used it for making meringues!

Electrolux also make electrical appliances, though their Warrant is specifically for suction cleaners and floor polishers. When their first factory opened in Luton in 1927 it was the first outside Sweden to make suction cleaners and refrigerators. Since then the company has made more than 17 million cleaners and 12.5 million refrigerators and freezers. King George V's Warrant followed only two years after the opening, thus confirming the sales slogan, 'Every Home an Electrolux Home'. At the time of writing the company was planning a book of its history and a museum of its products.

The manufacturer of painting and decorating brushes is Leslie G. Harris, who started his company in two rented houses in Birmingham at the very beginning of the thirties. His capital was borrowed from his father, the Depression was about to start and, on his own admission, he 'knew nothing of how to make brushes'. One might have thought this a straightforward enough business, but even making paint brushes at Stoke Prior Mills near Bromsgrove, where the firm moved in 1936, can be an exotic and fraught endeavour. There was a near catastrophe, for instance, a year after he was granted The Queen's Warrant in 1961, when the price of Chinese pig bristle almost doubled overnight due to drought in the country of origin. Because of this Harris and Co. started its own bristle factory – the only British brush factory to have one.

The first lift in a British Royal palace is said to have been a 'flying chair' installed at Windsor Castle for Queen Anne as evidence that anything the French could do at Versailles we could do better. Not until some 200 years later did the Express Lift Company install the passenger lift at Sandringham House on which their Royal Warrant is founded. At much the same time George Bernard Shaw was having one installed in his house at Ayot St Lawrence, though when I mentioned this to Shaw's official biographer, Michael Holroyd, he was incredulous, partly because he had never seen the lift, partly because the house was so small, and partly because Shaw was incredibly agile to the end of his days. In more recent times Express Lifts have installed twenty-two 1,400-feet-per-minute lifts in the National Westminster Bank Tower; twelve external observation lifts for Lloyd's of London and fifty-five Express Lifts in the Shun Tak Centre on the Hong Kong waterfront.

To try out this new generation of lifts the company erected a test tower at their headquarters at Northampton, opened by The Queen in 1982. It is fourteen feet higher than the spire of Salisbury Cathedral and a potent reminder of how far lifts have come since the days of the eighteenth-century 'flying chair'.

Marley Tiles may be found on the floor and on the roof of Royal dwellings, but the work of Norfolk Reed Thatchers of Henley-on-Thames can be found only above top-floor level. (The 'Norfolk' refers to the provenance of the reeds used in thatching rather than the firm's location.) Thatch is, on the whole, a domestic rather than a palatial form of finishing, but the late Harold Sallkild, whose firm's objects are 'to promote the interests of owners of thatched properties, to provide organised maintenance facilities and protect this ancient craft' did have The Queen's Warrant and also thatched 'The Queen's Little House' at Windsor.

Even in the best-ordered households things get broken or simply grow old. In houses containing so many beautiful and historic objects this poses particular problems and Royalty is lucky to be able to find skilful specialist solvers. Thus Clive Swindle, who works from his cottage in Kent, repairs the porcelain; Wilkinson and Son in London's East End, whose founder used to etch the BOAC symbol on all their glass, is responsible for restoring glass, notably the Monarch's majestic chandeliers; and Anna Plowden and Peter Smith hold the Warrant as restorers of 'Fine Art Objects'.

This wonderful catch-all phrase means that on any given day you are likely to find their workshop in St Ann's Hill, Wandsworth, absolutely stacked with vast marble columns, intricate pieces of Etruscan jewellery,

Belling still supply Royal electrical appliances

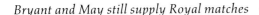

Bryant and May still supply Royal matches

heraldic beasts, sixteenth-century diptychs and even mediaeval iron coffin-handles. Any antique artefact seems to be grist to their particular mill.

They concede that clients are often surprised by the variety of skills available in their twenty-five ·strong workshop. They offer expertise in 'gold, silver, bronze and other metals; stone and marble; wax portraits and models; ceramics, mosaics and glass; wood, ivory and shell; frescoes and polychrome'. Anna Plowden came to the business from the Institute of Archaeology at London University and the Baghdad Museum; Peter Smith came from thirteen years in the Research Laboratory at the British Museum. They joined forces in 1966.

Christie's, Sotheby's, the National Trust, the V and A, the Metropolitan in New York . . . all the big names in the field are now among their clients, but a characteristic of their work is that it is not all sublime. They once restored a collection of 350 human tattoos taken from late-nineteenth-century sailors in the Dutch East Indies and they also claim responsibility for a Dog Collar Museum at Leeds Castle. They have held The Queen's Warrant since 1983.

The many priceless books in the Royal libraries do not break so much as come apart with age. When they do, they are rebound using beautiful leathers from the tannery of J. Hewit and Sons of Currie, Edinburgh. They have been serving the bookbinding industry for almost 200 years,

ABOVE Royal candles are made by Price's Patent Candle Co. at the Belmont Works in South London. These are specially guaranteed not to drip

OPPOSITE Shedding a little light – Bryant and May are the perfect match for Royalty

Richard Belling, the Belling grantee demonstrates how much technology has changed the face of kitchens since the 1931 Baby Belling pictured on page 225

tanning and dressing their selected skins specifically for books. Levant and Morocco Grain, Antique Calf and Sheep – the names and the appearance and the smell of these leathers are totally traditional. Yet 'progress' can break with tradition. For years the best goatskin came from South Africa. Then, around the last war, the quality dropped dramatically. All the skins were perforated with hundreds of tiny holes. An expert was sent to Africa to investigate and came back with a simple answer. The South Africans had just introduced barbed wire and their goats, rubbing up against it, were ruining the skins. Today the best-quality goatskins for rare and ancient books come from Botswana, where barbed wire is rare.

No less than a dozen of The Queen's Warrant Holders are listed under furnishing fabrics and the oldest known example of weaving – a Peruvian design showing a man holding up two severed heads, dating from before Christ – is in the archive of a Royal Warrant Holder. It belongs to G. P. and J. Baker of High Wycombe.

At Sudbury in Suffolk the Gainsborough Silk Weaving Company was only started in 1903 but is the heir to a tradition which goes back hundreds of years. In the late seventeenth century the persecution of the Huguenots meant that thousands of French Protestant silk workers fled to England, many settling in Spitalfields, then a village to the east of London. In 1774 the Spitalfields Act

was passed, enabling the Justices to set wages for the London weavers. Because of this the silk manufacturers began to set up country branches in East Anglia, where the new act had no force and they could pay lower wages. A prime beneficiary of this was Sudbury, where in 1844 there were said to be 600 looms. Some of these were still weaving 'buntings and drabbets' – a legacy of the old wool trade – but many more were engaged on 'silks, velvets and satins'.

Reginald Warner began the Gainsborough Company in a cottage with only two looms, but the firm prospered and soon attracted Royal patronage. An early newspaper report mentioned Queen Alexandra's dress for the Delhi durbar which was made of Gainsborough silk with a rose, thistle and shamrock design. Gainsborough silks were used in wall panelling, upholstery and curtains. For Windsor Castle they provided lengths of a quarter and an eighth of a mile and, like so many other surviving Warrant Holders, they were involved in the famous Queen Mary's doll's house, which went on exhibition at the Wembley Exhibition in 1924. They supplied miniature versions of their own wall hangings and carpets under the direction of Sir Edwin Lutyens. Wall panels for the House of Commons, for King Faroukh's Egyptian palace and for Hampton Court and curtains for Mr Sopwith's yacht – Gainsborough supplied them all. They even wove the silk which covered the seat of the chair on which, apparently, Winston Churchill sat while leading the nation during the Second World War.

More recently they have woven silk sashes for The

Royal Lodge, Windsor, thatched by Norfolk Reed Thatchers of Henley-on-Thames

Queen, The Queen Mother and Princess Margaret, and to prove it they have a photograph of the trio wearing them for the first time together. And they wove a beautiful deep Royal blue damask with oak leaves and acorns for new upholstery in Queen Alexandra's State Coach when it was used at The Prince and Princess of Wales's wedding.

Warner and Sons also have a strong Spitalfields and Huguenot connection, dating back to those extraordinary times when 15,000 Huguenots settled in London in a single year and parliament voted a staggering £200,000 to help them. Originally they were in scarlet dyeing and began weaving properly only in 1870. So successful have they been that when they celebrated their centenary the Victoria and Albert Museum honoured them with a special exhibition.

One of the earliest exhibits was a rose and thistle pattern woven for the new Ball Room at Buckingham Palace in 1859, though technically this was not a Warner work but one of Daniel Walters of Braintree, who were subsequently taken over by Warners.

Although the present Warrant is for "Silks and Furnishing Fabrics", this gives a slightly misleading impression, for the origins of Warners' association with the Royal Family stem from clothing. On Tuesday, 7 March 1893 Princess Mary Adelaide, Duchess of Teck, and her daughter Princess May, later Queen Mary, visited the Warner factory in Spitalfields. They were so impressed that they ordered the fabric for Princess May's wedding dress – a thick white satin with a Tudor rose and clusters of may. For the next forty years 'dress silks rather than furnishing silks were the subject of Royal orders and gifts'.

Warners wove the satin pall for the funeral of Queen Victoria and the cloth of gold for the symbolic pallium or mantle placed over King Edward VII's shoulders at his Coronation by the Dean of Westminster and clasped by the Lord Great Chamberlain. The company also provided cloth of gold and velvet for the coronations of George V, George VI and Queen Elizabeth II. The directors' report for 1953 reported to shareholders that 'The Company had the honour of weaving by hand purple, crimson and Garter blue velvets, and cloth of gold for Her Majesty's robes and other purposes including St Edward's Throne and the Royal crowns, crimson satins and damasks for the Throne, Chair of Estate, faldstools and chairs of the Royal Dukes.' The firm also wove 1,600 yards of silk warp fabric for frontals and hangings.

Many Royal rooms are now hung in Warner fabrics. The Royal Yacht had a special cotton, 'Elmsett', made for it in 1954, but other less regal surroundings contain Warner fabrics too. The proscenium curtain for Barking Town Hall was made by Warners and so were the blinds for the Hilton Hotel in Brussels.

In Scotland Jenners, the famous and still independent department store on Princes Street, holds a Warrant for furnishing materials. They celebrated their 150th birthday in 1988 and furnishing materials have never been their only link with Royalty. In the old days when debutantes were still presented at Holyroodhouse they used to make a speciality of ladies' headdresses consisting of three Prince of Wales plumed feathers. Like all Scots they will never willingly yield to their rivals south of the border and, after all, they pay higher rates per square foot than Harrods!

Henry Newbery and Co have been making furnishing trimmings, for which they hold The Queen's Warrant, since John Newbery set up his business in Upper Marylebone Street in 1782. The present Managing Director, Carol Newbery, is the sixth generation of the family to work in the company, which after a peripatetic two centuries is now in its own property in Newman Street, where Ms Newbery – she is married but works under her maiden name for the sake of family continuity – has set up a museum of trimmings – tassels, pelmet trimmings and the like – going back to Tudor times. They

*Skins being cured at J. Hewit and Sons of Edinburgh. Hewit supply leather for binding books in
the Royal libraries. The leather for binding the special edition of this book comes from them too*

Glass blowing at the Royal Brierley crystal factory. There is still no acceptable substitute for the human mouth

A 1940 screen printing from G.P. and J. Baker who have The Queen's Warrant for furnishing fabrics and wallcoverings

keep hundreds of different designs and they try to keep 300 m of each braid and fringe in stock just in case. 'It's amazing,' she says, 'how many people put a whole room together and then realise they've forgotten the trimmings.'

G. J. Turner and Co. also make furniture trimmings, at Scrutton Street in London, in workshops so authentically traditional that you might almost think that you had

The Duchess of Teck and Princess May visit Warner and Sons silk factory in 1893

walked on to a film set. When one of their ancient braiding machines breaks down they will manufacture a replica themselves, but they are not believers in discarding unnecessarily. Not long ago the textile museum telephoned to say that they understood Turners had a machine dating back to the early nineteenth century and might they have it as an exhibit? 'Certainly not,' responded Turners indignantly. 'We're still using it.' Small wonder that their trimmings are indistinguishable from the originals.

Some interior furnishings come from Martin Frost of George Street, Edinburgh, whose company was originally in bedding and baskets. The original Martin, the present Managing Director's great-grandfather, founded the firm with the money he won in a slander action against his erstwhile employers, the Royal Blind Asylum workshops, who sacked him in 1894.

Cole and Son have a Warrant for suppling The Queen with wallpaper and own a set of more than 3,000 antique wallpaper blocks. When the Houses of Parliament had to be restored it was Coles who were able to locate the Pugin original and reprint the designs just as they first were.

The Queen's ventilation equipment is from 'Vent-Axia', the company who say 'We've helped the world breathe a little easier.' They fitted their first ever extractor fan, 'The Silent Six', in 1936 and were granted the Warrant in 1985.

There are four Royal window cleaners, one with The Queen's, one with The Queen's and Prince of Wales's and two with the Queen Mother's Warrant. Of these last two the Mayfair Window Cleaning Company have been cleaning Royal windows for almost seventy years. They cleaned the Prince of Wales's windows at York House in 1921 and were awarded his Warrant three years. later. On 12 March 1953 their estimate for cleaning the windows at Clarence House was first accepted and they were given the Queen Mother's Warrant in 1959.

Any window cleaner wanting a ladder to stand on could find one at Drew, Clark and Co where Roger Drew is the third generation of a ladder-making family which has had the Queen's Warrant since 1960. Each ladder is numbered so that it can be identified with the craftsman who made it. They use silver spruce for the frames and birch for the rungs and still employ fewer than twenty people.

Most fundamental of all are the builders themselves – firms like Hall and Tawse of Aberdeen, who have worked on both Balmoral and Birkall, as well as churches, distilleries, hospitals and other great houses. They built

The Design Studio at the Royal Carpet Factory in Wilton

Marks and Spencer's in Aberdeen and Lochay Power Station and the Post Office in Kirkwall. When they restored Pluscarden Priory near Elgin, the Benedictine monks who moved back in were the first to live there in 300 years. Their most demanding and romantic achievement, however, was finding a huge chunk of granite in a quarry at Balmoral and shipping it to northern France, where it now stands at St Valery, a solid twenty-four-foot-high memorial to the men of the 51st Highland Division who made their last forlorn stand there during the retreat of 1940.

Matthew Hall, who hold The Queen Mother's Warrant, is now a multi-million-pound business with contracts involving the new underground railway in Melbourne, nuclear power stations, leisure complexes and car delivery centres in Swindon. Once, in 1848, all this was just one man – Matthew Hall, who came to London from Newcastle to set up a lead-work business in Lambeth. Next time you pass Westminster Cathedral, look up at the great lead cross that stands at its topmost point. It was cast in Matthew Hall's workshops and wrought to a design of Jack Woodbridge, who was taken on in the 1870s by Matthew himself as an apprentice leadworker.

The firm have been linked with Royalty ever since they had to install special plumbing for the guests at The Duke of Fife's funeral in Windsor. It was a rush job. 'We worked day and night to prepare,' recorded the site foreman. 'I contacted the office at 10 a.m. for many tons of nine-inch drain. It was put on a special train and arrived at Windsor at 3.30 the same day.'

Sinks and worktops have been a speciality of another Royal builder, Simmonds Brothers of Kensington, who even installed them for Sir Vivian Fuchs's Antarctic expedition in the fifties. They were founded by two teenage brothers who started their building careers in the late nineteenth century, working as a carpenter and bricklayer on the construction of the Natural History Museum. Today their clients include The Duchy of Cornwall, three other Dukes, a clutch of embassies, British Rail, the Russian Benevolent Society and, of course, Her Majesty The Queen.

When it comes to custom-built furniture, there are few more specialised and expert craftsmen than Swann of Heddon-on-the-Wall, near Newcastle-on-Tyne. This is the sort of business which confirms all one's preconceptions about the Royal Warrant Holders. Their

*ABOVE The Antique Room at Thomas Goode and Son, suppliers of glass and china to The Queen,
The Queen Mother and The Prince of Wales*

OPPOSITE Irish Linen from Givan's Irish Linen Stores. They are Linen Drapers to The Queen

stock-in-trade is the cabinet for storing small valuable objects, particularly coins and medals. Their standards are an eight-drawer and a sixteen-drawer, priced at the time of writing between £300 and £500. They are usually made from Brazilian mahogany, though if you want something rarer, like walnut or Honduran mahogany, the cost could double. Cuban mahogany, satinwood and rosewood are 'by special quotation'. The doors are covered in finest

Landscape with Chimneys – Leslie Scales, who holds the Royal Warrant on behalf of the London Brick Company

Morocco goatskin, all fittings are solid brass, the trays are fronted with Indian rosewood and you can have special knobs in ivory or leather numbered in gold leaf.

But Mr Swann really comes into his own with special orders. The entire Royal Mint coin collection is housed in eighty of his cabinets. He made the Bishop of London's pastoral staff and pectoral cross, in Rio rosewood, ivory and gold. The firm had a commission from a client in Bad Homburg which enabled them to stay in Princess Victoria's old room at Kaiser Wilhelms Bad. And this, immediately after being at Windsor Castle!

Mr Swann's work for Her Majesty The Queen began in 1975 when a complete reorganisation of the Royal coin collection was set in motion. All went well until the winter of 1988, when he discovered that the Indian government had banned the export of rosewood. As The Queen's cabinets are all made in that precious wood, this represented what Mr Swann concedes was 'a slight crisis'. He was hoping the Indian government would relent and allow a few logs out for The Queen. Luckily a friend of his, the Assistant Bishop of Newcastle, happened to be on a visit to Bangalore, spoke all the necessary local languages and was good at woodwork. He was being relied on to produce a minor miracle and somehow procure six good logs. Whether, on this occasion, the Lord did provide we do not know!

Nine companies are listed under the general heading of bedding and linen but few can have had a more intimate connection with the Royal Family than Staples, who now make bedsteads and bedding for The Queen 'in much the same way they always have been'. In 1982 they moved from their long-standing home at Staples Corner to a new factory in Huntingdon, but anyone wishing to get a first-hand idea of their work for the Monarchy has only to go to the Victoria and Albert Museum, where the firm's archive material is now stored, together with a bed they made specially for The King in the 1920s.

Also there is the original British patent for which Ambrose Heal, grandson of the founder of the Tottenham Court Road furniture store, paid £1,000 in 1895. It had originally been taken out by John Atkinson Staples of New York State. Staples had, in effect, revolutionised the mattress.

From the start the Staples mattress was advertised as the healthiest possible thing to sleep on. 'Don't crease your tummy!', 'Cannot sag', 'Be healthy, Buy a Staples' – these were the slogans that brought prosperity, so it was no surprise that when King George V had a bad riding

Clock repairing at Hamilton and Inches of Edinburgh, The Queen's silversmiths and clock specialists

accident in 1915 his doctors immediately advised the purchase of a Staples mattress. His horse had reared and fallen after being upset by cheering troops on a visit to France and his back was badly strained.

The King was so pleased with the bed that he ordered several more and allowed his 'satisfaction' to be recorded in Staples's future advertisements and other promotional literature. In fact, the bed now looks extraordinarily uncomfortable, but these were pioneering days.

In 1925 Sir Edwin Lutyens designed a special bed incorporating a Staples mattress for the Viceroy's residence in New Delhi. The British embassies, from Moscow to Washington, ordered Staples beds; so did Rhodesian railways; LNER put them in their first-class sleepers; and Cunard built them into the *Queen Mary*. During the Second World War Staples made a special bed for Winston Churchill; and there were special featherweight beds for Sir Sholto Douglas and General Montgomery to sleep on while flying about in a Dakota.

Immediately after the war Staples made a new bed for King George VI, who had had his first Staples bed in 1929. Other successes included a 'cantilever table' which was dubbed 'Granny favourite', a seven-foot-round bed for the Sultan of Oman's summer palace and a nine-foot square one for a person improbably described as 'a London journalist'.

Another Royal bed-maker is the invitingly named Hypnos of Princes Risborough.

The blankets on the bed are likely to come from Early's of Witney, who have held the Warrant only since 1969 but are members of the exclusive Tercentenarian Club, limited to those companies that can legitimately trace their history back for 300 years. In fact, the little Oxfordshire town has been weaving blankets – and Royal blankets at that – since the seventeenth century. The Witney Weavers, or wavers, presented James II with a pair of blankets fringed in gold. In 1711 the same Witney 'wavers' were formed into a company by Queen Anne. Their original seal is still preserved in Witney though they now employ far fewer weavers than before.

*Indian elephants in the window of Harold Higgins suggest, correctly, that though Higgins hold
their Royal Warrant for coffee they also supply tea*

THE STAFF OF LIFE

'Could we have some butter for the Royal slice of bread?'
(A.A. Milne: *The King's Breakfast*)

In A. A. Milne's plaintive lament, 'The King's Breakfast', as the Monarch keeps on to his wife and the dairymaid about what he wants on 'the Royal slice of bread', The Queen says to him, 'Talking of the butter for the Royal slice of bread, many people think that marmalade is nicer. Would you like to try a little marmalade instead?' She did not stipulate 'Frank Cooper's', and the King was so upset that he said 'Bother!' and went back to bed. This is not entirely surprising since that famous English breakfast preserve never held a King's Warrant until the reign of George VI. Queen Alexandra, in 1919, was partial to it and so was The Prince of Wales from 1920 to 1936, but not, apparently, Edward VII or George V.

For more than twenty years now 'Oxford' marmalade has been manufactured far from its original home. It began in 1874. Frank Cooper was the proprietor of The Italian Warehouse, a grocery at 84 Oxford High Street. One autumn his wife, Sarah, made a batch of 76 lb of marmalade from an old family recipe. This was surplus to the Cooper family's requirements and so Frank packed some of it in earthenware jars and put it in the shop window, where it attracted the attention of the dons from Queen's College just across the road.

Their product quickly caught on and became an institution. Demand was such that in 1900 the Coopers closed The Italian Warehouse and moved to a factory by the railway station. The Boat Race crew trained on their marmalade, Scott took it to the Antarctic and it was mandatory in 'nearly all the Naval and Military Messes'. Shortly before the factory was requisitioned in the Second World War they were selling 651,643 jars at 1s 6d a pound.

All this time it remained a family company, but in 1964 it was taken over by Brown and Polson, the cornflour

people. The familiar tale of take-over, merger and rationalisation has meant that production was moved to Paisley in Scotland and then Redditch in Worcester. There are no longer any Coopers working for the company, which is – along with fellow Warrant Holders Brown and Polson Cornflour and Mazola Corn Oil – part of the 'Best Foods Division' of CPC (United Kingdom) Ltd, with headquarters in Esher.

Not all multi-national conglomerates are soulless. It may be naïve to call it sentiment and more realistic to describe it as shrewd marketing, but Frank Cooper Ltd came back home in 1984. Not just to Oxford but to 84 The High, original site of The Italian Warehouse – and also, it

A miniature jar of Cooper's Oxford marmalade as supplied for Queen Mary's doll's house

is claimed, of the oldest coffee house in England, which was set up in 1650.

The Royal Warrants are displayed inside, as is the Royal arms. When they hung it outside in the usual fashion it was stolen, possibly as a prank, because it was later found in a field a few miles away. Here too are Sarah Cooper's original recipes – not just for marmalade but for jams and jellies of every conceivable fruit. They are very simple – not much more than 'fruit, sugar . . . boil' – and are written in fine Victorian copperplate. Even now, Fred Perry, who supervises the place for CPC, is laconic in describing the mystery of his marmalade. 'We use a lot of oranges,' he says.

They come from Seville and are pre-cut, unlike the old days, when they were carved up by local women in long aprons every autumn. There are lots of pictures of operations then and it does all look very primitive. The shop itself was a marvellous jungly Aladdin's cave, unlike the stylish, modern place, which attracts more than 20,000 purchasers a year and which now sells Cooper aprons, cakes and chocolates as well as the traditional marmalade. It is an interesting twentieth-century compromise, and the marmalade, they swear, is just like it was when Sarah Cooper boiled up that very first batch.

Not that Coopers is the only modern Royal marmalade. Baxters, the family firm which dominates the Speyside village of Fochabers, produce a wide variety of marmalade – Castle Orange, Vintage Orange, Fine Shred, Scotch Orange, Fine Shred Lemon and Three Fruits. But one must be careful here. Coopers have the Warrant for marmalade; Baxters are The Queen's 'Fruit Canners' and The Queen Mother's 'Purveyors of Scottish Food Specialities'.

They were bottling beetroot and canning pheasant when I called at Fochabers, which one visitor, a Justice of the Canadian Supreme Court no less, once called 'The happiest place in Scotland'. It does have a family atmosphere, which is hardly surprising since the Baxters still own 96 per cent of the shares. They intend, in the words of Chairman Gordon Baxter, 'to maintain our independence for as long as possible'. The company is so attractive that it sounds as if one of Mr Baxter's main tasks is repelling predatory boarders. At a recent guess he estimated that he had turned down 129 take-over bids. If you want to experience the feel of the place it is not a problem, for they are almost as much of a tourist attraction as a factory and have a modern visitors' centre with armies of trained guides. Annual attendance has risen to well in excess of 100,000 a year, which would, for

This creamery was a precursor of the Royal Warrant holding Express Dairies

instance, put Baxters well into the middle reaches of the stately home league if it were that sort of place.

What you would see being processed and cooked would depend on the time of year since, obviously, theirs is a seasonal business. Apart from the pheasant and beetroot I was also intrigued by some discreet unlabelled silvery cans which had a 'Q' stamped into the code on the base. 'Q' was for Queen. I had stumbled on the Victoria plums which Baxters supply exclusively to Her Majesty. What impressed me most was not the clanking machinery and high-tech automata but the naturalness of the product. Obviously, everything is very sophisticated – at 900 cans a minute it has to be – but despite the machinery, this was still recognisable as a kitchen. Real vegetables, real stock, real spoons, real smells, real cooks and the result is real food.

If the A. A. Milne example were followed and butter was insisted on for the Royal breakfast, it might come from Express, St Ivel or Unigate, or Kennerty Farm Dairies in Aberdeen. Nothing indicates the changes of the last two centuries better than the evolution of Express Dairies, who acquired their first Warrant from Queen Victoria in 1895 – a reward for all the advice they gave on the Royal farms at Windsor. Today they are part of Express Foods Group International, which in turn is part of the Grand Metropolitan Group, which is itself now big almost beyond belief. In 1827 Robert Barham started the dairy when he came up to London from Sussex and grazed a herd of cattle on the banks of the Thames, just about where the Savoy Hotel now stands. The Savoy is wonderful and holds two Warrants, one for flowers in the name of Edward Goodyear and one for Savoy coffee, but even so . . . One does not have to be an absolutely incurable romantic to wish that there were still dairy cows grazing on pastures in central London. If, in deference to what the Chairman of Van den Berghs calls 'the trend towards healthy eating', margarine is preferred to butter, it will come from Van den Berghs. Only they hold the Warrant for margarine.

Bread for the Royal toast might come from any of several bakers great or small, from Lyons at one extreme to someone like John Stopps of Egham at the other. Mr Stopps's grandfather started their family bakery in 1898 and they deliver to The Queen Mother at Royal Lodge, to the Queen at Windsor and to the boys at Eton College. Or there might be crispbread instead, for which Ryvita of Poole hold the Warrant.

If the Royal marmalade were preceded by cereal it

The PERFECT NIPPY

Cap correctly worn, monogram in centre.

Teeth well cared for.

Clean and well laundered collar correctly sewn in.

Dress clean and tidy.

All buttons sewn on with red cotton.

Clean and well laundered cuffs, correctly sewn in.

Point well pressed.

Clean, well laundered apron, correctly worn.

Dress correct length.

Well polished plain shoes. Medium heels for comfort.

Ribbon clean and pressed.

No conspicuous use of make-up. Hair neat and tidy.

Badge clean and securely sewn.

Fastening to have Hooks, Eyes and Press Studs, which should be securely sewn on and fastened.

Clean hands. Nails well manicured.

Plain Black Stockings.

J. Lyons & Co. Ltd.

No nippies now, but Lyons still hold the Royal Warrant

might be from Kelloggs, Quaker Oats or Weetabix, all of whom have Warrants. If sugar is taken with it there are two Royal sugar makers. British Sugar deal exclusively with British beet, while Tate and Lyle also import cane from all over the world and have cane sugar refineries in the UK, Canada, USA, Zimbabwe and Portugal. They also have beet sugar refineries in the USA.

The first known sugar beet was grown in the King of Babylon's vegetable garden in 722 BC and was called 'Silga'. The British lagged behind the rest of the world for over 2,500 years, but in 1912 a pioneer factory at Cantley was set up. Now more than 11,000 British farmers produce beet for British Sugar and the slightly improbable flagship of the British Sugar Industry is in Bury St Edmunds, where 12,000 tonnes of beet a day are handled during the annual four-month campaign from September to January. Next door is a packaging plant capable of handling 200 million kilogram packets of granulated sugar a year. All Silver Spoon Sugar for the south comes from here and British Sugar produces over half the nation's supply. There is no reason why it should not continue to do so, provided we do not succumb to the 'constant threat'

Gordon Baxter and his family in their shop at Speyside. Nearby they can the fruits and Scottish specialities which have earned them Royal Warrants from The Queen and The Queen Mother

Fortnum and Mason are famous for cake. The Piccadilly store provides groceries and provisions
for The Queen and leather and fancy goods for The Queen Mother

of rhizomania or 'root madness', a European disease as menacing to the sugar beet as rabies to wildlife.

The Royal eggs come from Goldenlay Eggs Ltd of Drighlington near Bradford, a co-operative of egg producers formed in 1934. The Royal bacon must come from one of the large number of sausage makers, butchers or provision merchants. Mattessons Wall's have the Warrant for sausages and meat pies and first held a Warrant, as plain Wall's, in 1812. Richard Wall joined a butcher named Cotterill as an apprentice in St James's Market in 1786, eventually took over the business and moved to 113 Jermyn Street in 1834. His son Thomas acquired The Queen's Warrant in 1838 and made a special 'chopping' of sausages once a week. The Buckingham Palace chef had his own seasoning recipe, which was sent down to Jermyn Street with a member of staff each time. The motive power for the mincing machines came from a single donkey on a treadmill in the cellar. Working closely with pork farmers

HP Sauce is 'By Appointment'

Wall's produced their own breed of pig and were also the first firm to introduce pre-packed bacon, rindless bacon and even, in 1983, frozen bacon steaks in sauce. A sausage maker who perhaps retains more of the old world than the rather high-tech atmosphere of Wall's is Greenstage, who make The Queen Mother's sausages by hand on their premises at Newmarket. Should ham be preferred it could be from Emmetts Store in Saxmundham or Anthony Worham of Nutfield, both of whom have The Queen Mother's Warrant. Or from Marsh and Baxter, Suppliers of York Ham to Her Majesty The Queen. The Royal mustard comes, predictably, from Colmans of Norwich, and has done since Queen Victoria's time.

One butcher who holds Warrants on behalf of two different companies is Colin Cullimore, the grantee at the huge high-street chain of Dewhursts and also at the more exclusive John Lidstone of Lower Belgrave Street. The latter supplies meat for The Queen Mother's as well as The Queen's table.

Sauce, if minded, might be from HP Foods, or their subsidiary Lea & Perrins, who make Worcestershire Sauce. Worcestershire Sauce, incidentally, was discovered, like so many of the best things in life, by mistake. Lea and Perrin were two chemists who went into partnership in Worcester selling a vast number of patent medicines, such as Essence of Sarsaparilla for scurvy. One day, Lord Sandys, a former Governor of Bengal, who had retired to his country estate at Ombersley Court not far away, dropped by and asked if they would make up a favourite sauce he had come across out East. Lea and Perrin had all the ingredients to hand and made up enough for Lord Sandys and a little for themselves. Sandys was well pleased but when Lea and Perrin tasted it they found it raw, revolting and far too hot. Instead of throwing it out, however, they put it in the cellar, where it stayed till the following year's spring clean. By then it had matured. It smelt excellent. It tasted better. They saved it, bottled it and sold it, and the rest is history. By 1855 they were selling 30,000 bottles a year.

Tea north of the border is likely to be from Melroses of Edinburgh. The founder of the firm, Andrew Melrose, was the first person to import tea direct when the clipper *Isabella* docked at Leith in 1835, twenty-three years after he had left the employ of a butcher named Robert Sheppard to start his own grocery in Canongate. Melroses were granted Queen Victoria's Warrant in 1837.

That was also the year that Richard Twining II of the Strand in London was granted the Victorian Warrant as

*The production line at Greenstage Ltd in Newmarket where the unique Royal Warrant holding
'Musk's sausages' come from*

Sam Twining, latest in a distinguished line of Royal teamen, in front of the original Twinings tea shop in the Strand

*Peter and John Renshaw with Alan Spilling, all of John F. Renshaw and Co. Ltd. of Mitcham in
Surrey. They purvey 'almond products' to The Queen and The Queen Mother*

The interior of Melrose's, Edinburgh, Royal teamen north of the border

'Purveyor of tea in Ordinary'. Twinings, however, were a very much older concern. They were originally founded in 1706 and are now the oldest ratepayer in the City of Westminster. Sam Twining can still be found at 216 The Strand, even though his company has long outgrown the shop and has its modern headquarters at Andover. This is where Twinings tea is sorted and sifted, tasted and tested, and exported to serious tea drinkers the world over. The Strand shop still sells an enormous range of more than 140 esoteric teas and coffees. The achievement is unique, says Sam Twining. No other family has traded so long in the same commodity from the same address. Or, as A. P. Herbert put it when the firm celebrated its 250th anniversary,

> Two-fifty years! Same trade – and same address –
> Same family! Is this a record? yes.

The company are almost compulsively innovative, whether experimenting with the new fruit-based caffeine-free infusions like their blackcurrant, which is so popular in the USA, or searching out special classics for commemorative issues like their 1981 275th anniversary tea. This was a tea from Yunnan, 'the kingdom of tea', possessing 'a bouquet of the finest fragrance matched only by a bouquet of utmost delicacy and refreshment'.

It seems certain that Twinings tea was enjoyed by several Monarchs before Queen Victoria, for the early ledgers are full of references to customers from the Court. There was Earl Cardigan, Master of Queen Anne's buck-hounds; Sir Brocus Gardner, a Commissioner of the Stamp Office in Queen Anne's reign; Lord Litchfield, sometime Gentleman of the Bedchamber; Lord Sussex, who carried the Golden Spurs at the Coronation of George I and officiated as deputy Earl Marshal of England at King George II's Coronation. They all drank Twinings.

In more recent years the company have consistently held Royal Warrants, and blended individual teas for Queen Mary, a regular visitor to the shop who allowed her name to appear on the packaging, and The Prince of Wales, and they will still produce special teas for special customers.

In the past the most special was the one made up for Earl Grey, now more famous for his tea than the 1832 Reform Bill passed when he was Prime Minister. Sam Twining says that although this blend was unquestionably made up by his ancestors and the Earl, nobody bothered to register it. 'As a result it has become a generic,' he says with feeling. 'Everybody produces an Earl Grey tea and some are ghastly.' Almost the only constant is oil of bergamot.

Perhaps in deference to changing popular taste there are twice as many coffee men with the Royal Warrant as there are tea men, though Melroses and Twinings appear under both headings.

One curiosity among coffee men is the Warrant granted to the Nairobi Coffee Company of Watford in 1931. Sir Christopher Coote, the senior extant Irish baronet and present grantee, was able to produce a letter from Buckingham Palace saying that the original Warrant appeared to be 'the first granted in recent years for which no application has been made'. The conditions of eligibility had been fulfilled and the authorities felt that the Warrant would come 'as a pleasant surprise'. In recent times it is more often the other way round. Companies are over-eager to apply and therefore risk an unpleasant rather than an agreeable surprise.

Like tea, coffee has followed the trend of wine and is becoming – at least at the Warrant Holding end of the market – a topic for the connoisseur. H. R. Higgins Ltd, of Duke Street, London, who has held The Queen's Warrant since 1979, has a coffee list which is remarkably like that of a particularly adventurous wine merchant with an eclectic taste.

His recommended 'best general purpose coffee available' is Kibo Chagga, discovered by the original H. R. Higgins himself just after the end of the last war. It is grown by the Wa-Chagga tribe of Tanzania, picked by hand and washed in the streams from the Kibo Glacier, then dried in the pure air of Mount Kilimanjaro. It is clearly much sought after, for the company says, 'We encounter fierce competition from other European buyers for this superb coffee.' If you want to know more about

A trio of Royal beverage conveyances

this or the remarkable Costa Rica from Tobias Umana Jimenez, who grows on Tarrazu Mountain in the San Marcos district, you could always ask Tony or Audrey Higgins, the present Directors, to come and give one of their lectures.

Luncheon tends to be less of a celebration than dinner and when one looks at the Royal calendar and diary, one sees that the most visible lunches tend to be those informal occasions where The Queen tries to meet an interesting cross-section of her subjects, drawn from different walks of life. Dinner is the grand white-tie affair to honour the visiting Head of State.

No one has the exclusive Warrant for soup, though companies such as Baxters and Heinz include soups among their products. There is, however, a Royal potted shrimp purveyor, James Baxter and Son of Morecambe. The Baxters have been potting local Morecambe Bay shrimps since 1799, and it is still a family business whose buttery recipe is still a family secret. They have been potting shrimps for The Queen and The Queen Mother since the early 1960s.

Nathaniel Hawthorne once said that 'Dr Johnson's morality was as English an article as a beefsteak', but it is not my purpose to enter into a controversy over the relative merits of Scottish and English meat. In this matter the granting of Warrants displays an admirable even-handedness, with meat for the Royal tables coming from both sides of the border. North of Hadrian's Wall there is not only the admirable Mr Sheridan of Ballater, with his special line in haggis and other Scots items; there is also, further down the Dee at Banchory, Aberdeen Meat Marketing, who have held The Queen's Warrant for supplying beef and lamb since the late 1970s.

This is a large, modern enterprise with an EEC abattoir on a five-acre site, 110 employees and an annual turnover of some 35,000 cattle and 20,000 sheep. John Lind, their Chief Executive, says they have been producing 'top-quality meat' for over twenty years to a wide variety of buyers, from supermarkets to international hotels. He has even launched an advertising campaign, designed to comfort the nation's eaters with its slogan promoting 'Aberdeen Premier Meat for Health, Fitness and Energy'.

In the south, meat is associated with Smithfield and here one finds the Royal coat of arms at Woodhouse, Hume, who supply some 800 to 900 customers in the hotel and restaurant trade as well as such upmarket establishments as the Bank of England and Lloyd's. They have had The Queen's Warrant since 1965 and started by supplying the

The ultimate home cure – Mr Jerrey of Emmetts stores takes one of his hams from the smoker in Peasenhall near Saxmundham, Suffolk. Emmetts are curers and suppliers of Sweet Pickled Hams to The Queen Mother

A typical market scene at Smithfield, London, where Woodhouse Home Ltd. hold three Royal Warrants for the supply of meat and poultry

Royal Yacht. Occasionally they get called in to supply meat for an overseas trip, such as the Lusaka Commonwealth Prime Ministers' Conference.

There are almost three times as many Royal fishmongers as there are butchers. Three are in Aberdeen, which is the fish capital of Britain, though you would hardly think so if you sat sipping tea and nibbling smoked monkfish with Ken Watmough in his tiny shop in a side street just off the city's main thoroughfare. Like all good fishmongers Mr Watmough is an enthusiast and an expert, always on the lookout for something new, different and above all fresh. Another, Campbells of Edinburgh, who were granted The Queen's Warrant in 1968, offer over thirty different varieties of whole fresh fish to the catering trade every day, adding that 'if you don't see it on this list – but you want it – we'll get it'. They even offer smoked quail and venison with dill alongside such staples as codlings and catfish, haddock and halibut, turbot and whiting. Ken Watmough, who supplies The Queen Mother, remarks that whiting is a particular favourite with The Queen Mother's chef, who turns it into a Birkhall speciality called 'Merlan en colère'.

Most fishmongers supply smoked fish but only Pinneys of Scotland hold the Warrant simply as Her Majesty's 'Purveyors of Smoked Salmon'. Theirs is smoked over oak in kilns at their headquarters at Brydekirk near Annan, Dumfries. The Chairman's wife, Annabel Stapleton, is no mean cook and has written a book of smoked fish recipes to prove it. It is a compilation of her own and customers' recipes. The Earl of Shelburne's 'Smoked Salmon Terrine for Cheats' is highly recommended and so is Mrs Stapleton's own Creamy Chicken Soup with Smoked Salmon, of which she comments (with justice): 'The marriage of whisky and smoked foods is excellent and makes this a very unusual soup.' A slightly deceptive-seeming grantee, however, is Scotts Fish Shop of Kirkwall, Orkney, most northerly of all British Warrant Holders. Mrs Watson, the grantee, does not hold the Warrant for fish, but for cheese, which they supply to Her Majesty The Queen Mother.

One might have thought the Royal Family would be virtually self-sufficient in fruit and vegetables but there are a number of 'Greengrocers and Fruiterers' with the Warrant. Paintons of Tetbury are one of the comparatively rare Prince of Wales Warrant Holders. Perhaps it is significant that The Prince should number three greengrocers among his grantees – only one fewer than The Queen herself. This fits with his reputation and

with the fact that he has not yet awarded a Warrant for butchery. In London The Prince's greengrocers are Hyams and Cockerton, who also supply The Queen. Knowles of Aberdeen have three Warrants. They use Harrodian green and gold livery plastic bags and supply Balmoral – and not just with vegetables. Mrs Cowie, the grantee's wife, has a thriving line in flower arrangements too.

When it comes to pudding The Queen Mother has granted her Warrant to Rowntree Mackintosh as 'Makers of Table Jellies'. There is a strong jelly tradition in British Royalty, for we know that Henry VIII included them in his 'banket viands' and Elizabeth I was partial to 'wine, brawn, chely and other vitails'. Queen Victoria's chef, Francatelli, once included thirty-six different 'moulds of jellies and creams' for a Ball Supper. Rowntrees started making them in 1923, in ten different flavours. Now there are eleven. Greengage and vanilla have gone; black cherry, grapefruit and pineapple have arrived.

Even The Queen Mother's Christmas puddings have an official manufacturer. In this case it is Premier Brands, alias Chivers. They provide puddings for Her Majesty herself and her household, but it is also her custom to send Christmas puddings to soldiers in those regiments, like the 9th/12th Lancers or the Black Watch, of which she is Colonel-in-Chief. Here a most traditional product conceals a highly contemporary phenomenon – the

Crosse and Blackwell – 'Purveyors of Preserved Provisions'

Mr A.T. Johnson, a Victorian sales rep for Rowntree Macintosh

management buy-out. In 1986 another Warrant Holder, Cadbury-Schweppes, decided to abandon its food operations. Premier Brands was created by nine directors, all of whom took out second mortgages on their houses to do so. If there are crackers to pull with the Christmas pudding, they will come from Tom Smith of Norwich, who hold three Warrants.

Some of the Royal provisions come direct from source, but others are ordered through intermediaries. Of these some, like Fitch and Son, first established in 1784 as grocers and provision merchants, are relatively unknown to the general public because they deal principally if not exclusively with the catering trade. Others are famous stores, like Fortnum and Mason in Piccadilly, who have held the Warrant ever since the Royal Warrant Holders' Association was first established 150 years ago. And as we have already seen, a regular daily order emanates from Harrods Food Hall when the family are in London and from a whole variety of local shops and suppliers when they are in the country.

Teatime means Twinings, Ridgways or Melroses again, but also biscuits. Eight different biscuit makers hold Warrants, though not all are of the teatime variety. We are still, it seems, a nation of biscuit eaters. The jam-and-cream-filled section of the British biscuit market alone has been valued at about £80 million a year, say Fox's, who make biscuits for The Queen Mother. This company began as a small shop in Batley, Yorkshire, in 1853, specialising in brandy snaps; in 1897 they added ginger buttons. They still make traditional brandy snaps, but the range of products has now increased out of all recognition and inventiveness never ceases. In 1987 they launched a black-cherry-jam sandwich cream biscuit to complement the same design in raspberry and increase still further their sales in that lucrative area.

Lyons Bakery near Barnsley bake The Queen's cakes. Sir Alex Alexander, at the time of writing Chairman of Lyons, says that his company 'has been honoured to hold the Royal Warrant of appointment since 1899'. Quite apart from cakes, Lyons Maid have the ice-cream Warrant and if you are lucky enough to be invited to a Royal garden party the odds are that it will be catered by Lyons, who were first appointed 'Refreshment Contractors' in 1904. Their records only go back to 1919, but that year they catered for the garden party on 27 June. There were five altogether that year and the largest was for 10,000 people.

Burton, Son and Sanders of Ipswich, founded in 1824, might also feature at tea. They make The Queen's fondant, though Mr Pryke, their Managing Director, explains that 'any type of cake can be made wholly from Burton-manufactured products – the board it stands on, the complete cake and the decorations on the top'.

If there is to be jam on toast or scones, James Robertson have the Warrant for preserves, and may indeed have cropped up at breakfast with a rival marmalade. They are famous for their marmalades – their registered office is actually called 'The Golden Shred Works' – and it was James and Marion Robertson's marmalade which was the foundation of their success in the mid-nineteenth century. The company has held the Warrant since King George V first granted it in 1933.

Mr Gladstone, no less, used to be an admirer of Wilkin and Sons' strawberry jam – which is still made from fruit grown in East Anglia in the land where the Catuvellauni marched with the Trinovantes. This place, Tiptree, is almost better known in a jam context than Wilkin itself and its fame has something to do with Gladstone, because

Royal fishmonger, Iain Campbell, with his salmon smoker in Edinburgh

Mr P. Wilkin of Wilkin and Sons, the Tiptree family firm who make jam and marmalade for The Queen

Tiptree jams helped to make the Empire great

it was the Grand Old Man who encouraged the first Wilkin to start the business. Most people laughed when the Prime Minister made a speech encouraging his tenants to go out and make jam but Arthur Wilkin took him at his word. The company has held a Warrant ever since receiving George V's in 1911.

With tea still in mind one should not forget Wilkin and Sons's contribution to the enjoyment of the Royal 'cuppa'. 'Table delicacies' have a faintly old-fashioned ring to them, which is only appropriate because the company which supplies The Queen is V. Benoist of London, who

used to hold Queen Victoria's Warrant. They also supply the more prosaically named 'General Groceries' to The Queen Mother and The Prince of Wales.

Teatime might also mean baked beans. On one occasion Prince Charles was visiting the factory of Royal Warrant Holders Aston Martin, when a five-year-old boy called Matthew Turvey suddenly grabbed a tin of beans from his mother's shopping bag and presented them to the Prince, asking if he'd like them for lunch. The Prince replied that he would, only he would eat them later. Because Beanz meanz Heinz, the company who introduced the baked

The Golden Shred marmalade works, Bristol in the 1920s.

bean to Britain in 1912 responded by screening a commercial with the following lyrics:

> What does a Prince have for his tea?
> It might be Heinz baked beans.
> I think Heinz baked beans are good enough
> For even Kings and Queens.
> They may not let him have them
> But I think that would be mean –
> He'd get them if he lived with us
> Or if my Mum were Queen.
> (I don't think she ever will be though.)

Although Heinz is an American company Her Majesty The Queen has knighted Henry J. Heinz II 'for his services to British-American relationships' and granted her Warrant to the company as 'purveyors of Heinz Products'. Which must mean beanz.

There is in some quarters, as we have already seen, a certain sensitivity about some Warrants. In an age which seems more alive than most to the dangers of smoking and alcohol abuse – and even to diet – there will be some who deplore any association at all between the Monarchy and tobacco and drink. Yet whatever one may think about it, the historical links are there for all to see and whatever their personal tastes, most people surely concede that it would be a pretty paltry Monarchy which offered its guests only nut cutlets and mineral water.

There are several Royal brewers and very properly so, for as Sydney Smith asked, 'What two ideas are more inseparable than Beer and Britannia?' Beer and Burton-on-Trent is one possible answer, for they have been making beer in Burton since the monks of Burton Abbey started doing it in 1002, soon after their foundation by Wulfric Spot, Earl of Mercia. In the sixteenth century Mary Queen of Scots was imprisoned at Tutbury Castle not far away and smuggled secret letters to her supporters

Another Royal sauce

ABOVE Paxton and Whitfield of Jermyn Street are cheesemongers to The Queen Mother

OPPOSITE Biscuits on the production line of Huntley and Palmers

Huntley and Palmers made Victorian biscuits too

in empty casks of the ale supplied to her by the Abbey Brew House. The loyal Burton brewer told Francis Walsingham, the Elizabethan equivalent of Ian Fleming's M, and the information led directly to the execution of her friend Babington and, later, of Mary herself.

Bass, the only Burton brewer with the Warrant, started brewing in 1777. By 1785 they were producing 800 thirty-six-gallon barrels; by 1832, 10,000. The coming of the railway in 1839 accelerated sales and they reached 100,000 a year in 1850 and 1 million in time for the centenary in 1877.

The Royal connection has never been quite as historically significant as it was in the sixteenth century. Before the Industrial Revolution most great houses and Royal Palaces would have brewed their own. Queen Victoria granted Bass a Warrant in 1860. And on 22 February 1902 the seemingly ubiquitous King Edward VII, a close friend of Michael Bass, MP, mashed The King's Ale in the new Bass brewery. Bottles of this strong ale still appear at auctions from time to time. Prices dropped dramatically when the firm gave many of its long-term employees souvenir bottles to mark the 1977 Jubilee. Twenty-seven years later his grandson, The Prince of Wales, mashed a Prince's Ale and in 1977 – The Queen's Silver Jubilee and the Bass bicentennial – the company laid down another strong ale – Jubilee. The present Princess Royal has mashed a Princess Ale and Earl Spencer, Prince William's grandfather, went to Burton to mash a Celebration Ale after his grandson's birth. This was sold for charity at £25 a bottle. These vintage Royal ales are said to be at their best about forty years on.

The red triangle, which used to be William Bass's shipping mark, was the first trademark ever registered under the Trade Marks Registration Act of 1875.

Newcastle claims to have been brewing even longer than Burton and Scottish and Newcastle Breweries also have the Warrant. Carlsberg of Denmark are the only foreign brewers, through their Northampton-based subsidiary. The Royal Brewery at Brentford, now part of the Courage Group, has the unusual privilege of displaying King William IV's coat of arms in perpetuity. This was a personal favour from the Sailor King to Sir Felix Booth, who owned the brewery and financed Ross's 1828 voyage to the Arctic. The Boothia peninsula and the Gulf of Boothia, west of Baffin Island, are both named after him!

Berry Brothers have been providing wine to the Royal Family from their sepulchral office and vaults at the bottom of St James's Street since 1910, though the association goes back much further and it is even alleged that in the old days there was a secret passage running through from Berrys to St James's Palace on the other side of Pall Mall.

The link between the company and the Monarchy came to fruition for a happy medicinal purpose. King Edward VII's doctor was concerned for His Majesty's health as he bowled along in his draughty Daimler. He approached Henry Berry at 3 St James's Street and asked if he could come up with something which might ward off the chill. Berrys accordingly produced what is now listed in their catalogue as 'The King's Ginger Liqueur'. Had you wanted a bottle for Christmas 1988 it would have set you back £13.20. The list description says it is 'a warming tipple to fortify The King after riding in his horseless carriage during the cold of winter'. It adds that 'the strong, yet smooth taste of ginger is so well-balanced and has such a reviving effect that this is surely the ultimate hip-flask filler.' Henry Berry's successors apparently swear that it is so versatile that it 'can as well be taken for its cheering effect before breakfast or mid-morning as at tea-time or late at night'. But it should, perhaps, be pointed out that it is 41 per cent volume. It is specially made for Berrys by Wynand Fockink in Amsterdam.

The special relationship was further cemented in 1923 when they were chosen to provide the wine for the cellar of the famous Queen Mary's doll's house, now on view in the public apartments at Windsor Castle. Francis Berry evidently had a fine time solving the problem of producing miniature miniatures. There were thirty-eight bottles in all and if a bottle claimed to contain Château d'Yquem, then Château d'Yquem was what it contained. There was a properly compiled tiny cellar-book to go with the collection and Berry made some extra bottles which can still be seen in the shop.

That same year the Berry Brothers came up with the idea of marketing their own brand of whisky under the name Cutty Sark. The famous clipper had just returned to England after years sailing under the Portuguese flag and over lunch in the parlour at 3 St James's Street they and their friend James McBey, the painter and sailor, thought of the name and McBey drew the original label design, which remains almost unchanged to this day. Cutty Sark is a key ingredient in the modern company's prosperity, as is their modern warehouse at Basingstoke, where they have room to store more than 300,000 cases of wines and spirits. But the shop remains almost unchanged, with the great weighing beams still in place and still operational. Behind them the ledgers record the weights of an extraordinary cross-section of society from Byron and Beau Brummel to Pitt and Peel. The first item in the Berry Bros list says, 'One aspect of Berry Bros. and Rudd is unashamedly old-fashioned – its standard of service.'

H. P. Bulmer of Hereford are one of The Queen's cider makers. Is there a disproportionate number of family firms among the Royal Warrant Holders? Does the fact that the Monarchy is a family business prompt imitation in others? Certainly there is no suggestion that Warrants are granted except on merit and yet there is a strange feeling of familiarity when one opens the Bulmer centenary brochure, published in 1987, and reads the Chairman, Esmond Bulmer, beginning his message with the words: '"If you are going into business let it be food or drink, they never go out of fashion" was the advice given by my great-grandmother to my grandfather.'

It was obviously sound advice and although there has been change and modernisation – Bulmer's distribute a great many other drinks, including Perrier Water – cider is still at the heart of the business. There are now 6,500

names on the share register and yet the family remains pre-eminent. It was Esmond's younger brother, David, who showed me round the factory at harvest time and as we walked among the 110 vast vats and the soggy lorryloads of bleeding apples newly arrived from the Herefordshire orchards, I had an enormously strong sense of continuity and empathy. Since 1977 the company have had an Employee Council with twenty-five elected members; they set up life assurance and pension schemes in 1920; they started a sports club in 1935 – they have a fine photo of the cricket team with Fred Bulmer in the middle; and they established an endowment fund before the war for sickness payments and child allowances which now pays out about £100,000 a year.

They have held the Royal Warrant since 1911 and The Queen still has the Wedgwood cider mug given to her by

A pre-war advertisement from Bulmer's, Royal cidermakers

261

John Marks, who holds the Royal Warrant as confectioner on behalf of Edward Sharp and Sons,
the toffeemakers, watches an army of Trebor Extra Strong Mints on the move

The Queen's chocolates – a golden display at the Winchester factory of Bendicks (Mayfair) Ltd.

David Bulmer, of H.P. Bulmer, The Queen's cidermakers, who have been making their Herefordshire cider in vats like these for over a century, 'Bertram' is named after Bertram Bulmer, a director of the company for more than sixty years.

Howard Bulmer when she came on a visit in 1957. She must have been impressed with what she saw because Prince Philip came a year later – at his own request.

Away on the other side of England, William Gaymer and Son also hold the warrant for 'Cyder' and claim that the east has been making alcohol from apples even longer than the west. They call in evidence a reference to a rent of 200 pearmain apples and four hogsheads of wine 'made from pearmains' being paid as rent at Redham and Stoksley in 1205. The last Prince of Wales evidently had a soft spot for Gaymers because he ordered it specially for his naval tours in the 1920s, and Gaymers still have a photograph of cyder crates saying, 'This side up. To HRH The Prince of Wales, HMS *Repulse*, Portsmouth. Gaymers Cyder. Keep away from Boilers.' In 1961 Gaymers was taken over by Showerings and is now part of Allied Lyons. When I attended the Sandringham AGM, however, William Gaymer was much in evidence and still Chairman of Gaymers at Attleborough in Norfolk, where they have been since 1896.

Harveys of Bristol, founded in 1796, are another of The Queen's wine merchants and also, *inter alia*, the biggest sherry company in the world. When The Prince of Wales, shortly to become Edward VIII, called at their cellars to sample the famous Bristol Milk sherry, his only recorded comment is: 'All I can say is you must have dam' fine cows.' The Royal connection goes back to Victorian times and burgeoned towards the end of The Queen's reign, when John Harvey II and the Master of the Royal Cellars, Colonel Thomas Kingscote, seem to have established a particularly cordial relationship. 'Tommy,' wrote Harvey in one letter, had placed an order for 115 cases of the '91 Medoc. Later Harvey attended the Jubilee and remarked, 'I will only say now that The Queen looked 20 years younger than her recent photos – I am afraid to say what she wore as I never remember ladies' dress but I think she wore a light colour – but the scene was so dazzling I may be mistaken.'

Justerini and Brooks were awarded their first Warrant by George III, before Harveys was even founded. Giacomo Justerini had come to London from Bologna in pursuit of a beautiful opera singer called Margherita Bellino. Soon after his arrival in 1749 he was set up in business, distilling delicious-sounding fruit ratafias and shrubs, by a theatrical impresario called Samuel Johnson (no relation). By the time George III granted his Warrant Justerini had returned to Italy and the company was, in effect, though not name, all Johnson. Early invoices to The Prince of Wales in 1799 and 1802 describe the firm as 'Johnson and Justerini, Foreign Cordial Merchants'.

The original Johnson died after his sedan chair overturned in Piccadilly as he was coming home from taking a large order from The Duke of Queensberry. In 1831 his son Augustus sold out to Alfred Brooks, and Brooks, a little ungraciously, crossed out Johnson's name from the firm and inserted his own after Justerini's. The company has remained J and B ever since.

During the nineteenth century Justerini and Brooks supplied The Prince of Wales with one particularly curious drink of which he was very fond. This was Pomeranzen, a sort of dry Curaçao produced in Latvia. In 1910 J and B placed a very large order for Pomeranzen but by the time it arrived the King, as he had become, was dead and no one wanted the stuff any more. For years it languished in the company's cellars under the arches at Charing Cross, until in 1942 alcohol-starved J and B customers were finally induced to consume it. It no longer features on the firm's otherwise comprehensive list!

In 1972 J and B became part of the Grand Metropolitan Group, but they continue to hold the Royal Warrant as they have done for nine successive reigns.

Although they continue to be successful wine merchants, J and B are well known for their J and B blended whisky and they also own four separate Highland distilleries. There are a number of other whisky-producing companies with the Warrant. Visiting one specimen – in my case, Lang Brothers of Glasgow, who hold the Queen Mother's Warrant – one is struck yet again by that typical Warrant Holding common denominator of a fusion between high tech and ancient craft. On the one hand, there were laboratories full of boffins in white coats, testing and analysing, and bulk-carrier trucks discharging malt and malted barley into three storage bins with a combined capacity of ninety-nine tonnes; and on the other, there was a beautiful old distillery in the Campsie Hills, and old copper stills and a director of the company, Jim Turle, telling me, as I contemplated the seventeen years that their most expensive whisky has to spend maturing in wood: 'There's nothing you can do to hurry the process.'

Every year now Langs sponsor a hill race. It is called the Glengoyne Gallop and is described by the organisers as 'the worst two-mile run in Scotland'.

The distillery lies fifteen miles north of Glasgow and is the most southerly of all Highland malt whisky distilleries. The Highland fault at this point is buried

Nineteenth-century wines in the cellars of Berry Brothers and Rudd Ltd., Royal wine and spirit merchants

Jacques and Georges Hine together with a cask of their cognac presented to The Prince and Princess of Wales as a wedding present and now maturing at Hine HQ in Jarnac, France

beneath the A81, which divides the distillery proper from the warehouses where the Scotch matures. The Blane valley is lush; the rhododendrons are in full flower; rucksacked walkers plod the disused railway line, which is now the West Highland Way; Ben Lomond looms on the horizon and immediately behind the distillery is a near vertical 1,100 feet of Campsie Hill called Dumgoyne. Shortly after lunch 126 slim, wiry people with knotted calves and thighs convene in the neighbourhood of the plaque commemorating Lord Tedder's birth – his father was the local excise officer from 1889 to 1892.

Alisdair Campbell, a civil engineer employed by Strathclyde Council, is the man most responsible. He runs an athletic club named Westerlands, which is clearly designed with strange people in mind. The club arranges a number of races, including night runs up Ben Lomond in the dead of winter, the Cort-ma Caw Hill race ('well-thought-out masochist event with a romp across the Campsie Fell plateau') and 'annual grudge matches against our East Coast rivals, Hunters Bog Trotters'.

Three years ago Alisdair approached Lang Brothers and asked if they would mind Westerlands staging an annual race up and down Dumgoyne. They would like to borrow the car park and use the distillery as a changing room. Jim Turle said they could do better than that. They'd lay on a barbecue, a wee dram or so and trophies and bottles for the winners.

It was a fine summer day; pheasants clucked in the woods; sheep did gently graze, their droppings peppering the hillside; a brook babbled. 'No a bad day, eh!' remarked a spindly figure with a white dappled ginger beard, the briefest of shorts hitched high over blue-veined shanks.

The field set off at three, started by the distillery Manager, Ian Taylor, with a blast of shotgun fire. A loop through field and sheep allowed the field to spread a little, then the procession dipped out of sight into dead ground before reappearing in a single multi-coloured file which slowly stretched up the mountainside. The first man hit the 1,100-foot summit after about sixteen minutes, before turning for the downhill belt home.

I only just got to the finish in time. It was by the pond fed by the burn which makes Glengoyne single malt the nectar it is. The last stretch was a vertical skid through woodland, followed by a few yards of almost horizontal tarmac. The first man home, one of the finest hill runners in Europe, an exiled Scot from Pudsey in Yorkshire named Jack Maitland, must have done the whole downhill trip in only a little over five minutes because he clocked in

with a new record time of twenty-two minutes and eight seconds.

The Scots have been charging up and down their mountainsides since King Malcolm put up a purse of gold at Braemar for a race up Creag Choinnich in 1040 to decide who was going to get the plum job of Royal Messenger. They have probably been distilling whisky for almost as long, though the first reference to it is only in 1494, when the Rolls of the Scottish Exchequer reveal that a friar called John Cor was granted 'eight bolls of malt' to make Aqua Vitae or, in Gaelic, Usque Beatha, 'the water of life'. I apologise for mentioning this, especially to the official historian of White Horse whisky (another Warrant Holder), who says he has heard it so often that his mind boggles to think about it. For almost 200 years, from 1644 to 1823, various governments tried, with virtually no success, to tax it, but eventually, after the discovery of no fewer than 14,000 illicit stills, a workable system of licensing was installed and the legitimate Scottish whisky industry began to evolve. Glengoyne, for instance, began distilling legally in 1833.

The taste for whisky was slow to take on outside its native Scotland, but despite such hiccoughs as the Depression and Prohibition in the States, Scotch has become a major export. Nowadays over 80 per cent goes abroad and in some years since the war it has actually been Britain's largest dollar earner. Which is one reason for being pleased to see the industry so well represented among those holding the Royal Warrant.

Historically it has always been alleged that Queen Victoria, under the influence of John Brown, was not averse to mixing it with claret. But The Duke of Windsor provided the best Royal whisky moment, which came soon after his abdication when the Viennese press ran a breathless scoop about a telegram the exiled monarch had sent home to England. According to the Austrians he had pleaded for 'the magnificent white horse which he had used as king' to be sent to him. The Viennese assumed this was a romantic nostalgia for a favourite steed. But actually the Duke was just asking for whisky.

Corney and Barrow of Helmet Row in the City of London supply wine for The Queen, The Queen Mother and The Prince of Wales, and are also able to boast that their grantee, Robin Kernick, holds the coveted and exalted post of 'Clerk to the Royal Cellars'.

Soft drinks come from Schweppes, who are now Cadbury-Schweppes, and therefore also responsible for The Queen's and The Queen Mother's cocoa and

PRORSUS

SCHWEPPERVESCENTIA   TOTUM POTUM DURAT

SCHWEPPSHIRE, COUNTY OF

The Schweppeshire Coat of Arms of the Royal mineral water makers

chocolate. Schweppes provided soda water for William IV and were confirmed as soda-water manufacturers by Queen Victoria only two months after she came to the throne in 1837. In 1927 Schweppes acquired Burrows of Great Malvern, their great rivals in the production of that famous English spring water and a company which had held Warrants since being granted one by Queen Mary's mother, Princess Mary Adelaide of Teck. Today, Malvern water is one of the few products which Royal observers always identify. It seems to be a constant companion on journeys abroad as a safe alternative to uncharted foreign waters.

The original Schweppe, Jacob, arrived from Geneva at the end of the eighteenth century and opened his first factory in Drury Lane. He owed his breakthrough largely to the patronage of a group of eminent philosophers, inventors and, most important, medical men. Like Bulmers cider, which used to be recommended for gout and rheumatism, the original Schweppes's soda water – a term first applied to his greatly superior product – was

widely acknowledged to have curative properties. Matthew Boulton, the Birmingham industrialist who manufactured Watt's first steam engine, was a great fan of Jacob Schweppe and wrote about him glowingly to Erasmus Darwin.

'Mr J. Schweppe,' he said, 'preparer of mineral waters, is the person whom you have heard me speak of and who impregnates it so highly with fixable air as to exceed in appearance Champaign and all other Bottled Liquors. He prepares it of 3 sorts. No. 1 is for common drinking with your dinner. No. 2 is for Nephritick patients, and No. 3 contains the most alkali and given only in more violent cases, but I know not the quantity of alkali in either. It is contained in Strong Stone Bottles and sold for 6s 6d per doz. including the Bottles.'

Over the years Schweppes have produced an extraordinary number of inventive advertising schemes. In 1966 Prince Philip was pictured laughing hugely as he unveiled a typically scatty Rowland Emett model of a Schweppes Bitter Lemon on an export drive in Chicago and a few years earlier they launched a campaign based on the imaginary county of Schweppshire. For this they conjured up a pastiche coat of arms for use in *Debrett's Peerage*. It bears distinct if irreverent similarities to the Royal arms themselves. Instead of the three lions which appear on the Royal shield there are three bowler hats; the lion 'sejant guardant proper' holds an 'armed umbrella sable' and is 'crowned bowler proper', the supporters are a padded-up cricketer and a 'Sherlock proper' with deer-stalker and meerschaum. In another advertisement for Sport in Schweppshire there is a picture of Edward the Confessor introducing golf to the county on horseback. Another example of humorous *lèse-majesté* – he looks more as if he is playing polo.

The company have also maintained a marginal Royal connection through their sponsorship of the Schweppes Gold Trophy at Newbury, won by Her Majesty The Queen Mother's horse Tammuz in 1975.

When the company celebrated its bicentenary in 1983 Basil Collins, the Chief Executive, declared, with an erudition entirely proper among Royal Warrant Holders, *Nunc est Schweppendum.*

Coca-Cola, whose production now reaches a billion gallons a year despite a slow start in Atlanta, Georgia, in 1886, also hold a soft-drink Warrant.

Edward Sharp and Sons hold The Queen's and The Queen Mother's Warrants for their toffees. The grantee is John Marks, who made a little piece of history in 1988 by

Whitbread Fremlins brew pale ale for The Queen Mother here at their brewery north of Maidstone, Kent.

Lang Brothers Ltd. produce their Royal Warrant Holding whisky in Scotland's most southerly Highland distillery at Glengoyne beneath the Campsie Hills near Loch Lomond.

Iain Campbell, of George Campbell and Sons, Suppliers of Fish and Poultry to The Queen, with a typical fishscape at his Edinburgh shop

Coca-Cola hold a Royal Warrant for soft drinks

from *Star Wars*, with a great clanking combine harvester conveying mint after mint after mint in a continuous flow of white nuggets, while overalled operators sit aloft. The whole place is bathed in white dust and suffused with the smell of peppermint.

'Trebor' is 'Robert' spelt backwards, appropriate because one of the original directors of the company when it was founded in 1907 was Robert Robertson.

The company was called Robertson and Woodcock at first and changed its name to Trebor in 1921. They began with sweets like the 'Farthing Dip', so called because it was in the nature of a lucky dip – if children found a thin red line down the middle they won a big quarter-pound sweet stick. The first mints were produced in 1935 and Sharp's Toffees were taken over in 1961.

There are a number of chocolatiers and yet another Edwardian tradition in The Queen's Warrant to Charbonnel et Walker, who personally persuaded Mme Charbonnel to leave the Chocolate House, Maison Boissier in Paris and open a rival establishment in London. Today Charbonnel et Walker chocolates are produced in the time-honoured, hand-crafted way by white-coated, chocolate-daubed specialists in a small factory at Tunbridge Wells. All their chocolates are numbered and they send out printed cards on which you may specify those you like, those you like better and those you like best. Zero is for 'orange', 46 for 'Falstaff' (chopped grilled almonds with maraschino flavour) and 103 for 'noisette cream'. 'Enrobed truffles' are as seasonal oysters and only available from September to Easter. This is a pity, because No. 61m, a strawberry truffle in white chocolate, was created specially for Wimbledon.

A Charbonnel et Walker 61 would, however, make a perfect end to a day of Royal gastronomy.

presenting a specially made stick of rock in the shape of an episcopal crook to the Bishop of Reading when he spoke at the Royal Warrant Holders' Association annual banquet at which Mr Marks was presiding. He is the head of the family firm of Trebor, owners of Sharps, but perhaps better known for their Extra Strong Mints, which are turned out in a spanking new, modern factory just outside Colchester. There is one incredible room, like something

Ken Whatmough, Royal fishmonger, in his tiny shop in Aberdeen

SELECT BIBLIOGRAPHY

Tradesmen to the Royal Household Past and Present, a slim volume presented to the Royal Warrant Holders by Betty Whittington in 1961, is a useful summary of the Warrant's history.

The Royal Shopping Guide by Nina Grunfeld, a Pan Original published in 1984, is a mine of information and, as far as I know, the only other recent book to deal with the Warrant Holders.

Other published sources include:

Hardy Amies, *Still Here*; Weidenfeld and Nicolson, 1984

Richard Beaumont, *Purdey's*; David and Charles, 1984

Patrick Beaver, *The Match Makers*; Henry Melland, 1985

Maura Benham, *The Story of Tiptree Jam*; Wilkin and Sons, 1985

Bryan Bland, *Hamilton and Inches – the First Hundred Years*; 1966

Jacqueline de Chimay (with a preface by Evelyn Waugh), *The Life and Times of Madame Veuve Clicquot*; Veuve Clicquot - Ponsardin, 1961

Count Bertrand de Vogue, *Madame Clicquot – Her peaceful conquest of Russia*; Veuve Clicquot-Ponsardin SA

Brian Dobbs, *The Last Shall be First*; Elm Tree Books, 1972

Robb and Ann Edwards, *The Queen's Clothes*; Elm Tree Books, 1976

Patrick Forbes, *The Story of The Maison Möet and Chandon*; 1972

Gail Franzmann, *By Appointment. The History of Hardy Brothers 1780–1980*; Macmillan, Australia, 1980

Leslie Gardiner, *Bartholomew, 150 Years*; John Bartholomew Ltd, 1976

Keith Geddes and Gordon Bussey, *The History of Roberts Radio*; Roberts Radio, 1988

Sir Ernest Goodale, *Weaving and the Warners*; F. Lewis Ltd, 1971

D. R. Grace and D. C. Phillips, *Ransomes of Ipswich*; Institute of Agricultural History, 1975

Leslie G. Harris, *Mixed Memoirs*; L.G. Harris & Co. Ltd, 1986

Bevis Hillier, *Asprey of Bond Street*; Quartet Books, 1981

Jack House, *The Spirit of White Horse*

Anthony Hugill, *Sugar and All That*; Gentry Books, 1978

G. Jukes (Ed.), *The Story of Belling*; Belling and Co. Ltd, 1963

Peter King, *The Shooting Field*; Quiller Press, 1985

Robert Lacey, *Majesty*; Hutchinson, 1977

Lord Montagu of Beaulieu, *Royalty on the Road*; Collins, 1980

Jackie Moore, *Rich and Rare. The Story of Dawson International*; Henry Melland, 1986

Hans Nadelhoffer, *Cartier*; Thames and Hudson, 1984

Alfred Plummer and Richard E. Early, *The Blanket Makers*; Routledge and Kegan Paul, 1969

Jan Read and Maite Manjon, *The Great British Breakfast*; Michael Joseph, 1981

Basil N. Reckitt, *The History of Reckitt and Sons Limited*; A. Brown and Sons, Ltd, 1965

Rentokil, *Fifty Years of Service*; Rentokil Group Ltd, 1977

Douglas A. Simmons, *Schweppes*; Springwood Books, 1983

Stephen H. Twining, *The House of Twining*; R. Twining & Co. Ltd, 1956

Wray Vamplew, *The Turf*; Allen Lane, 1976

David Wainwright, *Broadwood by Appointment*; Quiller Press, 1982

Andrew Whyte, *Jaguar*; Patrick Stephens, 1980

Frank Whitbourn, *Mr Lock of St James's Street*; William Heinemann, 1971

L. P. Wilkinson, *Bulmers of Hereford*; David and Charles, 1987

R. S. Williams-Thomas, *The Crystal Years*; Stevens and Williams Ltd, 1983

Louise Wright, *The Road from Aston Cross*; Smedley-HP Foods Ltd, 1975

Signed and sealed – a clutch of IRS notices from the Royal Sign and Notice Manufacturer wait to be baked in 'the cooker' at Swaffham, Norfolk

Dr Frank Mercer, who holds The Queen's Warrant for plastic mesh, examines some of his own Netlon at home in Blackburn

Mr Baxter of Farlow and Co., The Prince of Wales' supplier of fishing tackle and waterproof clothing. With a friend

Jeffery Pratt, who supplies the Prince of Wales with veterinary products, on the farm at Gaddesden, Herts. Also pictured with friends

ROYAL WARRANT HOLDERS

James Wiggins of Arnold Wiggins and Sons, picture frame makers to The Queen and The Queen Mother, pictured in one of his own frames

ROYAL WARRANT HOLDERS

ROYAL WARRANTS OF APPOINTMENT
TO
HER MAJESTY QUEEN ELIZABETH II

DEPARTMENT OF HER MAJESTY'S PRIVY PURSE

Abbey Rose Gardens, Rose Growers and Nurserymen, Burnham

Aberdeen Coal, Coal Merchants, Aberdeen

Ainsworths Homoeopathic Pharmacy, Chemists, London

Allan & Davidson, Interior Decorators and Painting Contractors, Aberdeen

Allen and Neale (Chemists) Ltd, Chemists, Heacham, Norfolk

Amies, Hardy, Ltd, Dressmakers, London

Anglia Telecomms Limited, Suppliers of Radio Telecommunications and Associated Services, March

Angus Chain Saw Service, Horticultural Engineers, Lawton, by Arbroath

APV Vent-Axia Limited, Suppliers of Unit Ventilation Equipment, Crawley

Archibald, James L. & Sons, Ltd, Cabinetmakers and Upholsterers, Aberdeen

Ardleigh Swift Ltd, Manufacturers of Agricultural Machinery, Ardleigh

Armitage Brothers, PLC, Pet Food Manufacturers, Nottingham

Armstrong Addison & Co. Ltd, Suppliers of Preserved Timber Fencing, Sunderland

Army & Navy Stores, Ltd, Suppliers of Household and Fancy Goods, London

Asprey PLC, Goldsmiths, Silversmiths and Jewellers, London

Atco Ltd, Manufacturers of Motor Mowers, Stowmarket

BBC Fire Protection Ltd, Purveyors of Fire Protection Systems, Norwich

BICC Pyrotenax Ltd, Manufacturers and Suppliers of Electric Cable, Hebburn

BOCM Silcock Ltd, Suppliers of Cattle Foods, Basingstoke

BP Oil Ltd, Purveyors of Motor Spirit, London

BACO-Compak (Norfolk) Ltd, Waste Disposal Contractors, Bawsey

Bamford, J. C. Excavators, Ltd, Manufacturers of Construction and Agricultural Equipment, Rocester

Barbour J, and Sons Ltd, Manufacturers of Waterproof and Protective Clothing, South Shields

Barnhams Electrical Co. Ltd, Electrical Contractor, Fakenham

Barrow Leather Ltd, Manufacturers of Royal Maundy Purses, London

Barton & Gant, Suppliers of Agro-Chemicals and Fertilisers, King's Lynn

Bartram Mowers Ltd, Suppliers of Horticultural Equipment, Norwich

Bell & Croyden, John Ltd, Chemists, London

Belling & Co. Ltd, Manufacturers of Electrical Appliances, Enfield

Bennett-Levy, Valerie M., Supplier of Nosegays, Haslemere

Bennett, R. S. & Co. Ltd, Suppliers of Agricultural Machinery and Farm Equipment, Downham Market

Bennett & Fountain PLC, Suppliers of Electrical Equipment, London

Benney, Gerald, Goldsmith and Silversmith, Beenham

Bentley, Joseph, Ltd, Suppliers of Horticultural Chemicals, Barrow-on-Humber

Berkshire Air and Hydraulics Ltd, Suppliers of Hydraulic Hose Assemblies, Windsor

Berthoud Limited, Manufacturers of Agricultural Crop Sprayers, King's Lynn

Bestobell Service Co. Ltd, Maintenance Engineers, Taplow

Billings & Edmonds, Ltd, Tailors and Outfitters, London

Blackhall, William, Tailor and Outfitter, Tarland

Blooms of Bressingham Limited, Suppliers of Hardy Nursery Stock, Diss

Blue Circle Industries PLC, Cement Manufacturers, London

Boiler Maintenance and Plumbing Repairs, Boiler Service Engineer, Newmarket

Bonk and Company Ltd, Suppliers of Multifuel Heating Appliances and Chimney Systems, Inverness

Booker Seeds Limited, Seedsmen, Sleaford

Boots Co. PLC, The, Manufacturing Chemists, Nottingham

Boots The Chemists, Ltd, Chemists, Nottingham

Bowden, M. D., Newsagent, Dersingham

Bridger & Kay Ltd, Postage Stamp Dealer, London

Bridon Fibres Limited, Manufacturers of Agricultural Twine, Doncaster

Brintons, Ltd, Carpet Manufacturers, Kidderminster

Britag Industries, Suppliers of Agricultural Chemicals, York

British Olivetti Limited, Manufacturers of Office Equipment, London

*Robert Baxter at the family potted shrimp shop in Morecambe. His potted shrimps contain
nothing but shrimps, butter and spices*

John Stopps with freshly baked bread fit for a Queen at his shop in Egham, not far from Windsor Castle

Milky Way – a lactic conveyor belt speeds Unigate milk into cartons at their West London plant.
Unigate hold The Queen and The Queen Mother's Warrants

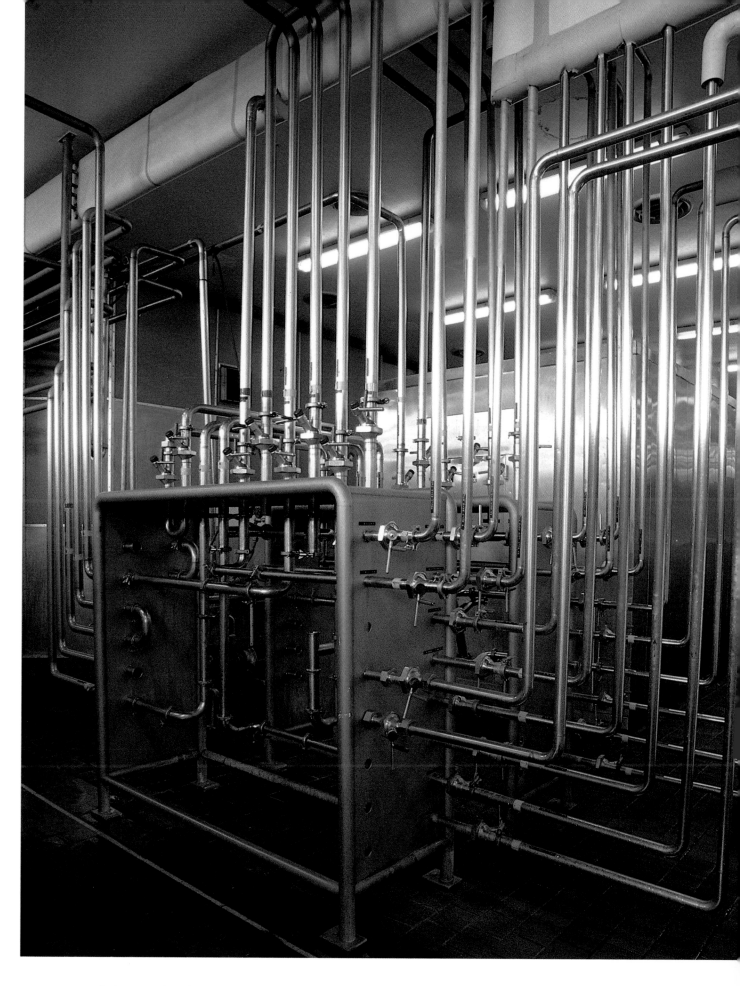

All change – the 'changing station' at Lyon's Maid, Ice Cream Manufacturers to The Queen,
switches from strawberry to vanilla to chocolate and back again…

Bruce, Simon Limited, Catering Equipment Consultants
and Suppliers, Norwich

Buckley, Anthony & Constantine Ltd, Photographers, London

Burberrys Ltd, Weatherproofers, London

Burgess, Ben and Company, Suppliers of Agricultural
Machinery, Norwich

Bynoth, H. C., Roofing Contractor, King's Lynn

Calders Fencing, Suppliers of Diamond Braced Field Gates,
Boston, Lincolnshire

Caleys (Cole Brothers Ltd), Suppliers of Household
and Fancy Goods, Windsor

Callander, R. F., Drystone Dyker, Finzean

Calman Links (Trading) Ltd, Furriers, London

Calor Gas Ltd, Suppliers of Liquefied Petroleum Gas, Slough

Car-Men Supplies Limited, Suppliers of Agricultural
and Industrial Equipment, Corby

Carters Tested Seeds Ltd, Seedsmen, Llangollen

Case International, Manufacturers of Agricultural Machinery,
Doncaster

Cash, J. & J., Ltd, Manufacturers of Woven Name Tapes,
Coventry

Cassie, Alistair, TV Suppliers and Engineer, Ballater

Cassie, William C., Pianoforte Tuner, Aberdeen

Century Oils Ltd, Suppliers of Agricultural
and Horticultural Lubricant, Stoke-on-Trent

Charrington-Hargreaves, Suppliers of Fuel Oils,
Bishop's Stortford

Charringtons Solid Fuel, Coal Merchants, Huntingdon

Chase, W. D. (Builder), Builder and Contractor,
King's Lynn

Child, G. E. & Son Ltd, Electrical Contractor, King's Lynn

Chubb Alarms Ltd, Installers of Intruder Alarms,
Walton-on-Thames

Chubb & Son's Lock and Safe Co., Ltd, Patent Lock
and Safe Makers, Feltham

Ciba-Geigy Agrochemicals, Manufacturers of Crop Protection
Chemicals, Cambridge

Clark, A. A. Ltd, Automobile Engineers, Windsor

Coalite Building Supplies, Suppliers of Building Materials,
King's Lynn

Cocker, James & Sons, Suppliers of Roses, Aberdeen

Coe, C. & C. (Bircham) Limited, Haulage Contractors, Bircham,
King's Lynn

Collie, Peter S., Suppliers of Game Food, Aberdeen

Collingwood of Bond Street Limited, Jewellers and Silversmiths,
London

Colt, W. H. Son & Co. Ltd, Suppliers of Pre-fabricated Timber
Framed Houses, Bethersden, Ashford

Coopers Animal Health Limited, Manufacturers of Animal
Health and Hygiene Products, Crewe

Countrywear, Field Sports Outfitter, Ballater

Cox, Harold & Sons (Jewellers), Ltd, Jewellers, Windsor

C. P. & B. (Haulage) Ltd, Suppliers of Woodshavings, Diss

Crawford, Robert H. & Son, Suppliers of Agricultural
Machinery, Boston, Lincolnshire

Crompton Parkinson Ltd, Manufacturers of Electrical Lamps,
Northampton

Crossley Builders Merchants Ltd, Suppliers of Building
Materials, Stockton-on-Tees

Crown Berger Europe Limited, Manufacturers of Paints
and Wallcoverings, Darwen

Culford Fencing Limited, Suppliers of Specialist Fencing,
Bury St Edmunds

Cyclax Ltd, Manufacturers of Beauty Preparations, London

Dacrylate Paints Limited, Manufacturers of Paint Varnishes and
Emulsions, Kirkby-in-Ashfield

Dale, Frank H. Ltd, Suppliers of Farm Buildings
and Tubular Equipment, Leominster

Dalgety Agriculture Ltd, Manufacturers of Animal Feeds, Bristol

Dalton Supplies Ltd, Manufacturers of Animal Identification
Equipment, Nettlebed

Daniel, Neville Ltd, Hairdressers, London

Darby Nursery Stock Ltd, Suppliers of Ornamental Shrubs and
Trees, Thetford

Day, Thomas Motors Ltd, Motor Vehicle Suppliers, Fleet

Deas, John D. and Company Limited,
Suppliers of Kitchen Equipment, Glasgow

Deere, John Ltd, Suppliers of Agriculture Equipment,
Nottingham

Delamore, R. Ltd, Suppliers of Chrysanthemum Stock, Wisbech

Dennison PLC, Suppliers of Gift Wrapping Material, Watford

DER Ltd, Suppliers of Television Receivers, Chertsey

Devlin Stuart Ltd, Goldsmith and Jeweller, Southwater

Dilloway, P. W. Ltd, Agricultural Engineers, Swindon

Dobbie & Co., Ltd, Seedsmen and Nurserymen, Lasswade

Dodson and Horrell Limited, Horse Feed Manufacturers,
Kettering

Double Paul Nurseries Limited, Tree Nurseryman, Ipswich

Dow Agriculture, Suppliers of Agricultural Insecticides,
Fungicides and Foliar Feeds, Hitchin

Drake and Fletcher, Ltd, Manufacturers of Agricultural Spraying
Machinery, Maidstone

Driscoll, Tailors, Eastbourne

Dunhill, Alfred, Ltd, Suppliers of Smokers' Requisites, London

Dynatron Radio Ltd, Manufacturers of Television
and Radiogramophones, West Molesey

Eastern Counties Farmers Ltd, Suppliers of Agricultural
Products, Ipswich

Edmondson, R. C. Ltd, Suppliers of Motor Vehicles
and Agricultural Machinery, Fakenham

Edwardes (Camberwell) Ltd, Suppliers of Mopeds, London

Eldernell Vehicles, Suppliers of Agricultural Vehicles,
Peterborough

Elliott, Thomas, Ltd, Suppliers of Fertilisers and Peat, Hayes,
Kent

Ellis and McHardy Oils, Oil Distributors, Aberdeen

Elsoms Seeds Ltd, Seedsmen, Spalding

En-tout-cas plc, Manufacturers of Tennis Courts, Leicester

Equiform Nutrition Ltd, Suppliers of Equine Vitamin
Supplements and Feed Additives, Grimsby

Eutectic-Co. Ltd, Supplier of Maintenance Welding Materials,
Feltham

Ewers, D. and G. Pet Supplies, Bird Seed Supplier, Windsor

Express Lift Co., Ltd, Manufacturers and Suppliers of Passenger
Lifts, Northampton

FMC Corporation (U.K.) Limited, Suppliers of Pea Harvesting
Equipment, Fakenham

FSL Bells, Ltd, Manufacturers of Animal Feed Supplements,
Corsham

FARGRO Ltd, Horticultural Sundriesmen, Littlehampton

Farm Health Limited, Suppliers of Animal Health, Dairy
Hygiene and Nutritional Products, Alton

A final finish is applied to a Papworth briefcase

Oriental enamel from a private collection being restored at Plowden and Smith's workshops in Wandsworth

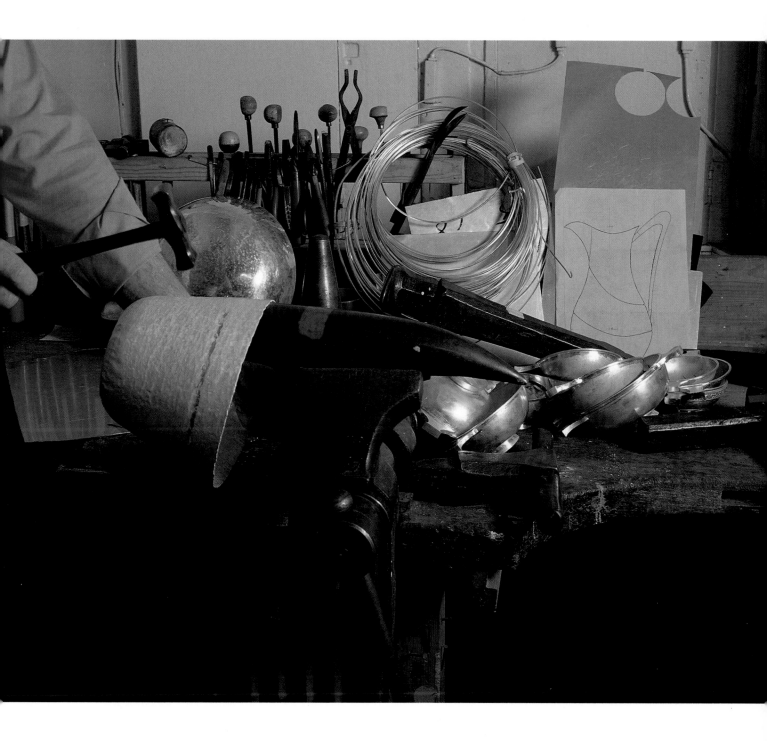

Hamilton and Inches specialise in modern versions of ancient Celtic drinking bowls

A brace of Royal hairdressers – Charles Martyn of Neville Daniel Ltd. (The Queen) and Gerald Blomfield of Maurice and Robert (The Queen Mother)

Farmwork Services (Eastern) Ltd, Agricultural
and Spraying Contractors, Holbeach

Fen Ditching Company, Land Drainage Contractors, Wisbech

Fisons PLC, Manufacturers of Horticultural Products, Ipswich

Fleming, John & Co. Ltd, Timber Merchants, Aberdeen

Forces Help Society and Lord Roberts Workshops, The,
Manufacturers of Fancy Goods, London

Fosroc Ltd – Timber Treatments Division,
Manufacturers of Wood Preservatives, Marlow

Fossitt and Thorne, Tyre Distributors and Service, Boston,
Lincolnshire

Fox, Frederick Ltd, Milliner, London

Fraser, G. R. & Co., Printers and Stationers, Aberdeen

Fyfe, John, Limited, Supplier of Quarry and Concrete Products,
Aberdeen

Gallyon & Sons, Ltd, Gunsmiths, Norwich

Gascoigne Milking Equipment Ltd,
Milking Machine Manufacturers, Reading

Gates Rubber Company Limited, The, Manufacturers of
Waterproof Rubber Footwear, Dumfries

General Trading Co. (Mayfair) Ltd, The, Suppliers of Fancy
Goods, London

Gibbons, Stanley Limited, Philatelists, London

Gibbs, J. Ltd, Suppliers of Agricultural Machinery
and Implements, Feltham

Gibson Saddlers Ltd, Suppliers of Racing Colours, Newmarket

Gilbertson & Page Ltd, Manufacturer of Dog and Game Food,
Colney Heath

Gladwell, H. G. & Sons Limited, Millers and Agricultural
Merchants, Ipswich

Goodyear, Edward Ltd, Florist, London

Grugeon, Peter Studio, Photographer, Reading

Guardian Window Co., Ltd, Manufacturers
and Suppliers of Double Glazing, King's Lynn

Halcyon Days Ltd, Suppliers of Objets d'Art, London

Hall and Tawse Scotland Limited, Building Contractors,
Northfield

Hallam (E. C. Engineering, Leicester) Ltd,
Manufacturers of Construction Machinery, Leicester

Hamblin, Theodore Ltd, Opticians, London

Hamleys of Regent Street Ltd, Toy and Sports Merchants,
London

Hardie, R. G. & C., Bagpipe Makers, Glasgow

Hardy Brothers, Ltd, Silversmiths, Sydney

Hardy Minnis, Mercers of Woollen Cloth, Stroud

Harris, L. G. & Co. Ltd, Manufacturers of Paint Brushes
and Painters Tools, Stoke Prior

Hartnell, Norman, Ltd, Dressmakers, London

Hatchards, Booksellers, London

Hayters PLC, Manufacturers of Agricultural Machinery,
Bishop's Stortford

Haythornthwaite & Sons, Ltd,
Manufacturers of Grenfell Garments, Burnley

Heaton, Wallace Limited, Suppliers of Photographic Equipment,
London

Hilleshög (United Kingdom) Limited, Seed Suppliers,
Docking

Hillier Nurseries (Winchester) Ltd, Nurserymen and
Seedsmen, Ampfield

Hilling Woodshavings, Suppliers of Baled Woodshavings,
Tushingham

Holme Park Game Hatcheries, Suppliers of Stock Game,
Wokingham

Horrockses Fashions, Ltd, Dressmakers, Milton Keynes

Horse Requisites Newmarket Ltd, Suppliers of Equine Products,
Newmarket

House of Fraser (Stores) Ltd, T/A Frasers, House Furnishers,
Edinburgh

Houseman (Burnham) Ltd, Specialists in Water Treatment
Services, Burnham, Buckinghamshire

Humber Fertilisers Limited, Fertiliser Manufacturers, Hull

Hydro Fertilizers Limited, Manufacturers of Agricultural
Fertilisers, Ipswich

I.R.S. Ltd, Sign and Notice Manufacturer, Swaffham

Imperial Business Equipment Ltd, Suppliers of Typewriters,
London

ICI Agrochemicals, Manufacturers of Crop Protection
Chemicals, Haslemere

ICI Fertilisers, Manufacturers of Fertilisers, Cleveland

ICI Seeds UK Limited, Seedsmen, Boston, Lincolnshire

Institution Supplies (Leeds) Ltd, Manufacturers of Luggage
Trolleys and Accessories, Leeds

James, Cornelia Ltd, Glove Manufacturer, Brighton

James and Son (Grain Merchants) Ltd,
Suppliers of Animal Feeding Stuffs, London

John, C. (Rare Rugs) Ltd, Suppliers of Carpets, London

Johnson Brothers, Manufacturers of Ceramic Tableware,
Stoke-on-Trent

Johnson, Herbert (Bond Street) Ltd, Hatters, London

Jollye, Leonard F. (Brookmans Park), Ltd, Forage Merchant,
Enfield

Kango Ltd, Suppliers of Electrical Equipment, London

Kardex Systems (UK) Limited, Manufacturers of Office
Machines and Equipment, London

Kemira Fertilisers, Manufacturers of Agricultural Fertilisers,
Chester

Kerner-Greenwood & Co. Ltd, Manufacturer of Waterproofing
Material, Mansfield

Keyline Builders Merchants (North) Ltd, Suppliers of Paint and
Wallpaper, Aberdeen

Kidd Farm Machinery Ltd, Manufacturers of Farm Machinery,
Devizes

Kilian & Crisp (Great Baddow) Ltd, Suppliers of Horticultural
Chemicals, Great Baddow

Kilian, H. Ltd, Manufacturer of Horticultural Packaging,
Great Baddow

King, John K. & Sons, Ltd, Seedsmen, Coggeshall

Kinloch Anderson, Tailors and Kiltmakers, Edinburgh

Knight, Peter (Beaconsfield) Ltd, Suppliers of Interior
Furnishings, Beaconsfield

Knight, Peter (Esher) Ltd, Suppliers of Fancy Goods
and Lighting, Esher

Kodak, Ltd, Manufacturers of Photographic Supplies,
Hemel Hempstead

LEP (Bloodstock) Ltd, International Bloodstock Forwarders,
Newmarket

Lambert, James & Sons, Ltd, Suppliers of Building Materials,
Snettisham

Lambourn Racehorse Transport Limited, Horse Transport
Contractors, Lambourn

Langton, W. E., Suppliers of Milking Machine Components,
Coventry

Latham, James PLC, Wood Merchants, London

Latter, G. P. and Company (Engineers) Limited, General Engineers, Windsor

Launer, S. & Co. (London) Ltd, Manufacturers of Handbags, Croydon

Leech, Ken Trees, Fruit Tree Nurserymen, Bulmer Tye, Sudbury

Lewis East Ltd, Manufacturers of Stationery, Leicester

Leyland DAF Ltd, Manufacturers of Commercial Vehicles, Preston

Leyland Paint Company, The, Supplier of Decorative Paints, Batley

Lidstone, Midwinter Limited, Suppliers of Animal Feed, Seed, Fertiliser and Crop Protection Chemicals, Newbury

Lilliman and Cox, Ltd, Dry Cleaners, London

Lillywhites, Ltd, Outfitters, London

Lincolnshire Drainage Co. Ltd, Drainage Contractors, Boston

Lindisposables Ltd, Suppliers of Cleaning and Catering Disposable Products, Boston

Lister Shearing Equipment Limited, Manufacturers of Animal Health Care Products, Gloucester

Lock, S., Ltd, Embroiderers, London

London Brick Company Limited, Brick Makers, Bedford

Longmire, Paul, Ltd, Supplier of Jewellery and Leather Goods, London

Luda Pet Food Limited, Dog and Game Food Manufacturers, Louth

Lusher, W. S. & Sons, Ltd, Building Contractor, Norwich

M. K. Electric Limited, Manufacturers of Electrical Equipment, London

Malloch, P. D., Suppliers of Shooting and Fishing Equipment, Perth

Mann, Egerton & Co. Ltd, Automobile Engineers, Norwich

Marley Building Systems Limited, Building Manufacturers and Constructors, Godalming

Marley Floors Ltd, Suppliers of Floor Tiles, Maidstone

Marley Roof Tile Co. Ltd, The, Suppliers of Roof Tiles, Sevenoaks

Massey Ferguson (U.K.) Limited, Manufacturers of Agricultural Machinery, London

Maxwell, Henry & Co. Ltd, Bootmakers, London

May & Baker Ltd, Manufacturers of Agricultural Herbicides, Dagenham

May, H. (Ascot) Ltd, Automobile Engineers, Ascot

McArthur Group Limited, Suppliers of Fencing, Wire Products and Ironmongery, Bristol

Meadham and Rampton, Builders, Kingsclere

Merryweather & Sons, Ltd, Fire Engineers, Hyde, Cheshire

Meyer and Mortimer, Ltd, Military Outfitters, London

Mill Feed Company Limited, The, Mobile Compounders and Suppliers of Animal Feed, Lincoln

Minns Bros. Ltd, Builders, Sedgeford, Hunstanton

Mirman, Simone, Milliner, London

Mobil Oil Co. Ltd, Suppliers of Petroleum Fuels and Lubricants, London

Moir, W. Clock Repairer, Aberdeen

Morris, Green Machinery (Sussex) Ltd, Manufacturers of Agricultural Machinery, Worthing

Mowlem, John & Co., PLC, Building Contractors, Brentford

Murkett Brothers, Ltd, Suppliers of Motor Vehicles, Huntington

Murray, J. & D., Chemists, Ballater

NCR Limited, Suppliers of Electronic Accounting Systems, London

NDS Animal Feeds, Suppliers of Dogfood, Nairn

NEI International Combustion Ltd, Cochran Boilermakers, Annan

NRS Limited, Manufacturers of Refrigerating Machinery, Newbury

National Foaling Bank, Supplier of Foster Mares for Orphan Foals, Newport, Shropshire

Netlon Ltd, Manufacturers of Plastic Mesh, Blackburn

Newey & Eyre Ltd, Suppliers of Industrial and Domestic Electrical Equipment, Edgbaston

Nickerson Seeds Ltd, Seed Merchants, Lincoln

Norfolk Seeds Ltd, Seedsmen, Fakenham

Norfolk Steel Stockholders Ltd, Suppliers of Steel Products, King's Lynn

Northern Heating Supplies Limited, Suppliers of Central Heating Equipment, Aberdeen

Notcutts Nurseries Ltd, Nurserymen, Woodbridge

Nu-way Ltd, Manufacturers of Combustion Equipment, Droitwich

O'Hanlon & Co. Ltd, Wm, Suppliers of Window Shade Fabrics, Manchester

Office International (Eastern Counties) Limited, Suppliers of Office Stationery and Equipment, King's Lynn

Olympia Business Machines Co. Ltd, Suppliers of Office Equipment, London

Page, J. & E. (London) Ltd, Florist, London

Papworth Group, Travel Goods Makers, Cambridge

Parker Pen UK Ltd, Manufacturers of Pens, Pencils and Ink, Newhaven

Patman of Cambridge, Clock Repairer, Cambridge

Pattrick and Thompsons Limited, Timber Merchants, King's Lynn

Pauls Agriculture Ltd, Manufacturers of Animal Feeding Stuffs, Ipswich

Peden International Transport Limited, Bloodstock Shipping Agents, Newbury

Pedigree Petfoods, Manufacturers of Canned Dog Food, Melton Mowbray

Pertwee Holdings Limited, Suppliers of Horticultural Chemicals, Colchester

Pilkington Glass Ltd, Manufacturers and Suppliers of Glass, St Helens

Planned Maintenance Painting Limited, Painter and Decorator, Glasgow

Plaspak (UK) Ltd, Polyethylene Film and Bag Manufacturers, Swindon

Pleyer and Morton Limited, Manufacturers of Equine Products and Equipment, Telford

Pratt & Leslie Jones Ltd, Suppliers of Fancy Goods, Windsor

Price, Arthur & Co. Ltd, Cutlers and Silversmiths, Lichfield

Pringle, J., Motor Engineer, Ballater

Pringle of Scotland, Limited, Manufacturers of Knitted Garments, Hawick

Protim Services Ltd, Damp Proofing and Timber Treatment Specialists, Hayes

Purdey, James & Sons, Ltd, Gun and Cartridge Makers, London

Rank Xerox Ltd, Manufacturers and Suppliers of Xerographic Copying Equipment and Materials, Marlow

Ransoms Sims and Jefferies, PLC, Manufacturers of Agricultural and Horticultural Machinery, Ipswich

Rayne, H. & M. Ltd, Shoemakers and Handbag Manufacturers, London

Elizabeth Hanley of Clare House Ltd., supplier of lampshades to The Queen

A word processor from Royal Warrant Holder British Olivetti Ltd

Redmayne, S. Ltd, Tailors, Wigton

Reekie Engineering Ltd, Suppliers of Agricultural Machinery, Arbroath

Reid, Ben & Co. Ltd, Nurserymen and Seedsmen, Aberdeen

Remploy Ltd, Manufacturers of Knitwear, London

Rentokil Ltd, Pest Control and Timber Preservation Services and Products, Felcourt

Rexel Business Machines Limited, Manufacturers of Security Shredding Machines, Aylesbury

Rexel Limited, Suppliers of Office Equipment, Aylesbury

Rigby, John & Co. (Gunmakers) Ltd, Rifle and Cartridge Makers, London

Rigby and Peller, Corsetières, Croydon

Riverside Garage, Automobile and Electrical Engineers, Ballater

Roberts Radio Co., Ltd, Radio Manufacturers, West Molesey

Rony, Belt Maker, London

Ross Breeders Ltd, Suppliers of Ross Live Poultry, Newbridge, Midlothian

Rowe, Frank, Suppliers of Chrysanthemum Stock, Wellington, Somerset

Royal Albert Limited, Manufacturers of Paragon Fine Bone China, Stoke-on-Trent

Royal British Legion Poppy Factory Ltd, The, The Royal British Legion Poppy Manufacturers and Supplier of Rosettes, Richmond

Russell, Gordon Ltd, Manufacturers of Furniture, Broadway

Sanderson, Arthur & Sons Ltd, Suppliers of Wallpapers, Paints and Fabrics, Uxbridge

Sanderson (Forklifts) Limited, Manufacturers of Material Handling Equipment, Skegness

Schering Agrochemicals Limited, Manufacturers of Agrochemicals, Hauxton

Scottish Agricultural Industries PLC, Manufacturers of Fertilisers and Seeds, Edinburgh

Securicor Ltd, Express Parcel Carriers, Sutton

Sellers, Derek Home Choose Carpets Limited, Carpet and Floor Covering Supplier, Ingoldisthorpe

Semex (UK) Sales Ltd, Suppliers of Cattle Breeding Services, Dalrymple, Ayrshire

Simmonds Brothers and Sons Limited, Building Contractor, London

Simpson (Piccadilly) Ltd, Outfitters, London

Smith, James (Scotland Nurseries), Ltd, Nurserymen, Matlock

Smith W. and Son, Ltd, Seedsmen and Nurserymen, Aberdeen

Smythson, Frank, Stationers, London

Solignum Ltd, Manufacturers of Wood Preservatives, Crayford

Southern Tree Surgeons Ltd, Tree Surgeons, Crawley

Sovereign Chemical Industries Limited, Building Material Manufacturers, Barrow-in-Furness

Spencer (Aberdeen) PLC, Manufacturers of Paints and Putties, Aberdeen

Spey Pheasantries, Suppliers of Ex Laying Pheasants and Pheasant Poults, Grantown-on-Spey

Spink & Son, Ltd, Medallists, London

Spratt's Patent Ltd, Suppliers of Dog Foods, New Maldon

Stanton Hope, Ltd, Suppliers of Forestry Equipment, Laindon

Star Horse Transport, Horse Transporter, Ely

Steinway & Sons, Pianoforte Manufacturers, London

Stenner of Tiverton Ltd, Manufacturers and Suppliers of Sawmilling Machinery, Tiverton

Store Design Ltd, Shopfitters, Dunfermline

Stuart, A. G. Limited, Suppliers of Timber Buildings, Insch

Suttons Seeds Ltd, Seedsmen, Torquay

Tate, Anthony, Chemist, London

Taylor O. A. & Sons Bulbs Ltd, Bulb Growers, Holbeach

Technoproof, Ltd, Roofing Contractors, Newbury

Thwaites and Reed Ltd, Turret Clockmakers, Hastings

Thomas, Ian, Dressmaker, London

Thorn Lighting Ltd, Manufacturers of Electric Lamps, Enfield

Timber, H. G. Ltd, Suppliers of Timber Products, Hayes

Valentines of Dundee Ltd, Suppliers of Christmas Cards and Calendars, Dundee

Vitax Limited, Manufacturers of Fertilisers and Insecticides, Skelmersdale

Wallace, Cameron & Co. Ltd, Manufacturers and Suppliers of Ultraplast First Aid Dressings, Glasgow

Wartski Ltd, Jewellers, London

Weatherill, Bernard, Ltd, Riding Clothes Outfitters and Livery Tailors, London

West Norfolk Super Lime Company, Ltd, Suppliers and Distributors of Agricultural Lime, Hillington, King's Lynn

Wigg & Plowright– Dalgety Engineers Ltd, Suppliers of Agricultural Machines, Fakenham

Wilder, John (Agricultural) Ltd, Suppliers of Agricultural Machinery, Wallingford, Oxon.

Wilson, William & Co. (Aberdeen) Ltd, Suppliers of Plumbing, Electrical and Building Materials, Aberdeen

Wimpey Asphalt Ltd, Road Surfacing Contractors, London

Witney Blanket Co., Ltd, Bedding Manufacturers, Gateshead

Wood, William & Son, Ltd, Garden Contractors and Horticultural Builders, Taplow

Wright, Rain Ltd, Manufacturers of Irrigation Equipment, Ringwood

DEPARTMENT OF THE MASTER OF THE HOUSEHOLD

Abels of Watton Limited, Removals and Storage Contractor, Thetford

Aberdeen Meat Marketing Ltd, Suppliers of Beef and Lamb, Banchory

Afia Carpets Ltd, Carpet Suppliers, London

Agma PLC, Manufacturers of Cleaning and Hygiene Products, Northumberland

Airwick (UK) Limited, Manufacturers of Airwick, Hull

Angostura Bitters (Dr J. G. B. Siegert & Sons), Ltd, Manufacturers of Angostura Aromatic Bitters, Trinidad

Ardath Tobacco Co., Ltd, Suppliers of Cigarettes, London

Arden, Elizabeth, Ltd, Manufacturers of Cosmetics, London

Armstrong World Industries Ltd, Manufacturers of Floor Covering, Uxbridge

'At-A-Glance' Calendar Co. Limited, Calendar Manufacturers, London

Baker G. P. and J. Ltd, Suppliers of Furnishing Fabrics and Wallcoverings, High Wycombe

Balls Albert (King's Lynn) Ltd, Wholesale Fish and Shellfish Merchant, King's Lynn

Barnard and Westwood Limited, Printers and Stationers, London

Bartholomew, John & Son Ltd, Suppliers of Maps, Edinburgh

Bass Brewing Ltd, Brewers, Burton-on-Trent

OPPOSITE Mountain landscape – cross-section of a mattress from Sleepeezee, bedmakers to The Queen and The Prince of Wales

ABOVE Making a pile – looms at the Royal Carpet Factory in Wilton near Salisbury

Baxter, G. G. Ltd, Suppliers of Pork Sausages, Birchington-on-Sea

Baxter, James & Son, Purveyors of Potted Shrimps, Morecambe

Baxter, W. A., & Sons Ltd, Fruit Canners, Fochabers

Beecham Products, Suppliers of Lucozade and Shloer, Brentford

Bendicks (Mayfair), Ltd, Manufacturers of Chocolates, Winchester

Benoist, V. Ltd, Purveyors of Table Delicacies, London

Benson & Hedges Limited, Tobacconists, London

Berkel Ltd, Manufacturers of Slicing Machines, Leicester

Berry Bros. & Rudd, Ltd, Wine and Spirit Merchants, London

Black & Edgington Hire Ltd, Tent and Flag Makers, London

Bollom, J. W. & Co. Ltd, Trading as Henry Flack Ltd, Manufacturers of French Polishes and Lacquers, Beckenham

Booth's Distilleries Ltd, Gin Distillers, London

Brentfords, Bedlinen Suppliers, Cramlington, Northumberland

British Sugar plc, Manufacturers of Sugar, Peterborough

British Van Heusen Company Ltd, The, Shirt Makers, Taunton

Britvic Soft Drinks Ltd, Manufacturers of Fruit Juices & Soft Drinks, Chelmsford

Broadwood, John & Sons Ltd, Pianoforte Manufacturers, Milton Keynes

Bronnley, H. & Co., Ltd, Toilet Soap Makers, London

Brooks W. & Son (UYC Foods Ltd), Purveyors of Frozen Food, London

Bryant & May Ltd, Match Manufacturers, High Wycombe

Buchanan, James & Co., Ltd, Scotch Whisky Distillers, London

Bulmer, H. P. Limited, Cider Makers, Hereford

Burgess, John & Son, Ltd, Manufacturers of Pastes and Condiment Sauces, London

Burton Son & Sanders, Ltd, Manufacturers of Fondant, Ipswich

Bury Cooper Whitehead Ltd, Felt and Carpet Manufacturers, Bury

C.P.C. (United Kingdom) Ltd, Manufacturers of Corn Oil and Cornflour, Esher

Cadbury Limited, Cocoa and Chocolate Manufacturers, Bournville

Campbell Brothers, Purveyors of Meat and Poultry, Edinburgh

Campbell, George & Sons (Fishmongers) Ltd, Suppliers of Fish and Poultry, Edinburgh

Carlsberg Brewery Ltd, Suppliers of Lager Beer, Northampton

Carnell, J. W. Limited, Coach Hirers, Sutton Bridge, Spalding

Carr's of Carlisle Ltd, Biscuit Manufacturers, Carlisle

Castle Pharmacy, Pharmaceutical Chemists, Windsor

Cerebos, Suppliers of Table Salt and Pepper, London

Chalmers, David Limited, Fruit and Vegetable Supplier, Elgin

Champagne J. Bollinger, S. A., Purveyors of Champagne, Ay-Champagne

Champagne Heidsieck & Co., Monopole, S. A., Purveyors of Champagne, Reims

Champagne Lanson Pere et Fils, Purveyors of Champagne, Reims

Champagne Louis Roederer, Purveyors of Champagne, Reims

Champagne Moet & Chandon, Purveyors of Champagne, Epernay

Charbonnel et Walker Ltd, Chocolate Manufacturers, London

Clare House Limited, Suppliers of Lampshades and Fittings, London

Clyde Canvas Goods & Structures Ltd, (Trading as Purvis Equipments), Manufacturer and Hirer of Marquees, Leith

Coca-Cola Great Britain Limited, Suppliers of Soft Drinks, London

Cole and Son (Wallpapers) Ltd, Suppliers of Wallpapers, London

Coloroll Carpets Limited, Carpet Manufacturers, Kidderminster

Colmans of Norwich, Manufacturers of Mustard and Sauces, Norwich

Cooper, Frank, Ltd, Marmalade Manufacturers, Esher

Cope & Timmins Ltd, Brass Finishers and Spring Makers, London

Corney & Barrow Limited, Wine Merchants, London

County Window Cleaning & Steam Carpet Beating Company, The, Window Cleaners, Reading

Crawford, D. S. (Catering), Caterers, Edinburgh

Crawford, William & Sons, Ltd, Biscuit Manufacturers, Edinburgh

Cromessol Company Limited, Manufacturers and Suppliers of Disinfectants and Detergents, Glasgow

Cross Paperware Ltd, Manufacturers of Disposable Tableware, Dunstable

Crosse and Blackwell, Purveyors of Preserved Provisions, Croydon

Darville & Son, Ltd, Grocers, Windsor

Davies, Bruce Limited, – Trading as Robert Bruce, Fruit and Vegetable Merchant, London

De Blank, Justin (Provisions) Ltd, Baker, London

Dewar, John & Sons, Ltd, Scotch Whisky Distillers, Perth

Dewhurst J. H. Ltd, Butcher, London

Dobbins, J. T. Limited, Suppliers of Household Cleaning Materials, Liverpool

Domecq (U.K.) Ltd, Suppliers of Domecq Sherry, London

Donaldson, Andrew, Ltd, Suppliers of Fish and Ice, King's Lynn

Drew, Clark & Co., Ltd, Manufacturers of Ladders, London

Dubois Chemicals Ltd, Suppliers of Dishwashing Compounds and Controls, High Wycombe

Early's of Witney PLC, Manufacturers of Blankets, Witney

Electrolux Ltd, Suppliers of Suction Cleaners and Floor Polishers, Luton

Express Foods Group Ltd, Dairy Suppliers, South Ruislip

Fenland Laundries Limited, Launderers and Cleaners, Skegness

Ferrari, S. & Sons (Soho), Ltd, Suppliers of Kitchen Equipment, London

Findlater Mackie Todd & Co. Ltd, Wine and Spirit Merchants, London

Findus, Suppliers of Frozen Food, Croydon

Fitch and Sons, Limited, Provision Merchants, London

Floris, J. Ltd, Perfumers, London

Footsure South Eastern Limited, Safety Footware Supplier, London

Fortnum & Mason PLC, Grocers and Provision Merchants, London

Foster, John & Co. Ltd, Suppliers of Furnishing Fabrics, London

Frigicold Limited, Suppliers of Freezer Ware Packaging, Shipley, West Yorkshire

Gainsborough Silk Weaving Co, Ltd, The, Manufacturers of Furnishing Fabrics, Chilton, Sudbury

Gaskell Textiles Ltd, Manufacturers of Carpet Underlays, Bacup

Gaunt, J. R., and Son Ltd, Ribbon Suppliers, Birmingham

Gaymer, William, & Son Ltd, Cyder Manufacturers, Attleborough

Givan's Irish Linen Stores Limited, Linen Drapers, London

Gloag, Matthew & Son Ltd, Scotch Whisky Blenders, Perth

A soft touch – felt-tip pens being assembled in King's Lynn at Berol, Manufacturers of Writing Instruments to The Queen

John Mackaness, maker and supplier of charcoal to The Queen, supervises charcoal burning on his Northamptonshire estate

Goddard, J. & Sons, Ltd, Manufacturers of Silver
and Metal Polishes, Camberley

Goldenlay Eggs Ltd, Supplier of Eggs, Drighlington

Goode, Thomas & Co. Ltd, Suppliers of China and Glass,
London

Gray, James & Son (Ironmongers & Electricians) Ltd,
Suppliers of Cleaning Materials, Edinburgh

Guinness PLC, Brewers, London

H. P. Foods Limited, Manufacturers of HP Sauces,
Market Harborough

Hamilton & Inches Ltd, Silversmiths and Clock Specialists,
Edinburgh

Harris, C. & T. (Calne) Ltd, Manufacturers of Bacon
and Sausages, London

Harrods Ltd, Suppliers of Provisions and Household Goods,
London

Harvey, John & Sons Ltd, Wine Merchants, Bristol

Hawker, James, & Co. Ltd, Purveyors of Sloe Gin, Wokingham

Heal & Son Ltd, Upholsterers and Suppliers of Bedding, London

Heering, Peter F. Purveyors of Cherry Heering, Haslev,
Denmark

Heinz, H. J., Company Ltd, Purveyors of Heinz Products,
Hayes, Middlesex

Higgins, H. R. (Coffee-man) Ltd, Coffee Merchants, London

Hill Brush Co. (Mere), The,
Manufacturers of Household Brushware, Mere

Hill Thomson & Co. Ltd, Scotch Whisky Distillers, Edinburgh

Hine, Thomas & Co. Suppliers of Cognac, Jarnac, France

Hodgkiss H. and Son Limited, Fishmonger, Windsor

Hoover PLC, Manufacturers of Vacuum Cleaners
and Laundry Equipment, Merthyr Tydfil, South Wales

Hunter and Hyland Limited, Suppliers of Curtain Rails
and Upholstery Fittings, Leatherhead

Huntley & Palmers Ltd, Biscuit Manufacturers, Reading

Hyams & Cockerton Ltd, Purveyors of Fruits and Vegetables,
London

Hypnos Limited, Upholsterers and Bedding Manufacturers,
Princes Risborough

Ind Coope Ltd, Brewers of Ale and Lager, London

Jacob & Co., W. & R. (Liverpool) Ltd, Biscuit Manufacturers,
Liverpool

Jaeggi, Leon & Sons, Ltd, Suppliers of Catering Utensils
and Equipment, London

Jenners, Princes Street, Edinburgh, Limited,
Suppliers of Furnishings Materials, Edinburgh

Jet Carpet Cleaners Ltd, Carpet Cleaners, Uxbridge

Johnson Wax Ltd, Manufacturers of Wax Polishes,
Cleaner and Hygiene Products, Camberley

Jones, Yarrell & Co., Ltd, Newsagents, London

Justerini & Brooks Ltd, Wine Merchants, London

Kellogg Company of Great Britain Limited,
Purveyors of Cereals, Manchester

Kennerty Farm Dairies Ltd, Suppliers of Milk
and Dairy Products, Aberdeen

Kent, G. B. and Sons PLC, Brush Makers, Hemel Hempstead

Kirkness & Gorie, Supplier of Honey, Kirkwall

Kleen-Way (Berkshire) Co., Chimney Sweepers, Bracknell

Knight's Gallery, Mount Cutters and Picture Framers, Luton

Knowles & Sons (Fruiterers) Ltd, Purveyors of Fruit
and Vegetables, Aberdeen

Krug, Vins Fins de Champagne S. A., Purveyors of Champagne,
Reims

Lampitt, Henry, Ltd, Suppliers of Hardware, London

Lansing Lindel Ltd, Manufacturers of Industrial Trucks,
Basingstoke

Lea & Perrins Ltd, Purveyors of Worcestershire Sauce,
Worcester

Leith, G. & Son, Bakers and Confectioners, Ballater

Lever Brothers Limited, Soap and Detergent Makers,
Kingston-upon-Thames

Lidstone, John, Butchers, London

Lingwood Richard A., Gold Leaf Manufacturer, South Ruislip

Lister & Co. plc, Manufacturers of Furnishing Fabrics, Bradford

Lyons Bakery Ltd, Manufacturers of Cakes, London

Lyons, J. & Co. Ltd, Caterers, Alperton, Middlesex

Lyons Maid Ltd, Manufacturers of Ice Cream, Greenford,
Middlesex

M. & R. – Martini & Rossi Ltd, Suppliers of Martini Vermouth,
London

John Mackaness, Maker and Supplier of Charcoal, Northampton

Mackay Hugh plc, Manufacturers of Wilton Carpeting, Durham

Magnolia Manufacturing Ltd, Manufacturers of Picture Frame
Mouldings, Loughborough

Manns & Norwich Brewery Ltd, Brewers, Northampton

Marsh & Baxter, Ltd, Suppliers of York Ham, Northallerton

Martin & Son Edinburgh Ltd (Trading as Martin & Frost),
Interior Furnishing Specialist, Edinburgh

McCarthy, D. & F. Ltd, Fruit and Vegetable Merchants, Norwich

McVitie & Price Ltd, Biscuit Manufacturers, Edinburgh

Mappin & Webb Ltd, Silversmiths, London

Mattessons Wall's Limited, Suppliers of Sausage and Meat Pies,
Banbury

Mayfair Trunks Limited, Suppliers of Luggage, London

Medway Sacks, Suppliers of Domestic Refuse Sacks, Maidstone

Melroses Limited, Purveyors of Tea and Coffee, Edinburgh

Milevac Scientific Glass Ltd, Manufacturers of Vacuum Flasks,
Hemel Hempstead

Minton Limited, China Manufacturers, Stoke-on-Trent

Modern Fibre Glass Products Ltd, Manufacturers of Fibre Glass
Carrying Cases, Tonbridge

Morny Limited, Manufacturers of Soap, London

Mumm, G. H. & Cie, Purveyors of Champagne, Paris

Myland, John Limited, Manufacturers of French Polish,
Stains and Wax Polish, London

Nairobi Coffee & Tea Co. Ltd, Coffee Merchants, Watford

Nestlé Company Ltd, The, Manufacturers of Instant Coffee,
Croydon

Newbery, Henry & Co. Ltd, Suppliers of Furnishing Trimmings,
London

Norprint Ltd, Manufacturers of Baggage Labels, Boston,
Lincolnshire

North, James & Sons Ltd, Suppliers of Safety Footwear, Hyde

Office Cleaning Services Ltd, Cleaning Contractor, Sanderstead

Parry Tyzack Limited, Supplier of Hand Tools
and Portable Electric Tools, London

Pears, A. & F. Ltd, Soap Manufacturers, London

Peek, Frean & Co. Ltd, Biscuit Manufacturers, London

Percheron, H. A. Ltd, Suppliers of Furnishing Fabrics, London

Picreator Enterprises Ltd, Supplier of Products for Restoration
and Conservation, London

Pilgrim Payne & Co. Ltd, Cleaners of Soft Furnishings and Carpets, London

Pinneys of Scotland, Ltd, Purveyors of Smoked Salmon, Dumfries

Plastona (John Waddington) Ltd, Manufacturer of Disposable Plates, Leeds

Porter Nicholson, Upholsterers' Warehousemen, London

Preedy J. and Sons Limited, Supplier of Glass Table Tops, London

Prestat Ltd, Purveyors of Chocolates, London

Price's Patent Candle Company Ltd, Candlemakers, London

Procter and Gamble Limited, Manufacturers of Soap and Detergents, Newcastle upon Tyne

Quaker Oats Limited, Suppliers of Quaker Products, Southall

R & L Packaging, Suppliers of Plastic Bags, London

Reckitt & Colman, Products Ltd (see Colmans of Norwich)

Rickett & Colman Pharmaceutical Division, Manufacturers of Antiseptics, Hull

Renshaw, John F. Ltd, Purveyors of Almond Products, Mitcham

Ridgways, Tea Merchants, London

Robertson, James & Sons Preserve Manufacturers Ltd, Preserve Manufacturers, Manchester

Roger & Gallet SA, Manufacturers of Soap, Paris

Rose, L., & Co. Ltd, Suppliers of Lime Juice Cordial, London

Ross, John Jnr. (Aberdeen) Limited, Fish Merchants and Curers, Aberdeen

Royal Brierley Crystal Ltd, Suppliers of Table Glassware, Brierley Hill, West Midlands

Royal Doulton Limited, Manufacturers of China, Stoke-on-Trent

H. & L. Russell Ltd, Manufacturers of Garment Hangers, London

Russell, Donald Limited, Supplier of Meat and Poultry, Inverurie

Ryvita Company Limited, The, Manufacturers of Crispbreads, Poole

SDL Limited, Manufacturers of Sewing Machines, Basingstoke

Saccone & Speed Ltd, Wine Merchants, London

St Ivel, Ltd, Suppliers of Butter and Cheese, Swindon

Sandeman, Geo. G. Sons & Co. Ltd, Wine Merchants, London

Sanderson, William & Son Ltd, Scotch Whisky Distillers, London

Savoy Hotel Coffee Department, The, Suppliers of Coffee, London

Schweppes International Limited, Soft Drink Manufacturers, London

Scoles, R. F. & J., Butchers, Dersingham

Scott Limited, Manufacturer of Disposable Tissues, East Grinstead

Scottish & Newcastle Breweries Plc, Brewers, Edinburgh

Sekers Fabrics, Ltd, Manufacturers of Furnishing Fabrics, London

Sharp, Edward & Sons Ltd, Confectioners, Maidstone

Sharwood, J. A. & Co. Ltd, Manufacturers of Chutney and Purveyors of Indian Curry Powder, London

Shaw, Elizabeth, Ltd, Manufacturers of Confectionery, Bristol

Sheridan H. M., Purveyor of Meat and Poultry, Ballater

Shirras, Laing & Co. Ltd, Ironmongers, Aberdeen

Sinclair Melson Designs Limited, Upholsterers, Feltham

Sleepeezee Limited, Bedding Manufacturers, London

Slumberland Ltd, Bedding Manufacturers, Oldham

Smith, Tom Group, Ltd, Suppliers of Christmas Crackers, Norwich

Spink R. R. and Sons, Fishmongers, Arbroath

Spode, Manufacturers of China, Stoke-on-Trent

Sproston, W. F., Ltd, Suppliers of Fish, London

St Jude's Laundry, Launderers, Edinburgh

Staples & Co., Ltd, Manufacturers of Bedsteads and Bedding, Huntingdon

Stewart, J. & G. Ltd, Suppliers of Scotch Whisky, Edinburgh

Still, W. M. & Sons, Ltd, Manufacturers of Kitchen Equipment, Hastings

Stoddard, Carpets Limited, Carpet Manufacturers, Johnstone, Scotland

Strachan, George, Ltd, General Merchants, Crathie

Sturtevant Engineering Co., Ltd, Manufacturers of Vacuum Cleaners, Brighton

Swindle, Clive Restorations, Porcelain Restorer, Westerham, Kent

Sycamore Laundry & Dry Cleaners (Leman Brothers), Launderers and Dry Cleaners, London

Szell, Michael Limited, Suppliers of Furnishing Fabrics, London

Tanqueray, Gordon, & Co. Ltd, Gin Distillers, London

Tate & Lyle PLC, Sugar Refiners, London

Telephone Rentals plc, Suppliers of Dictograph Telephones, Milton Keynes

Temple & Crook Ltd, Suppliers of Brushes and Hardware, London

Terry, Joseph & Sons, Confectionery Manufacturer, York

Thermos Ltd, Manufacturers of Vacuum Vessels, London

Thewensum Co. plc, Livery Tailors, London

Thresher & Glenny Limited, Shirtmakers, London

Tissunique, Ltd, Suppliers of Furnishing Fabrics, London

Turner, G. J. & Co. (Trimmings) Ltd, Manufacturers of Furnishing Trimmings, London

Twining, R. & Co. Ltd, Tea and Coffee Merchants, London

Unigate Dairies Limited, Suppliers of Dairy Produce, London

Van den Berghs, Manufacturers of Margarine, Burgess Hill

Vantona International Linen Co. Ltd, Suppliers of Linen, London

Veuve Clicquot-Ponsardin, Purveyors of Champagne, Reims

Vileda Limited, Suppliers of Nonwoven Cleaning Materials, Cleckheaton

Vitopan Limited, Suppliers of Mopping Equipment, Sanderstead

Waddington's Playing Card Co., Ltd, Manufacturers of Playing Cards, Leeds

Walker, H. & T. Ltd, Suppliers of Canned Foods, Sevenoaks

Walker, John & Sons, Ltd, Scotch Whisky Distillers, London

Walley Ltd, Suppliers of Crockery and Glassware, Grays

Warner Fabrics plc, Suppliers of Silks and Furnishing Fabrics, London

Watney Truman Limited, Brewers, London

Weetabix Ltd, Manufacturers of Breakfast Cereals, Burton Latimer

Wensum Co. plc, The, Livery Tailors, London

Western Quilters Limited, Quilters, London

Whitbread & Co., PLC, Brewers, London

Whitbread Wessex, Purveyors of Beers, Spirits and Mineral Water, Portsmouth

White Horse Distillers Limited, Scotch Whisky Distillers, Glasgow

James Campbell Reed and his son David, Decorators and Furnishers to Her Majesty The Queen, at the headquarters of Whytock and Reed in Edinburgh

A family of Royal Fire Extinguishers from Chubb Fire Security Ltd.

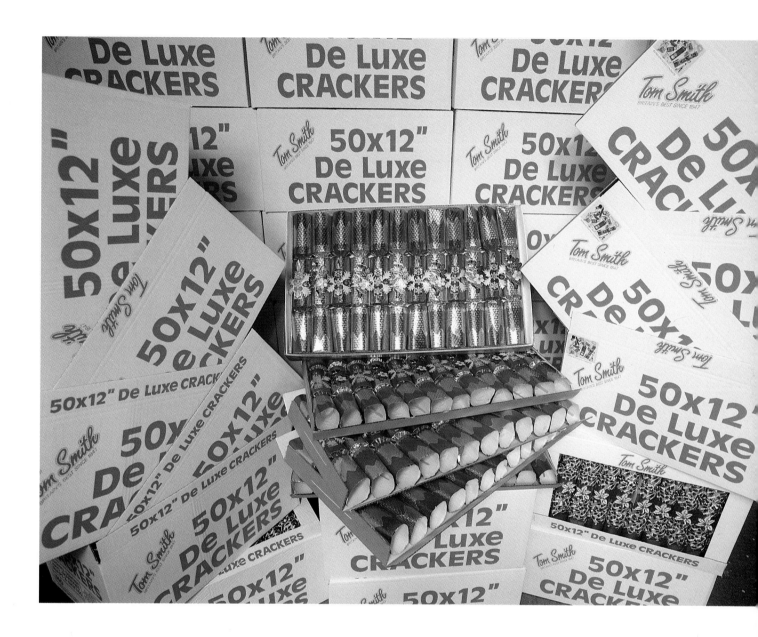

A different sort of motto – the Royal Christmas crackers come from Thomas Smith of Norwich

At ease in one of his drawing-room suites, Michael Archibald of Aberdeen, Cabinet Maker and
Upholsterer to The Queen

White, John, Footwear Ltd, Footwear Manufacturers, Wellingborough

Whitworths Ltd, Manufacturers of Provisions and Dried Fruit, Wellingborough

Whytock & Reid, Decorators and Furnishers, Edinburgh

Wilkin & Sons, Ltd, Jam and Marmalade Manufacturers, Tiptree

Wilkinson, R. and Son, Glass Restorers, London

Wilson, Andrew & Sons Ltd, Catering Equipment Hirers, Edinburgh

Wilton Royal Carpet Factory Limited, The, Carpet Manufacturers, Wilton

Windsor Glass Company Ltd, Glass Merchants, Windsor

Wolsey Division, Courtaulds Textiles Ltd, Manufacturers of Hosiery and Knitwear, Leicester

Woodhouse Hume Ltd, Suppliers of Meat and Poultry, London

Worcester Royal Porcelain Co., The, Manufacturers of China and Porcelain, Worcester

Yardley & Co. Ltd, Manufacturers of Soap, London

LORD CHAMBERLAIN'S OFFICE

Alden & Blackwell (Eton) Ltd, Booksellers, Windsor

Alliance Engraving & Lettering Co. Ltd, Engravers, Bristol

Atlantis Paper Company Ltd, Fine Art and Archival Suppliers, London

Barcham Green & Co. Ltd, Hand-Made Papermakers, Maidstone

Beam Office Equipment Limited, Photocopying Oxford, Suppliers of Photocopying Equipment, Thame

Berol Ltd, Manufacturers of Writing Instruments, King's Lynn

Burn, James International, Suppliers of Office Binding Equipment, Esher

Carters Coaches Ltd, Coach Hirers, Maidenhead

Carvers and Gilders, Carvers, Gilders and Restorers, London

Collings, Denis Vere, Calligrapher, New Barnet

Compton, J., Sons & Webb, Ltd, Uniform Makers, London

Connolly Bros. (Curriers) Ltd, Leather Tanners and Curriers, London

Conservation Resources (UK) Limited, Manufacturers of Archival Storage Material, Cowley

Cooper, A. C., Ltd, Fine Art Photographers, London

Cooper, A. C., (Colour) Ltd, Fine Art Colour Photographers, London

Dege, J. & Sons Limited, Tailors, London

Ede & Ravenscroft, Ltd, Robe Makers, London

Farris, Charles Ltd, Chandlers, London

Firmin & Sons plc, Button Makers, London

Garrard & Co., Ltd, Goldsmiths and Crown Jewellers, London

Greenaway-Harrison Ltd, Printers, London

Harrild, W. L. and Partners Ltd, Suppliers of Bookbinding Equipment, London

Harris, Aubrey Ltd, Suppliers of Printing and Stationery, London

Hewit, J., & Sons Ltd, Manufacturers of Leather, Edinburgh

Hill, William, & Son, and Norman & Beard, Ltd, Organ Builders, London

IBM United Kingdom Limited, Suppliers of Electric and Electronic Typewriters, Portsmouth

Maggs Bros. Ltd, Purveyors of Rare Books and Manuscripts, London

Petersfield Bookshop, Picture Framer and Supplier of Art Materials, Petersfield

Phoenix Fine Art, Suppliers of Fine Art Services, London

Plan Conservation Limited, Restorer of Drawings, Windsor

Plowden & Smith Limited, Restorer of Fine Arts Objects, London

Polybags Limited, Polythene Bagmakers, Greenford

Rogers, T. & Co. (Packers) Ltd, Packers and Transporters of Works of Art, London

Ryder, G. and Company Limited, Specialist Box Makers, Milton Keynes

Securicor Cleaning, Ltd, Office Cleaning Contractors, Walton-on-Thames

Skinner A. E. & Company, Jewellers and Silversmiths, London

Stothers & Hardy (Henley) Ltd, Manufacturers of Computer Software, Henley-on-Thames

Swann: Heddon-on-the-Wall, Cabinet Maker, Newcastle-upon-Tyne

Tortoiseshell and Ivory House Ltd, The, Restorers of Objets d'Art, London

Toye, Kenning & Spencer Ltd, Suppliers of Gold and Silver Laces, Insignia and Embroidery, London

Unisys Limited, Suppliers of Computer Systems, London

Walker, J. W. & Sons Ltd, Pipe Organ Tuners and Builders, Brandon

Watkins & Watson Ltd, Organ Blower Manufacturers, Wareham

Watts & Company Limited, Ecclesiastical Furnishers, London

Wiggins, Arnold & Sons Ltd, Picture Frame Makers, London

Wilkinson Sword Ltd, Sword Cutlers, High Wycombe

Wilson & Son, Piano and Harpsichord Tuners, Edinburgh

ROYAL MEWS DEPARTMENT

Allen J.A. & Co. (The Horseman's Bookshop) Limited, Suppliers of Equine and Equestrian Literature, London

Anstee & Company, Ltd, Forage Merchants, Ware

Arnolds Veterinary Products Limited, Suppliers of Equine Veterinary Pharmaceuticals, Leighton Buzzard

Asbridge, James (Greenwich) Ltd, Repairer and Painter of Horse Drawn Vehicles, London

Austin Rover Group Ltd, Manufacturers of Rover Cars & Austin Cars, Coventry

Betts and Broughton, Suppliers of Safety Footwear, Sutton-in-Ashfield

Birr, H.H., Suppliers of Riding Clothing, Leicester

British Nova Works Ltd, Manufacturers of Floor Maintenance Products and Waxes, Southall

Bullens Limited, Road Transport Contractors, Borehamwood

Campbell, Smith & Co. Ltd, Decorators, London

Car Care Products Group, Supplier of Vehicle Polishes and Cleaners, Liphook

Carpenter, J.W. Ltd, Suppliers of Cleaning Stores, Thame

Carr & Day & Martin Ltd, Manufacturers of Saddlery Care Products, Wilmslow

Castrol Limited, Manufacturers of Motor Lubricants, Swindon

Champion Sparking Plug Co., Ltd, Suppliers of Sparking Plugs, Upton, Wirral

Chapman, Albert E. Limited, Upholsterers, London

Chubb Fire Ltd, Manufacturers of Chubb Fire Extinguishers, Sunbury-on-Thames

Coppermill Limited, Manufacturers of Industrial Cleaning Cloths, London

Croford Coachbuilders Ltd, Wheelwright and Coachbuilders, Ashford

Curzon, G.E., Forage Merchants, Wraybury

D & H Horse Feeds, Horse Feed Supplier, Cirencester

Day Son and Hewitt Limited, Manufacturers of Veterinary Products, Lancaster

Eastern Counties Leather PLC, Manufacturers of Chamois Leather, Cambridge

Esso Petroleum Company, Ltd, Purveyors of Motor Spirit, London

Forbo-Nairn Ltd, Manufacturers of Floor Covering, Kircaldy

Ford Motor Company, Ltd, Motor Vehicle Manufacturers, Brentwood

Frames Rickards Ltd, Road Transport Contractors, Brentford

Francis, G.C. Heraldic Artist, North Lancing

Gardiner & Co., Suppliers of Protective Clothing, London

Gidden, W. & H. Ltd, Saddlers, London

Gieves & Hawkes Ltd, Livery and Military Tailors, London

Gliddons Gloves & Leatherwear Ltd, Suppliers of Gloves, Yeovil

Godfrey Davis Europcar Ltd, Motor Vehicle Hirers, London

Harvey, Matthew & Co. Ltd, Bitmakers, Walsall

Hawkins, G.T. Ltd, Riding Footwear Manufacturers, Northampton

Henleys (London) Limited, Coachbuilders, London

Hutton, E.H. (Coachbuilders) Ltd, Manufacturers and Repairer of Horseboxes, Melton Mowbray

Incorporated Association for Promoting the General Welfare of the Blind, The, Suppliers of Stable Mats, etc, and Renovators of Mattresses, London

Jaguar Cars Limited, Supplier of Motor Cars, Coventry

Jeyes' Group PLC, Manufacturers of Hygiene Products, Thetford

K Shoes Limited, Bootmakers, Kendal

Keep, John T. & Sons Ltd, Paint Manufacturer, London

Kenning London, Motor Car Distributors, London

Land Rover UK Ltd, Manufacturers of Land Rovers and Range Rovers, Solihull

Lobb, John Limited, Bootmaker, London

Lucas, Joseph, Ltd, Manufacturers of Electrical Equipment, Birmingham

Luxford, Keith (Saddlery) Ltd, Saddlers, Horse Clothiers and Harness Makers, Teddington

McArthur Gray (Stamford) Ltd, Suppliers of Shoeing Iron and Farriers' Equipment, Stamford, Lincolnshire

Mason, Joseph, PLC, Manufacturers of Coach Paints, Derby

Metropolitan Window Cleaning Co, Ltd, Window Cleaners, London

'Mordax' Studs Ltd, Makers of 'Mordax' Studs, Burnley

National Benzole Co., Ltd., Suppliers of Motor Spirit, London

Newsham, Stuart Photography, Photographer, Stourport-on-Severn

North, W.A. & Son, Forage Merchants, Bourne

Offord, Gordon J., Coachbuilders, Thames Ditton

Owen, Charles & Co. (Bow) Ltd, Protective Headwear Manufacturer, London

Parker, F. & Sons Ltd, Suppliers of Garden Materials, Bagshot

Patey, S. (London) Ltd., Manufacturers of Hats, London

Pettifer, Thomas & Co. Ltd, Manufacturers of Animal Health and Nutrition Products, Barking

Plessey Company, PLC, The, Suppliers of Car Radios, Ilford

Poole, Henry, & Company (Savile Row) Ltd, Livery Outfitters, London

Pratt, Jeffery A., Supplier of Animal Health and Veterinary Products, Rickmansworth

Reckitt Household Products, Manufacturers of Air Fresheners, Polishes and Cleaners and Laundry Products, Hull

Redwood and Feller, Tailors, London

Rolls Royce Motor Cars Limited, Motor Car Manufacturers, Crewe

Scottish Midland Co-operative Society Limited, Coach Painters, Edinburgh

Sandicliffe Garage Ltd, Suppliers of Motor Horse Boxes and Automobile Engineers, Stapleford

Sandicliffe of Stapleford (see Sandicliffe Garage Ltd)

Shell U.K. Ltd. Purveyors of Motor Spirit, London

S.P. Tyres UK Limited, Motor Vehicle Tyre Suppliers, Birmingham

Sleigh, W.L. Ltd, Motor Vehicle Hirers, Edinburgh

Sturgess, Walter E. & Sons Ltd, Suppliers of Horse and Carriage Conveyances, Leicester

Swaine, Adeney, Brigg & Sons, Ltd., Whip and Glove Makers, London

Tropical Plants Display Ltd, Installers and Maintainers of Plant Displays, London

Turner-Bridgar, Saddler and Harness Maker, Goring-on-Thames

Vauxhall Motors, Ltd, Motor Vehicle Manufacturers, Luton

Westway, Mark & Son, Manufacturers of Horse Forage, Marldon, Devon

Still life with fruit and chintz – A.L. Taylor of Arthur Sanderson and Sons Ltd., suppliers of Wallpapers, Paints and Fabrics, in his Uxbridge showroom.

Two generations of Royal jeweller – father David and son Andrew Bosford of Cartier

ROYAL WARRANTS OF APPOINTMENT
TO
HER MAJESTY QUEEN ELIZABETH THE QUEEN MOTHER

Ackermann's Chocolates Ltd, Confectioners, London

Addis Limited, Suppliers of Plastic Housewares, Hertford

Ainsworths Homoeopathic Pharmacy, Chemist, London

Amor, Albert Ltd, Suppliers of Fine Porcelain, London

Aquascutum, Limited, Makers of Weatherproof Garments, London

Arden, Elizabeth, Ltd, Manufactuers of Cosmetics, London

Army and Navy Stores, Ltd., Suppliers of Household and Fancy Goods, London

Asprey and Co., PLC, Jewellers, London

'At-A-Glance' Calendar Company Limited, The, Calendar Manufacturers, London

Avon Tyres Limited, Tyre Manufacturers, Melksham

Bandaville Ltd, Conveyors of Motor Vehicles, London

Bass Brewing Ltd, Brewers, Burton upon Trent

Baxter, G.G. Ltd, Suppliers of Pork Sausages, Birchington-on-Sea

Baxter, James & Son, Purveyors of Potted Shrimps, Morecambe

Baxter, W.A. & Sons, Ltd, Purveyor of Scottish Specialities, Fochabers

Begg, Graham Limited, Radio and Television Suppliers, Wick, Caithness

Bell & Croyden, John Ltd, Chemists, London

Benney, Gerald, Goldsmith, Silversmith and Enameller, Beenham

Benoist, V. Ltd, Purveyors of General Groceries, London

Black & Edgington Hire Ltd, Flag Makers, London

Brannam, C.H., Limited, Pottery Makers, Barnstable

Bremner, F. & J., Haulage Contractors, Castletown, Caithness

British Cable Services Ltd, Suppliers of Rediffusion, Guildford

Britvic Soft Drinks Ltd, Manufacturers of Fruit Juices & Soft Drinks, Chelmsford

Broadwood, John & Sons, Ltd, Pianoforte Tuner, Milton Keynes

Bronnley, H. & Co., Ltd, Toilet Soap Makers, London

Budgens, Grocers, Ruislip

Burley's Newsagents, Newsagent and Tobacconist, Englefield Green

Cadbury, Ltd, Cocoa and Chocolate Manufacturers, Bournville, Birmingham

Caithness Glass PLC, Glassmakers, Wick, Caithness

Caleys (Cole Bros. Ltd), Suppliers of Household and Fancy Goods and Millinery, Windsor

Calman Links (Trading) Ltd, Furriers, London

Calor Gas Limited, Suppliers of Liquefied Petroleum Gas, Datchet, Slough

Campbell & Co., Tweed Mercers, Beauly

Carrington & Company, Limited, Jewellers and Silversmiths, London

Carters (J. & A.) Ltd, Invalid Furniture Manufacturers, Westbury, Wiltshire

Carters Tested Seeds Ltd, Seedsmen, Llangollen

Cartier Ltd, Jewellers and Goldsmiths, London

Cassie, Alistair, Television Supplier and Engineer, Ballater

Castrol, Ltd, Purveyors of Motor Lubricants, Swindon

Chapman & Frearson Limited, Suppliers of Protein Balancers, Vitamin and Mineral Supplements, Grimsby

Chess, Mary Ltd, Perfumers, London

Collingwood of Bond Street Limited, Jewellers, London

Coombs & Sons (Guildford) Ltd, Suppliers of Motor Cars, Guildford

Corner Fruit Shop, The, Fruiterer and Greengrocer, Thurso

Corney and Barrow Limited, Wine Merchants, London

Cox, Harold & Sons Jewellers Ltd, Clockmakers and Silversmiths, Windsor

Cromessol Co. Ltd, Manufacturers and Suppliers of Disinfectants and Detergents, Glasgow

Crosse & Blackwell, Purveyors of Preserved Provisions, Croydon

Daimler Cars, See BL Cars Ltd

DER Limited, Suppliers of Television Receivers, Chertsey

Dettlyn Limited trading as Egham Mower Service, Suppliers of Horticultural Machinery, Egham

Dipre, D., & Son, Cutlery Servicers, Knifegrinders and Suppliers of Kitchen Equipment, London

Dreamland Appliances PLC, Manufacturers of Electric Blankets, Hythe

Dunnet, John, Agricultural Contractor, Seater

Ede & Ravenscroft Ltd, Robermakers, London

Egham Animal Food Supplies, Corn and Animal Feed Merchants, Egham

Emmetts Store, Curers and Suppliers of Sweet Pickled Hams, Peasenhall

Farris, Charles Ltd, Candlemakers, London

Findus, Suppliers of Frozen Foods, Croydon

Firmin & Sons Ltd, Button Makers, London

Forces Help Society and Lord Roberts Workshops, The, Furniture Makers, London

Ford Motor Co. Ltd, Motor Vehicle Manufacturers, Brentwood

Ford Oliver, Ltd, Decorators, London

Fortnum & Mason, PLC, Suppliers of Leather and Fancy Goods, London

Foster, John & Co., Suppliers of Furnishing Fabrics, London

Fox's Biscuits Limited, Biscuit Manufacturers, Batley

Frederick, John, Ltd, Carpet Cleaners, London

Garrard & Co, Ltd, Jewellers and Silversmiths, London

General Trading Co. (Mayfair) Ltd, The, Suppliers of Fancy Goods, London

Gestetner Limited, Suppliers of Reprographic Office Equipment, London

Gibson Saddlers Ltd, Suppliers of Racing Colours, Newmarket

Goddard, J. and Sons Ltd, Manufacturers of Silver and Metal Polishes, Camberley

Goode, Thomas & Co. Ltd, Suppliers of Glass and China, London

Goodyear, Edward, Ltd, Florist, London

Green Stage Ltd, Suppliers of Musks Sausages, Newmarket

Greenaway-Harrison Ltd, Printers, London

Grover Clyne, Carpet and Vinyl Floor Covering Supplier, Wick

H.P. Foods Ltd, Manufacturers of H.P. Sauces and Canned Foods, Market Harborough

Haggart, P. & J. Ltd, Tartan and Woollen Manufacturers, Aberfeldy

Halcyon Days Ltd, Suppliers of Objets d'Art, London

Hall, Matthew Ltd, Mechanical and Electrical Engineers, London

Hamblin, Theodore, Ltd, Opticians, London

Hancocks and Co. (Jewellers) Ltd, Goldsmiths and Silversmiths, London

Hardy Minnis, Mercers of Woollen Cloth, Stroud

Harris Aubrey Limited, Suppliers of Stationery and Office Equipment, London

Harris, D.R. & Company, Limited, Chemist, London

Harrods, Limited, Suppliers of China, Glass and Fancy Goods, London

Hartnell, Norman, Limited, Dressmakers, London

Harvey Nichols & Company, Limited, Drapers, London

Hatchards, Booksellers, London

Heaton, Wallace Ltd, Suppliers of Photographic Equipment, London

Hillier Nurseries (Winchester) Ltd, Nurserymen and Seedsmen, Winchester

Holt, Ray (Land Drainage) Ltd, Land Draining Contractors, Thurso

Hoover PLC, Suppliers of Vacuum Cleaners, Merthyr Tydfil, South Wales

Hubbard Refrigeration Ltd, Suppliers of Automatic Ice Making Machines, Woodbridge

Huntley & Palmers Ltd, Biscuit and Cake Manufacturers, Reading

Hypnos Limited, Upholsterers and Bedding Manufacturers, Princes Risborough

Jacob, W. & R. & Co. (Liverpool) Ltd, Biscuit Manufacturers, Liverpool

Jaguar Cars, Manufacturers of Daimler and Jaguar Cars, Coventry

Jeyes Group plc, Manufacturers of Hygiene Products, Thetford

Johnson Brothers, Manufacturers of Ceramic Tableware, Stoke-on-Trent

Johnson Wax, Ltd, Manufacturers of Wax Polishes, Cleaner and Hygine Products, Camberley

Jones, Peter, Draper and Furnisher, London

Jones, Yarrell & Co., Ltd, Newsagents, London

K Shoes Limited, Bootmakers, Kendal

Kleen-Way (Berkshire) Co., Chimney Sweepers, Bracknell

Knight, J.W. (Fisheries) Ltd, Fishmonger and Poulterer, Virginia Water

Knowles & Sons (Fruiterers) Ltd, Fruiterers and Greengrocers, Aberdeen

Land Rover UK Ltd, Manufacturers of Land Rovers, Solihull

Lang Brothers Ltd, Scotch Whisky Distillers, Glasgow

Leigh, G. & Son, Bakers and Confectioners, Ballater

Lentheric, Ltd, Manufacturers of Perfumery Products, Camberley

Lever Brothers Limited, Soap and Detergent Makers, Kingston-upon-Thames

Levy, M. (London Wall) Ltd, Fruiterers and Greengrocers, London

Leyland Cars, See BL Cars Ltd

Liberty PLC, Silk Mercers, London

Lidstone, John, Butchers, London

Lilliman and Cox, Ltd, Dry Cleaners, London

Longmire Paul Limited, Supplier of Silver and Presentation Gifts, London

Lyons, J. & Co. Ltd, Caterers, Alperton, Middlesex

McCallum & Craigie Ltd, Suppliers of Lan-Air-Cel Blankets, Huddersfield

M & R–Martini & Rossi Ltd, Suppliers of Brandy and Martini Vermouth, London

Mattessons Wall's Limited, Suppliers of Sausages and Meat Pies, Banbury

Maurice & Robert, Hairdressers, London

Mayfair Trunks Ltd, Suppliers of Luggage, London

Mayfair Window Cleaning Co., Ltd, Window Cleaners, London

Menzies, John & Co. PLC, Booksellers, Edinburgh

Milne John & Sons, Clockmaker, Wick, Caithness

Mirman, Simone, Milliner, London

Morny, Ltd, Manufacturers of Soap, London

Mowbray, A.R. & Co. Ltd, Suppliers of Fine Bindings, London

Moyses Stevens Ltd, Florists, London

Murray, J. & D., Chemists, Ballater

NRS Limited, Manufacturers of Refrigerating Machinery, Newbury

Nairobi Coffee and Tea Company, Ltd, The, Coffee Merchants, Watford

National Benzole Co., Ltd, Suppliers of Motor Spirit, London

Nestlé Company Limited, The, Manufacturers of Nestlé Products, Croydon

Papworth Group, Trunk and Cabinet Makers, Cambridge

Parker's, Saddlers, Horsham

Paxton & Whitfield Ltd, Cheesemongers, London

Pears, A.F. Ltd, Soap Manufacturers, London

John Peck (1982) Ltd, Suppliers of Overalls and Chefs Clothing, Liverpool

Peek, Frean & Co. Ltd, Biscuit Manufacturers, London

Petrie E., Painters and Decorators, Thurso

Phillips, S.J., Ltd, Antique Dealers, London

Phonotas Service Ltd, Telephone Cleaners and Sterilisers, Tunbridge Wells

Player, John & Sons, Tobacco Manufacturers, Nottingham

Plessey, Co. plc. The, Suppliers of Motor Car Radio Equipment, Ilford

314

Peter Keen of Hypnos Limited in Princes Risborough demonstrates one of his beds. He holds The Queen's and The Queen Mother's Warrants as 'furnisher, upholsterer and bedding manufacturer'

Pow, Kathy Beauty Care, Manicurist, Chalfont St Peter

Pratt & Leslie Jones Ltd, Suppliers of China, Glass and Fancy Goods, Windsor

Premier Brands UK Limited, Manufacturers of Christmas Puddings, Birmingham

Pringle John, Suppliers of Motor Spirit, Oil and Accessories, Ballater

Pringle, of Scotland Ltd, Manufacturers of Knitted Garments, Hawick

Procter & Gamble, Ltd, Manufacturers of Soaps, Detergents and Shortening, Newcastle-upon-Tyne

Prowse, Keith & Company Limited, Theatre Ticket Agents, London

RTC Mechanical Services Ltd, Heating Equipment Engineers, Ewell

Rayne, H, and M., Ltd, Shoemakers and Handbag Manufacturers, London

Reid C.J. (Eton), Chemist, Eton

Renshaw, John F. Ltd, Purveyors of Almond Products, Mitcham

Reynier, J.B. Limited, Wine Merchants, London

Ridgways, Tea and Coffee Merchants, London

Roberts Radio, Manufacturers and Suppliers of Radio Receivers, West Molesey, Surrey

Robertsons of Tain Limited, Supplier of Agricultural and Horticultural Machinery, Tain

Rowntree PLC, Makers of Table Jellies, York

Royal Albert Limited, Manufacturers of Paragon Fine Bone China, Stoke-on-Trent

Royal British Legion Disabled Men's Industries Ltd, The, Makers of Leather and Fancy Goods, Maidstone

Royal Crown Derby Porcelain Co., Ltd, Manufacturers of Fine Bone China, Derby

Royal Hotel (Caithness) Ltd, The, Victuallers and Vintners, Thurso

Rudolf, Milliner, London

Russell, Gordon, Limited, Suppliers of Furniture and Furnishings, Broadway

Sanderson, Wm. & Son, Ltd, Scotch Whisky Distillers, London

Scott Limited, Manufacturers of Disposable Tissues, East Grinstead

Schweppes International Ltd, Soft Drink Manufacturers, London

Scott's Fish Shop, Cheesemonger, Kirkwall

Semex (UK Sales) Limited, Supplier of Cattle Breeding Services, Dalrymple, Ayrshire

Sharp, Edward, & Sons Ltd, Suppliers of Confectionery and Confectionery Novelties, Maidstone

Sheridan, H.M. Purveyor of Meat and Poultry, Ballater

Ships Wheel, The, Furniture and Picture Restorer, Thurso

Sleigh, W.L., Ltd, Motor Vehicle Hirers, Edinburgh

Slumberland, Limited, Bedding Manufacturers, Oldham

Smith, H. Allen Ltd, Wine Cooper and Merchant, London

Smith, Tom Group Ltd, Suppliers of Christmas Crackers, Norwich

Smith, W. & Son Ltd, Seedsmen and Nurserymen, Aberdeen

Sparks, John, Ltd, Antiquaries of Chinese Art, London

Spink R.R. and Sons, Fishmongers, Arbroath

Sproston W.F. Ltd, Fishmongers, London

Steiner Products, Cosmeticians, London

Steven, James L., Plumbing and Heating Engineer, Wick, Caithness

Stopps, J. & Sons Ltd, Bakers and Confectioners, Egham

Stowells of Chelsea, Wine and Spirit Merchants, Dorking

Strachan, George Ltd., General Merchants, Crathie

Suttons Seeds Ltd, Seedsmen, Torquay

Swaine, Adeney, Brigg & Sons, Limited, Umbrella Makers, London

Sycamore Laundry & Dry Cleaners (Leman Brothers), Launderers and Dry Cleaners, London

Tanqueray Gordon and Company Limited, Gin Distillers, London

Telephone Rentals PLC, Suppliers of Dictograph Telephones, Milton Keynes

Thomas, J. Rochelle Inc., Dealers in Works of Art, Hamilton, Bermuda

Thomas Window Cleaning, Window Cleaner, Englefield Green

Thomson, Donald, Grocer, Castletown, Caithness

Thorn Lighting Limited, Manufacturers of Electric Lamps, Enfield

Thresher & Glenny, Ltd, Shirtmakers, London

Trianco, Redfyre, Ltd, Manufacturers of Domestic Boilers, Sheffield

Twining, R. & Co., Ltd, Tea and Coffee Merchants, London

Unigate Dairies (London) Ltd, Suppliers of Dairy Produce, London

Valentines of Dundee, Ltd, Suppliers of Christmas Cards and Calendars, Dundee, Scotland

Vernons Electrical Limited, Electrical Engineers, Sunningdale

Veuve Clicquot-Ponsardin, Purveyors of Champagne, Reims

Wallace, Cameron, & Co., Ltd, Manufacturers of Ultraplast First Aid Dressing, Glasgow

Want, Albert & Co., Ltd, Suppliers of Household Hardware and Garden Sundries, Englefield Green

Wartski Ltd, Jewellers, London

Watmough, Ken, Fishmonger, Aberdeen

Weatherill, Bernard, Ltd, Livery Tailors, London

Weetabix Limited, Manufacturers of Breakfast Cereals, Burton Latimer

West, R. & C., Greengrocer and Fruiterer, Sunningdale

Whitbread Fremlins, Brewers, Maidstone

Whitworths Ltd, Processors and Packers of Food Products, Wellingborough

Wholesale Fittings, PLC, The, Suppliers of Electrical Equipment, Dagenham

Wicks, E.J., Saddler, Lambourn

Wiggins, Arnold and Sons, Limited, Picture Frame Makers, London

Wolsey Division, Courtaulds Textiles Limited, Manufacturers of Hosiery and Knitwear, Leicester

Wood, William & Son Ltd, Garden Contractors and Horticultural Builders, Taplow

Woodhouse Hume Ltd, Suppliers of Meat and Poultry, London

Worham, Antony, Ltd, Suppliers of Tudor Queen Hams and Tongues, London

Yardley and Co., Ltd, Perfumers and Manufacturers of Soap, London

ROYAL WARRANTS OF APPOINTMENT
TO
HIS ROYAL HIGHNESS THE DUKE OF EDINBURGH

Allen, J.A. & Co. (The Horseman's Bookshop) Ltd, Equine and Equestrian Bookseller, London

Artistic Iron Products, Carriage Builder, Newark

Ashley and Blake Ltd, Shirtmakers, Manchester

Autoscan Limited, Manufacturers of Power Filing Systems, London

Barbour, J. & Sons, Ltd, Manufacturers of Waterproof and Protective Clothing, South Shields

Beken of Cowes, Ltd, Marine Photographers, Cowes, I.W.

Bell & Croyden, John Ltd, Chemists, London

Benney, Gerald, Goldsmith and Silversmith, Beenham

BOS Software Ltd, Computer Software Manufacturers, London

British Equipment Co. Ltd, Suppliers of Office Machinery, Warlingham

Buckley, Anthony & Constantine Ltd., Photographers, London

Ede & Ravenscroft Ltd, Robe Makers, London

Gates Rubber Company Limited, The, Manufacturers of Waterproof Rubber Footwear, Dumfries

General Trading Co. (Mayfair) Ltd, The, Suppliers of Fancy Goods, London

Gieves & Hawkes Ltd, Naval Tailors and Outfitters, London

Goodyear, Edward, Florist, London

Grant, Pat, Hairdresser, Aberdeen

Greenaway-Harrison Ltd, Printers, London

Halcyon Days, Supplier of Objets d'Art, London

Hamblin, Theodore Ltd, Opticians, London

Harrods Ltd, Outfitters, London

Hatchards, Booksellers, London

Heaton, Wallace Limited, Suppliers of Photographic Equipment, London

Holland & Holland Ltd, Rifle Makers, London

Jekmoth Ltd, Manufacturers of Garment Bags and Wardrobe Accessories, Watton

Johns & Pegg Ltd, Military Tailors, London

Jones, Yarrell & Co., Ltd, Newsagents, London

Kardex Systems (UK) Ltd, Manufacturers of Office Equipment, London

Kinloch Anderson Limited, Tailors and Kiltmakers, Edinburgh

Land Rover (UK) Limited, Vehicle Manufacturers, Solihull

Lobb, John Limited, Bootmakers, London

Lock, James & Co., Ltd, Hatters, London

Longmire, Paul Limited, Supplier of Jewellery and Presentation Gifts, London

Lyle & Scott Limited, Manufacturers of Underwear and Knitwear, Hawick

Penhaligon's Ltd, Manufacturers of Toilet Requisites, London

Philips Electronic and Associated Industries Limited, Suppliers of Electrical Goods, London

Purdey, James & Sons Ltd, Gunmakers, London

Simpson (Piccadilly) Ltd, Outfitters, London

Spink & Son Ltd, Medallists, London

Stephens Brothers Ltd, Shirt Makers and Hosier, London

Sycamore Laundry & Dry Cleaners (Leman Brothers), Launderers and Dry Cleaners, London

Symtec Computers Ltd, Suppliers of Computer Equipment, Southampton

Weatherill, Bernard Limited, Livery Tailors, London

Wilkinson Sword Ltd, Sword Cutlers, High Wycombe

A miniature rain forest from Tropical Plants Display of West London

ROYAL WARRANTS OF APPOINTMENT
TO
HIS ROYAL HIGHNESS THE PRINCE OF WALES

Anderson and Sheppard Limited, Tailors, London

Asprey and Co. plc, Jewellers Goldsmiths and Silversmiths, London

Aston Martin Lagonda Ltd, Motor Car Manufacturer and Repairer, Newport Pagnell

Atco Limited, Manufacturers of Motor Mowers, Stowmarket

Australian Dried Fruits (Europe) Limited, Purveyors of Dried Fruits, London

Barbour, J. & Sons Limited, Manufacturers of Waterproof and Protective Clothing, South Shields

Bell & Croyden, John Ltd, Chemists, London

Bennett & Fountain plc, Suppliers of Electrical Equipment, London

Benney, Gerald, Goldsmith and Silversmith, Beenham

Benoist, V. Ltd, Purveyors of Fine Foods and General Groceries, London

Bradfield Garages Limited, Automobile Engineers and Suppliers of Motor Fuel, Tetbury

Bronnley H., and Company Limited, Toilet Soap Makers, London

Collingwood of Bond Street Limited, Jewellers and Silversmiths, London

Corgi Hosiery Limited, Knitwear and Hosiery Manufacturer, Ammanford

Corney and Barrow Ltd, Wine Merchants, London

Crerar, Robert, Gold and Silversmith, Cellardyke

DER Limited, Suppliers of Television Receivers, Chertsey

Dipre, D. & Sons, Suppliers of Kitchen and Catering Equipment, London

Ede & Ravenscroft Limited, Robemakers, London

Eximious Limited, Manufacturers of Monogrammed Accessories, London

Farlow, C. and Co. Ltd, Suppliers of Fishing Trade and Waterproof Clothing, London

Findus, Suppliers of Frozen Foods, Croydon

Five Trees Garden Centre and Nursery Limited, Supplier of Gardening Materials, Tetbury

Floris, J. Limited, Manufacturers of Toilet Preparations, London

Ford Motor Co. Ltd, Motor Vehicle Manufacturers, Brentford

General Trading Company (Mayfair) Ltd, The, Suppliers of Fancy Goods, London

Gieves & Hawkes Limited, Tailors and Outfitters, London

Goode, Thomas & Co. Ltd, Suppliers of China and Glass, London

Goodyear, Edward Ltd, Florist, London

Grugeon, Peter Studio, Photographer, Reading

Halcyon Days, Supplier of Objets d'Art, London

Hall, Frank (Market Harborough) Ltd, Tailors, Market Harborough

Hardy, House of Ltd, Manufacturers of Fishing Tackle, Alnwick

Harris, Aubrey Limited, Suppliers of Stationery and Office Equipment, London

Harris Office Systems, Office Systems Division, Suppliers of Dictation Equipment, Winnersh

Harrods Ltd, Outfitters and Saddlers, London

Harvey Nichols and Company Ltd, Suppliers of Household and Fancy Goods, London

Hatchards, Booksellers, London

Heaton, Wallace Ltd, Suppliers of Photographic Equipment, London

Hyams & Cockerton Ltd, Purveyors of Fruit and Vegetables, London

IBM United Kingdom Ltd, Suppliers of Typewriters and Word Processing Equipment, Portsmouth

Jaguar Cars Limited, Supplier of Motor Cars, Coventry

Johns & Pegg Limited, Tailors, London

Johnson Herbert (Bond Street) Ltd, Hatters, London

Jones, Peter, Draper and Furnisher, London

Jones Yarrell & Company Limited, Newsagents, London

Kenning London, Motor Car Distributors, London

Kinloch Anderson Limited, Tailors and Kiltmakers, Edinburgh

Knowles and Sons (Fruiterers) Ltd, Purveyors of Fruit and Vegetables, Aberdeen

Land-Rover UK Limited, Motor Vehicle Manufacturers, Solihull

Leith, George & Son, Bakers and Confectioners, Ballater

Lilliman & Cox Ltd, Dry Cleaners, London

Lobb, John Ltd, Bootmakers, London

Luxford, Keith (Saddlery) Ltd, Saddlers and Horse Clothiers, Teddington

Lyons J. & Company Ltd, Caterers, Alperton, Middlesex

Mann Egerton and Company Limited, Suppliers of Bentley Motor Cars and Automobile Engineers, Leicester

Mappin & Webb Limited, Silversmiths, London

Metropolitan Window Cleaning Company Limited, Window Cleaners, London

Murray J. & D., Chemists, Ballater

Nicoll, B. (Shops) Limited, Fishmongers, Aberdeen

North, W.A. & Son, Forage Merchants, Bourne

Paintons, Greengrocer and Florist, Tetbury

Palmer, David, Building Contractors Limited, Building Contractors, Chippenham

Penhaligon's Limited, Manufacturers of Toilet Requisites, London

Poplak, Dudley Limited, Interior Designers, London

Pratt, Jeffery A., Suppliers of Animal Health and Veterinary Products, Rickmansworth

Price, Arthur and Company Limited, Cutlers and Silversmiths, Lichfield

Purdey, James & Sons Ltd, Gun and Cartridge Makers, London

Rank Xerox Limited, Manufacturers and Suppliers of Xerographic Equipment and Materials, Marlow

Roberts Radio Co. Ltd, Manufacturers and Suppliers of Radio Receivers, West Molesey, Surrey

Royal Brierley Crystal Ltd, Suppliers of Crystal Table Glassware, Brierley Hill, W. Midlands

Royal Doulton Limited, Manufacturers of Fine Bone China, Stoke-on-Trent

Russells of Tetbury, Dry Cleaners, Tetbury

Salter, J. & Son, Manufacturers of Polo Sticks, Aldershot

Sandicliffe Garage Limited, Suppliers of Motor Horseboxes and Automobile Engineers, Nottingham

Sheridan H.M., Purveyor of Meat and Poultry, Ballater

Simpson (Piccadilly) Ltd, Outfitters, London

Sleepeezee Ltd, Bedding Manufacturers, London

Sleigh, W.L., Ltd, Motor Vehicle Hirers, Edinburgh

Smith, Tom, Group Limited, Christmas Crackers, Norwich

Spink and Son Ltd, Medallists, London

Sproston W.F. Ltd, Suppliers of Fish, London

Start-rite Shoes Limited, Shoemakers, Norwich

Stephens Brothers Limited, Hosier, London

Strachan George Ltd, General Merchants, Aboyne

Swaine Adeney Brigg & Sons Limited, Suppliers of Leather Goods, London

Sycamore Laundry & Dry Cleaners (Leman Brothers), Launderers, London

Tate, Anthony, Chemist, London

Telephone Rentals PLC, Suppliers of Loudspeaking Telephones, Bletchley

Tricker, R.E., Limited, Shoe Manufacturers, Northampton

Turnbull & Asser Limited, Shirtmakers, London

Vantona International Linen Company Limited, Suppliers of Bed and Table Linen, London

Wallace, Cameron & Co, Ltd, Manufacturers and Suppliers of Ultraplast First Aid Dressings, Glasgow

Wartski Limited, Jewellers, London

Woodhouse Hume Ltd, Supplier of Meat and Poultry, London

PHOTOGRAPHIC ACKNOWLEDGEMENTS

All pictures by Jorge Lewinski and Mayotte Magnus except for the following:

CHAPTER 1

12 Mansell Collection, 13 Firmin & Sons plc, 21 Mansell Collection

CHAPTER 2

24 Royal Warrant Holders Association, 25 Jerry Cinamon, 29 Royal Warrant Holders Association

CHAPTER 3

40 Royal Warrant Holders Association, 49 Popperfoto

CHAPTER 4

69 Gieves & Hawkes, 72 Connolly Brothers (Curriers) Ltd., 77 Royal Warrant Holders Association, 85 Royal Doulton, 88 Spode/City Museum & Art Gallery Stoke on-Trent, 89 Popperfoto, 93 Black & Edgington Hire

CHAPTER 5

99 (right and left) National Motor Museum, 100 (left) Ford, 100 (right) Vauxhall Motors Ltd., 101 National Motor Museum, 104 Esso, 105 (left) Patrick Stephens (from *Jaguar*), 105 (right) John Bartholomew & Son Ltd, 112 The Boots Company plc, 113 Lever Brothers Ltd, 116 Dollond & Aitchison Group Ltd, 117 Parker Pen UK Ltd

CHAPTER 6

132 Suttons Seeds Ltd, 133 Hillier Nurseries (Winchester) Ltd

CHAPTER 7

136 Camera Press, 137 (left) Hulton-Deutsch Collection, 140 Popperfoto, 141 Wolsey, 145 Asprey plc, 176 (left) Aquascutum Ltd, 176 (right) Burberry Ltd, 148 & 149 (top) Cartier Ltd, 156 Daily Express, 157 Austin Reed, 161 Bernard Weatherill Ltd

CHAPTER 8

164 Hatchards, 173 Armitage's Brothers plc, 180 Royal Warrant Holders Association, 181 Roberts' Radio Company Ltd/ Illustrated London News, 181 C. Farlow & Co. Ltd

CHAPTER 9

208 John Lewis Partnership

CHAPTER 10

212 (left) Forbo-Nairn Ltd, 212 (right) Chubb Fire Security Ltd, 224 Rentokil Ltd, 225 (left) Hackney Archives Department, 225 (right) Belling and Company Ltd, 229 Norfolk Reed Thatchers, 232 G. P. & J. Baker Ltd, 232 (bottom) Warner & Sons Ltd

CHAPTER 11

239 Frank Cooper Ltd, 240 Express Food Group UK Ltd, 241 & 249 (top) J. Lyons & Company Ltd, 272 HP Foods Ltd, 248 & 249 (centre) Melroses Ltd, 249 (bottom) R. Twining & Co. Ltd, 252 *Anchovy Paste* by F. George, 253 Rowntree Mackintosh plc, 256 Wilkin & Sons Ltd, 257 (top) Wearne Public Relations/ James Robertson & Sons Preserve Mnfrs Ltd, 257 (bottom) H.J. Heinz & Co. Ltd, 260 Nabisco Group Ltd, 261 H.P. Bulmer Ltd, 269 Schweppes Great Britain, 273 Coca-Cola Great Britain ("Coca-Cola" and "Coke" are registered trade marks which identify the same products of the Coca-Cola Company)

One final rung. Roger Drew of Drew Clark and Co. makes The Queen's ladders at his 'Diamond Patent Ladder Works' in London

INDEX

'Mandatum novum de vobis' Valerie Bennett-Levy and her team make up the traditional posies for Maundy Thursday

The modern face of breakfast – Royal Warrant Holder, Richard George, in front of his Weetabix Mills in Kettering, Northants

A different sort of dinner service – Malcolm Macpherson of Cross Paperware Ltd., manufacturers of The Queen's disposable tableware

A true conserve – Frank Cooper's Oxford marmalade now back where it began, opposite the Queen's College in the City of Lost Causes

John Hillier, Nurseryman and Seedsman to The Queen and The Queen Mother, in a sea of sticks and leaves at his HQ in Romsey, Hants

Patrick Hackett of J. and E. Page Ltd., early one morning at Covent Garden Market. He holds The Queen's Royal Warrant as florist.

Index compiled by Lyn Greenwood

ABOVE After the Rose, the Nose… Bernard Hine sniffs samples of the eponymous Royal brandy at the family home in Jarnac

OPPOSITE Some like it hot – A Warholesque display of Royal Thermos interiors guaranteed to warm the inner person.